the greatest story

BIBLE INTRODUCTION

the greatest story

BIBLE INTRODUCTION

leader guide

THE GREATEST STORY
BIBLE INTRODUCTION
Leader Guide

Maps, charts, and other tools referred to in this book are available on *The Greatest Story Leader Reference CD* (Augsburg Fortress, 2011), ISBN 978-1-4514-0159-2.

ISBN: 978-1-4514-0151-6

Writers: Susan M. Lang, Thomas M. Lang
Review team: Dixon Kinser, St. Bartholomew's Episcopal Church, Nashville, TN; Drew Ludwig, Lafayette Ave. Presbyterian Church, Buffalo, NY; Becky Sechrist, Good Samaritan United Methodist Church, Edina, MN
Cover design: Alisha Lofgren
Interior design: Ivy Palmer Skrade
Typesetting: PerfecType, Nashville, TN

The paper used in this publication meets the minimum requirements of American National Standard for Information Sciences—Permanence of Paper for Printed Library Materials, ANSI Z329.48-1984.

Manufactured in the U.S.A.

13 12 11 1 2 3 4 5 6 7 8 9 10

CONTENTS

INTRODUCTION

WELCOME

Welcome to **the greatest story**, an introduction to the Bible! This course is for anyone who wants to get a big-picture overview of the Bible, its story, and how that story connects with our personal stories. It has been developed especially for young adults and adults, particularly those who are new to Bible study.

Through this study you will embark on a journey that starts at the very beginning of God's good creation and quickly moves to describe the tragic effects of sin on a fallen humanity. You will be introduced to the first family of faith, who God blesses and calls to be a blessing to all people. The stories of the Bible are very human stories. We see the most heroic and important ancestors in the faith struggle with sin and evil. Both the Old and New Testaments describe God's persistent efforts to reconcile with God's rebellious people. These efforts take a surprising twist in the life, death, and resurrection of Jesus Christ, who conquers both sin and death for all time. After Jesus' resurrection the story continues with the appearance of the Holy Spirit and the birth of Christ's church called to witness in his name. That means we're part of the story, too! The story lives on through our witness!

This course will engage the participants in the biblical story through actual storytelling, visual sand art presentations, and reflections on selected psalms. Questions accompanying each section of the session are intended to help participants reflect on the meaning of the story and how they live in the story and the story lives in them. You will also notice that every session encourages the use of charts, maps, illustrations, and diagrams found on the Leader Reference CD that accompanies this leader guide. Plan on using these resources during the sessions. They can be projected or photocopied for class use.

LEADING THE SESSIONS

Making participants feel welcome

Some people are actually frightened of the Bible and intimidated by idea of Bible "study." Let's face it: the Bible is an old book written by writers living in times and places very different from our own. The Bible's imagery and language isn't contemporary, so it can seem difficult to understand. Keep this in mind as you begin the course and as you invite people to participate. Assure them that it is perfectly fine to come with fears and questions. This course is not about memorizing obscure details or testing prior Bible knowledge. It simply aims to introduce the story and let it speak for itself. Invite God's Spirit to do the work to make the story come alive in each participant.

As leader, you have an important part to play in welcoming and encouraging learners, especially those who might be a little nervous about engaging in Bible study for the first time. Remind learners that it's not about what they already know about the Bible that counts. What's really important is what they will learn and how they will be transformed by connecting with the greatest story. Keep in mind that many participants in this study may not be familiar with biblical characters who may be quite familiar to you, people like Moses, King

David, or the apostle Paul. Don't take anything for granted. And remember to focus on the story experience itself rather than focusing on the minute details in each story.

If possible, choose a location for the class that is warm and inviting. Avoid using the church sanctuary unless you plan on taking in chairs to arrange in a semicircle. Using a sanctuary or formal classroom setting can stifle conversation. It can also project the image that you, as facilitator, are imparting knowledge while the learners are merely there to take it in.

Make sure whatever setting you are in is arranged with chairs or seating in more of a semicircle to encourage conversation and comfort. Since watching a DVD is part of each class session (and you'll definitely want to use it!) make sure that the chairs are arranged so that everyone can see the TV screen. As always, take into consideration the room's accessibility for those who may have issues with mobility or other challenges that could prevent them from more fully participating in the sessions.

Make sure you are in the classroom five or ten minutes prior to the start of the session so you can greet and welcome learners as they enter.

Experiencing the story

The methodology of this course offers participants the opportunity to experience the greatest story of God's love for humanity in a variety of ways. The story comes alive through hearing, seeing, praying, conversation, and even creating. Adult learners have a variety of preferred learning styles. This course recognizes that people do not learn and take in information in exactly the same way. So, each session employs teaching and learning options to engage the visual, auditory, and kinesthetic senses.

Visual learners learn best by seeing or drawing images that help them connect with the story. Two of the learning segments of the greatest story will be especially helpful to visual learners. Joe Castillo's dramatic sand art presentations on the DVD (Picturing the Story) will likely captivate all participants, but this is especially true of learners in this category. The Creative Corner options will give participants a chance to experience the story through creative reflection, including making drawings, videos, Bible character resumes, and a variety of other visual representations of the story.

Use the Creative Corner options to engage the kinesthetic, or tactile, participants who learn best by doing or moving around. It is often hard for these learners to sit still for long periods of time because they prefer movement to sitting listening to a lecture. These learners may also prefer to physically act out one of the story scripts when reading it.

Auditory learners are those who learn through the sense of hearing. Each session begins with some form of storytelling. Because not all participants will read the story summaries in the participant book ahead of time, it is crucial that the session begin with a telling of the story. Everyone loves a good story, especially if it is told in a compelling way.

This course has two equally important goals: (1) to provide an overview of the Bible story and (2) to connect the greatest story with our story. God's Word comes alive in the gathered community. First we hear the story. Then we reflect upon what it draws out of each of us. Together, our shared stories carry meaning and combine to build and strengthen faith.

The story of faith told in the Bible also comes through in the songs and prayers found in the psalms. Each session ends with an invitation to hear God's people speak through these ancient prayers and songs. We hear joy, sadness, anger, celebration and invitations to remember God's mighty deeds. And as we listen to and speak these words we are reminded that the greatest story is experienced in private times of devotion and in public times of worship.

Each learning component works in its own way to more deeply connect us to the greatest story.

A word about Bibles

Each session of the greatest story includes suggested Bible readings. Encourage all participants to have a Bible, or purchase a number of copies of the same Bible for participants to use during the course.

A study bible would work best with this course. Study Bibles generally contain overviews of the Old and New Testaments, introductions to groups of books (such as the Pentateuch) and individual books, as well as notes, maps, and other study tools.

This course uses the New Revised Standard Version (NRSV) of the Bible, but participants can use other translations that they find meaningful. They might also want to consult The Message, an interpretation of the Bible that many people find meaningful and easy to read.

The greatest story Leader Reference CD

The Leader Reference CD, designed for this course and other courses in the greatest story series, contains charts, maps, and other tools. Use this reference material as the story is told, project it during discussion, or incorporate it in handouts for group members.

Storytelling Tips

The first part of each core session includes a retelling of the portion of the greatest story covered in the participant book. As leader, you may choose to tell the story, or you may wish to choose a storyteller, or several storytellers, to tell the story. Suggested storytelling options are repeated in each session plan.

Here are a few general things to remember:

- Learn one or more of the story scripts well enough to be able to read it dramatically. Read over the script as many as five or six times until you can feel the story coming alive within you. As you read it over and over, increase your excitement for the high points of the story and your sense of anticipation during the lower points. Highlight key parts or images of the story so that you can see them coming as you read and be prepared to emphasize them. Allow your excitement and anticipation to show through your reading.
- Try reading the story breathing from your abdomen and not just from your lungs. Put your hand on your stomach and breathe in and out as deeply as you can. This is where your voice needs to come from.
- An interesting effect can be created by having different voices read the narrative. Alternate by sentence, by paragraph, by change of subject, or by character focus. Or have one reader read the narrative all the way through and have a second reader do the same. Different voices with different inflections may help listeners to hear different parts of the story in different and revealing ways!
- Have participants get comfortable enough to listen well, but not so comfortable that they might be tempted to doze off. This means sitting with backs straight, both feet on the floor and arms in a relaxed position hanging at one's side or resting gently in the lap. Some listeners may want to look directly at the storyteller. Others may want to close their eyes and picture the story in their minds. Either way, the key to good listening is to tune out all other noise and thoughts and focus on the story.
- You can invite listeners to focus on the physical elements of the story. What muscles did the characters engage? How did your muscles feel during and after the reading?
- Invite listeners to focus on the spiritual elements in the story. How did they see the Holy Spirit working through the story characters? How did they feel the Spirit working in themselves during the hearing of the story?
- Ask listeners to focus on the emotional elements of the story. How were they feeling as the story was read? How do they think the characters in the story were feeling? Why? Did listeners feel any discomfort in their bodies? Where? Why?
- Ask listeners to focus on the intellectual elements of the story. What do they think the different characters in the story were thinking? What were the listeners thinking? Why? Where might such thinking lead the listeners? Where did it lead the characters in the story?
- Suggest that the listeners use their senses to really get a sense of being there in the story. What did they see? hear? smell? taste? touch?
- Put another twist on the senses by narrating the story with appropriate background music. Or with total silence. Take a walk or project images as the story is told. Provide appropriate odors or taste appropriate foods. Pass around an object relevant to the story to be seen, smelled, tasted, felt.

THE SESSION PLAN AT A GLANCE

Each session in this leader guide will provide a Core Session plan and an Our Story conversation plan.

Core Session (60 minutes)

- *Gathering (10 minutes)*
  - Think of yourselves as fellow sojourners through the Bible. Coming together each week offers an opportunity to reconnect with each other prior to reconnecting with God's greatest story. Take time for a welcome and quick catch-up, which might include sharing insights from the suggested Mark It Bible readings.
  - Now take a few moments to share the session overview that links last week's session to this week's.
- *Telling the Story (15 minutes)*
  - Each session starts with Scripture and prayer to center learners in God's Word. A designated storyteller(s) will also tell or read the story at the beginning of each session. This is an important part of the class because you will be hearing the story in community, where God's Word is meant to be heard. Before moving on to Picturing the Story, give participants a few moments to share initial reactions and questions raised by the story.
- *Picturing the Story (20 minutes)*
  - Following the hearing of the story learners will have the unique opportunity of seeing sand artist Joe Castillo tell the story through his free-flowing sand art. This is an incredible and moving way to actually see the story unfold before your eyes.
  - You'll want to encourage conversation each week about how this particular segment touched each person. Additional reflection questions are provided to help participants respond to the segment of the story featured in the session.
- *Singing and Praying the Story (10 minutes)*
  - The selected psalms touch on themes addressed in the session. Be sure to read one or both of these aloud either responsively as a group or by a solo reader. Additional instructions for doing this are given in each session.
- *Looking Ahead (5 minutes)*
  - Many participants will want to know where they are headed next. This segment gives you an opportunity to introduce the next session briefly, and encourage participants to do the Mark It Bible reading activity for the week and read the suggested introductory material in a study Bible.

Our Story (45-60 minutes)

This time for group conversation and discussion may immediately follow the Core Session or be offered at different times and locations.

- *Welcome (5-10 minutes)*
  - Provide refreshments if appropriate.
  - Begin with prayer.
  - Invite general questions and observations from the Core Session.

- *Conversation (40-50 minutes)*
    - Have the participants discuss the questions found in the participant book in order to connect them to the story in more intimate ways.
- *Creative Corner (optional)*
    - Since some learners learn best by hands-on experiences, this segment offers an opportunity to do just that! If hands-on creativity isn't one of your strengths, consider recruiting someone else in the group to lead Creative Corner activities. You may substitute the Creative Corner activity for the Conversation, or extend the session further.

COURSE PLANNER

Any successful adult course offering requires advance planning. Here are a number of key things to keep in mind. Start early and invite others to share these tasks.

Leadership and recruitment

The leadership role is an important one for any course. Because the greatest story is a Bible introduction, it will be helpful for the leader to have some prior experience with the Bible. But leading this course does not require someone who is a biblical scholar. The leader's role deals with coordinating and facilitating. Assuring that the story is told is important, but being able to draw out the questions, wisdom, and thoughts of the group is key. Good leadership also requires knowing your particular context and recognizing what elements of the course need to be adapted for your setting. Pay attention to the options this course offers.

Here are some additional roles and characteristics of a good facilitator:

- Exhibits excellent listening skills and the ability to pay attention to group dynamics.
- Recognizes who is and isn't participating in group discussions and gracefully invites each person into the conversation without forcing anyone to participate.
- Synthesizes and summarizes discussions for the group.
- Moves the group along when it appears to be stuck.

While the leadership of class sessions can be divided among two or more people, the course leader will be the one to coordinate these responsibilities and involve others as needed. The course offers a variety of ways that others can be invited to share in leadership. Some of the roles that others might share include:

- *Small group discussion facilitators*
  If your group is large you'll need more than one small group facilitator. Optimal small group size is six to ten people. Pay attention to the list of roles and characteristics of a good facilitator when looking for someone to lead a small group. You don't want someone who will dominate and lecture the group. You'll need someone who is more skilled at listening and moving the conversation along. Share the "Guidelines for Small Group Discussion" (p. 17) with small group leaders to help them focus on their task. Connect with each small group leader on a regular basis to make sure he or she feels comfortable. Checking in also offers an opportunity to find out how the group is getting along.

- *Storytellers*
  People recruited as storytellers should be encouraged to be expressive when reading the story scripts. Be sure to copy and give each storyteller the list of storytelling tips (p. 10) to guide them. Encourage storytellers to practice telling the story several times prior to the class so that it will feel more natural.

- *Hospitality providers or coordinators*
  Invite people to play the role of hospitality coordinators prior to the start of the class, or play this role yourself the first time and ask for volunteers who would like to serve in this capacity. See the Hospitality section in this guide (p. 15) for additional ideas.

- *Invitations and course promotion*
  When selecting someone to handle invitations and course promotion be attentive to selecting those with good communication skills. Discuss the Inviting section of this leader guide (p. 14) with whoever serves as the communications person.

Scheduling the course

The Greatest Story: Bible Introduction offers flexibility and options for scheduling. The Core Session and Our Story conversation time can be offered back-to-back with a short break for refreshments, or these two main segments can be split up. The Core Session might be offered at a time when it is easiest for the largest number of people to be in attendance, such as a Sunday morning. In a split scenario, the Our Story conversation could take place later in the week and be flexible according to the needs of each particular small group. Small groups may meet at church, in homes, or in welcoming, comfortable public places.

Strongly encourage each participant to commit to being part of a small group conversation with six to ten people. This is where the greatest story can really come alive in the sharing of personal stories. But consider your specific context and the option that will work best for you. If you have already identified a group of participants who plan to attend this course, you might include them in a conversation about when it is best to schedule the sessions.

Items to consider when scheduling the course:

- Is it more effective to offer the Core Session and Our Story conversation back-to-back or in split sessions? How might split sessions affect young adult and adult participation in your particular context?
- What are the advantages and disadvantages of offering all or part of the course in a member's home?
- If meeting in a home for all or part of the course, will there be sufficient parking for the group?
- If meeting in a home for all or part of the course, will you stick with one location or rotate to other members' homes in order to share the hosting responsibilities?
- Check the church calendar to make sure the class doesn't conflict with major events or meetings.
- If offered at the church, consider context specific situations such as days or nights when the building might be in use by outside groups.
- Check the church sign-out sheet for audiovisual equipment to assure that a DVD player and TV will be available for your sessions.

- Will you provide babysitting for participants' young children? Consider soliciting youth group members to offer babysitting. Be sure to follow your church's child safety policies and procedures in doing this.
- Include the pastor and other congregational leaders in the scheduling conversation.

Inviting participants

Often when congregations offer a class or program the only "inviting" they do is through the Sunday bulletin and monthly newsletter. While these are important ways of getting the word out, don't forget about more personal invitations, especially to new members, those not previously involved in the adult education program in your church, and friends outside the congregation.

Here are some things to consider when promoting the course:

- Be sure the pastor is included in the promotion process. Solicit his or her ideas regarding whom you might personally invite and about other ways you might invite those in the church and community. Ask for a list of recent new members and anyone in a new members class and personally invite them to the class.
- Announce the class on your congregation's outdoor marquee to attract community attention. Hang or post a large banner announcing the class on the church property weeks in advance of the start of the course.
- Hang posters in the church announcing the class. Inquire about hanging a poster in your local grocery store. In many areas grocery stores permit nonprofit groups to hang posters.
- Post information about the class on the congregation's Web site.
- Get the word out further by posting information on your congregation's Facebook page. Include a link on Twitter. Don't have a Facebook page or congregational Twitter account? Get one! These are great ways to witness to the Internet community and they're free!
- Hold a congregational and community storytelling event with an experienced biblical storyteller. Promote the class as part of the event. To locate an experienced biblical storyteller visit the Web site of The Network of Biblical Storytellers International (www.nbsint.org).
- Announce information about the class in worship, emphasizing that this is a biblical overview for those new to Bible study, but it's also a great refresher and big-picture look at the Bible.

Promotional sample

Everybody loves a great story. In the Bible God has given us the greatest story ever told! It's a tale of God's love and faithfulness throughout the generations. Come join us as we take a look at The Greatest Story: Bible Introduction. In sixteen sessions you'll get a complete overview of the story and message of the Bible. This class is great for both those unfamiliar with Bible study and for those who want a refresher.

Join us beginning on XXX from XXX -XXX . Call or e-mail XXX at XXX for more information or to join the class.

Hospitality

In any kind of small group setting one of the most important things to tend to is hospitality. This helps create a warm, welcoming environment in which members of your group can relax and get to know each other. That's called building community! You also want people to feel comfortable so they'll return each week and perhaps even invite a friend to join them.

The first task is to secure a setting for the class that is welcoming for everyone—whether it is at the church or in a member's home. Make sure there will be good lighting and comfortable seats arranged so all can see and participate in the conversation. You'll want a location that is free from noise and distractions.

Be sure someone is designated to greet people as they arrive each week and to offer name tags so participants get to know each other. The course leader could serve in this capacity, or another person could be designated as hospitality coordinator with the task of greeting people and coordinating refreshments. Ask the group if they'd like to sign up to bring light refreshments each week and pass around a sign-up sheet if they do. Another option is to ask participants to donate a small amount of money so the hospitality coordinator can buy light, healthy snacks each week.

Here are some other things to consider:

- Provide healthy food options for refreshments. Check with the class to see if anyone has special dietary needs. Are there diabetics or gluten intolerant people in the group?
- Check with the group to see if anyone has environmental concerns such as allergies to strong perfume. If meeting in a home with pets, check to see if anyone has pet allergies.
- Provide babysitting so couples with young children can attend.
- If you decide to meet in a small group in someone's home, consider meeting at the church and traveling together so everyone feels at ease with the transition from church to an unfamiliar home.
- If you are hosting a small group in your home, pretend you are a first time visitor and walk around the room you'll be gathering in to see if there are any distractions or odors that might bother others.
- Tend to the room setting so all can see the DVD player. You might consider moving into a circle for discussion so everyone can see and hear each other.
- Does your particular context offer hospitality challenges? If so, what are they and how can you overcome them?
- Ask participants to silence their cell phones prior to the start of each session.

Leading small groups

In *Starting Small Groups—and Keeping Them Going* (Augsburg Fortress, 1995), authors Rochelle Melander and Harold Eppley point out that small groups aren't content-oriented but instead are focused on the relationships that develop within them. Just as God's relationship with humanity is central in the greatest story, relationships are central in small groups too. The relationships within the group must be tended regularly in healthy and appropriate ways. Remember that each small group will take on its own identity because connections and bonds will be different in each one.

Leadership in a healthy small group is actually shared among the members, though some common roles need to be acknowledged in each group. First, someone needs to lead, or facilitate, the group. This person coordinates the group and oversees advancing the conversation through asking questions and soliciting follow-up from group members. He or she may also summarize the conversation to draw it to an end. The facilitator will pay attention to the flow and tone of the conversation to ensure each person is respected and that things don't get heated or out of hand. For additional tips and practical advice see the DVD called *Leading in Faith: Guiding the Conversation* (Augsburg Fortress, 2009).

Participants have an active role, too, since they produce and take part in the majority of the conversation. As they engage in the discussion, they need to respect other group members and their stories by quietly listening when others are speaking. Have small group leaders go over the Guidelines for Small Group Discussion (p. 17) when small groups meet initially.

Guidelines for Small Group Discussion

- Remember that small groups are intended to provide a safe place for conversation and discussion.
- Maintain confidentiality in small groups in order to build trust and healthy relationships. Keeping communication confidential means not sharing the details of a person's story without his or her permission. The course or session leader should remind the group of confidentiality at the beginning of each session—especially if a new person has joined the group.
- Facilitators should encourage conversation among members, not dominate the group. A good facilitator will keep the flow of the conversation going.
- Small group members honor each person's story or opinion by listening respectfully and asking thoughtful questions to learn more about the speaker's perspective. It is never appropriate to attack another group member for saying something with which you don't agree.
- Stories that are shared among group members should be appropriate and not violate anyone else's confidentiality or be injurious to anyone.
- Provide an opportunity for each group member to engage in the conversation but never force anyone to participate.
- At the end of each group session have a group check-in to ask how the members thought things went. This also offers an opportunity to solicit ongoing feedback.

Celebrating milestones

Celebrating milestones in your group's time together keeps people connected to each other and to the process. You'll want to be sure to do this to keep participants engaged in all sixteen sessions. That's a lot of time to commit to a study, and you run the risk of losing people over time.

The most obvious milestone is the transition from the Old Testament to the New Testament. However, if your group is really into celebrating you could also divide the sixteen sessions into four units and celebrate after you've completed each unit. You might also create a simple chart and color in each of the books of the Bible as you've completed the sessions. This will give participants a visual of how far they've actually come in their biblical overview. Consider polling the group at your first session to see which option members prefer.

Here are some suggestions for how to celebrate milestones:

- Create a chart of the Bible and color in each book after it's been covered. Another option is to do this in the form of a timeline.
- Invite a local biblical storyteller to tell a story from the Old Testament to the class in the transition from the Old to New Testaments. Seeing someone who has internalized a story can have a dramatic effect on people. Check the directory of the Network of Biblical Storytellers International at their Web site (www.nbsint.org) for storytellers to invite.
- Serve refreshments from biblical times to celebrate. Early in the course, invite one or two people to do a little research into foods from biblical times. Then ask for volunteers to sign up to bring a food item for your celebration.
- At the transition from the Old to the New Testament and at the end of the class take time to reflect on and talk about which Bible story each person felt most connected to. Consider taping this to share with others either in worship or during a special event. This is a great way to spark interest in the Bible and encourage others to attend future sessions!
- Brainstorm with your group to come up with your own celebration ideas.
- Consider "commissioning" and saying prayers in worship for groups as they begin the course. Celebrate and give certificates of recognition to those who complete the course.

Evaluating the course

When offering any educational event it is always important to spend some time evaluating the process, the course material, and the group experience itself. This gives you the chance to see what worked and what might be tweaked the next time the course is offered.

You can also engage in regular ongoing evaluation by having a check-in at the end of each session. You might simply ask how people experienced the session that day. Ask whether or not they have suggestions for future sessions based on this one. Encouraging them to engage in regular evaluation not only builds group identity, but you might get some valuable input, too! It's also a good idea for the course leader to spend time after each session evaluating both their effectiveness as a leader and how things appear to be going in the group. Here are some questions to help you focus:

- How did today's session go? What went well? What might be tweaked?
- Are all members of the group actively participating in the conversation? (Pay attention to body language, which will indicate how engaged quieter group members are. Remember you don't need to talk all the time to be actively engaged in a group conversation.)
- Are there any questions that came up today that I might need to research further?
- Have I checked-in with other small group leaders or hospitality people to see if they have questions or need additional support?
- Has anything occurred within the dynamics of the class that the pastor needs to be notified of?
- What additional support or guidance do I need to more effectively do my job as coordinator?

Consider making an evaluation form that can be handed out to all participants so they have some time for reflection. Here are some questions you can use at the end of the class to evaluate the sessions:

- What did you like the most about this class? What would you have changed?
- How has this class changed the way you think about or approach the Bible?
- How has the greatest story transformed the way you see your story being lived out? How have you been transformed?
- If we offer this course again, would you consider being involved as a leader in some capacity? If so, how?

Offering the course again

The greatest story offers people who are not very familiar with the Bible an opportunity to get more accustomed to its stories, witness, and overarching theme of God's love and faithfulness for God's people. Plan to offer this course more than once as a starting point for people to engage in Bible exploration. Imagine a congregation of people transformed by how God's story is active in each of their lives! Who doesn't want to invite that to happen?

Here are some ideas on how to keep the course going:

- Check with the pastor to see if current class members can give one (or more) announcements during worship on what they are learning in the class about the greatest story and how it is transforming their lives. Invite members who might be interested in learning more about the course to contact them.
- Create a video highlighting comments from class members. Play the video in worship or other settings as a way to encourage interest in the course.
- Enlist someone from the class to write regular newsletter articles about what you're learning together. Ideas can be brainstormed at the end of the class or you can use some of the ongoing evaluation comments, but be sure to get permission before you publish others' comments.

- Speak with the pastor and develop a list of people he or she thinks might be interested in participating in this course. Make personal invitations to each one.
- Invite those participating in new member classes to join in the course. Let them know when you plan to offer it.
- Ask each member of the current class to identify and contact someone who they think might enjoy the course. Remind them this doesn't have to be someone who is already a church member! Make sure each person reports back by a designated time.
- Solicit the participation of current class members to assist with future classes. They might serve as small group leaders, promotions people, or work with hospitality. Someone who has already been through the course might also consider serving as a course leader.

Additional Resources

Here are some additional resources you may find helpful in planning or implementing the course, or in going deeper once the course is completed.

- Check with your pastor and in your church library for Bible commentaries, concordances, dictionaries, and other reference material that you might find helpful to use in your preparation.
- Visit the Web site of the Network of Biblical Storytellers International (www.nbsint.org) for additional storytelling resources. For example, see *How to Tell and Learn a Bible Story: Step by Step Instruction,* a DVD by the Network of Biblical Storytellers (NBS Productions) and *Let the One Who Has Ears to Hear, Hear*, a "how-to" DVD with instructions for telling biblical stories by Tracey Radosevic and Thelma Thomas at www.nbsint.org/store.
- The *Leading in Faith Series* includes instructional DVDs called *Guiding the Conversation* and *Foundational Training* (Augsburg Fortress, 2009) for anyone teaching the Bible.
- *Starting Small Groups—And Keeping Them Going*, edited by Rochelle Melander and Harold Eppley (Augsburg Fortress, 1995). This is an older resource but filled with helpful small group leadership ideas.
- *Story Journey: An Invitation to the Gospels as Storytelling* by Thomas E. Boomershine (Abingdon Press, 1988).
- *The Bible in Ancient and Modern Media: Story and Performance* (Biblical Performance Criticism) edited by Holly E. Hearon and Philip Ruge-Jones (Cascade Books, 2009).

THE STORY
Introducing the Bible

1

The story behind the greatest story

SESSION PREPARATION

OVERVIEW

Stories are powerful. They both shape us and give us an identity. The Bible is God's story of love for humanity. Through it we learn about God's intense desire for a two-way relationship with us. It's also our story because it continues and lives through us today. This session provides an overview of the Bible and its story to help you and your learners begin to explore the greatest story ever told.

Materials for this session available on the Leader Reference CD:

- Bible History Timeline (CHART)
- Different Canons of the Hebrew Bible (Old Testament) (CHART)

Scenes in this Session

Tell Me a Story
The Bible Has a Story, Too
The Bible Is God's Story
The Bible Is Our Story
Your Part in the Greatest Story

What's the Story?

The story of the Bible started the way most stories we're familiar with start—by being spoken by one person to another. Most of the Old Testament stories were told for generations before they were recorded by authors inspired by God to record them. Even the New Testament stories about Jesus were shared several decades before they were recorded. An important detail to remember about how these stories were written is that the authors of these texts were each influenced by what was happening in their own culture and time period. That means when we study the books of the Bible we need to also know a little about the time in which they were written.

STORY KEYS

- The Bible is God's greatest story.
- The Bible developed over 1,000 years and was told before it was written down.
- The Old Testament focuses on God's promises to the Israelites.
- The center of the New Testament is Jesus, God's son.
- We're part of the greatest story, too.

Once these books were recorded they underwent a process called *canonization* in which the church, inspired by the Holy Spirit, made the decision to include them in one volume called the *Bible*. The word *Bible* originates from a Greek word meaning "books." The books of the Old Testament were collected into a canon over centuries, with the books being gathered into the Jewish Tanakh, which had three main sections: Torah (the Law), Prophets, and Writings. Though the books belonging to these categories don't match up with what we would call the Protestant Old Testament, the content of the books is the same. The Jewish Scriptures were the Scriptures of Jesus and his followers. The canon of New Testament books was debated for centuries. The list of twenty-seven books we currently include is the same list that church leader Bishop Athanasius named in his Easter letter in 367 C.E.

God speaks to humanity through the Bible. That makes it a holy collection of writings. And although each of the books was written by a human being, they are God's Word because it was God's Holy Spirit that inspired each person to write the words. Most importantly, for Christians, the Bible points to Jesus Christ as God's revelation of love for all humankind.

We call the Bible a book of faith because it originates from faith communities inspired to collect these writings to create one holy book. We also read it in faith with the expectation that it will transform us and give us a new identity as the children of God. It is read for faith because it is meant to be shared. After all, that is how it all started—one person telling another. The story comes alive as it is shared.

What's the Message?

The central message of the greatest story reveals the depth of God's desire to be in relationship with humanity and the whole creation. The story begins with the relationship established in creation. Humanity is created in the image of God, but the story also reminds us that sin deeply affects this relationship established at creation. We share the struggle that all human beings have experienced throughout time. We rebel against God and bring pain to one another and to God's good creation. How can the relationship we have with God and with one another be restored? That's the key plotline in the story. God is concerned about restoring and healing all of creation, and God calls on humanity to help with this restoration.

The Old Testament focuses on God's relationship with the Israelites and the promises made to them. Its message is recorded in a variety of forms. The thirty-nine books of the Old Testament are comprised of the Pentateuch, Historical Books, Writings, and Prophets. The first five books of the Bible comprise the Pentateuch, which is also called the Torah (translated as "law" or "teaching") by Jewish people. It begins with creation and winds through the wilderness journey of the Israelites to the promised land. The Historical Books begin with the entry of the Israelites into the promised land and tell of the eventual fall of Israel to control by the Persians. The books of Ruth and Esther are additions that focus on women who made a difference in the lives of the Israelites.

The Writings of the Old Testament include everything from liturgies and prayers in the Psalms to love poetry in Song of Solomon, and the wisdom literature of Job, Proverbs, and Ecclesiastes that deals with issues of daily living.

Finally, the books of the Prophets record the messages that God has called specific people to deliver to the people of God at certain times in history.

The New Testament focuses on the revelation of God's love for humanity made known through Jesus Christ, God's son. It tells the incredible story of Jesus' birth, ministry, death, and resurrection. God came in the flesh to restore the relationship between God and all creation that sin and evil seek to destroy.

The Gospels record the story of the "good news" about Jesus and his ministry on earth. Acts picks up following Jesus' resurrection and ascension, and records the start of the early church and its gradual spread. This is followed by the Letters of Paul which are actually the earliest writings of the New Testament. These are Paul's letters of support to the churches that he helped birth as he traveled from place to place. They deal with contextual issues that each church faced. Not all of the letters attributed to Paul were actually written by him.

Finally, the New Testament includes the General Letters written as the church struggled to acknowledge that it lived in the time in between Jesus' resurrection and his promised second coming. These were not addressed to any specific church or group. Instead they were intended for a much more general audience.

MATERIALS NEEDED

- Extra copies of the Bible
- Participant books
- Computer or DVD player; projector or TV monitor
- Course DVD
- Reference materials
- Creative Corner materials (optional)
- Name tags
- Refreshments (optional)

PREPARE

1. Review chapter 1 in the participant book.
2. Review the overview and session plan for session 1 in the leader guide.
3. Watch the DVD segment for session 1.
4. Have extra Bibles available for those who did not bring one.
5. Have equipment for projecting or viewing the DVD set up and ready to go.
6. Consider distributing handouts or projecting images of reference materials (see list on p. 21) in the session. You might want to do this during Telling the Story or while discussing the Background Files.
7. If you are having the class do the Creative Corner activity, gather any materials suggested.
8. Pray for your class members and for God's presence and guidance as you gather in God's Word.

LEADER PRAYER

O Loving God, in the Bible you presented us with your greatest story of hope and forgiveness. As I prepare for this first session inspire me with this story so that I discern how I am both part of it and transformed by it. Arouse within all participants in this class a holy curiosity and deep desire to engage in the greatest story. Amen.

CORE SESSION PLAN

The Core Session Plan is designed for use in one 60-minute period. The Core Session Plan can be extended 45-60 minutes by incorporating the group reflection time called Our Story, found at the end of the Core Session Plan. Suggestions for alternative settings and schedules are provided on page 13 of this guide.

GATHERING (10 MINUTES)

Welcome and check-in

Provide name tags as you welcome participants to the session. If you are serving refreshments, have them set out ahead of time. You might consider having participants introduce themselves briefly and ask them to share either why they have decided to participate in the class or one thing they hope to learn or take away from the class. Listen to and record the responses, but don't take time to comment. Use the expectation list to guide you as you prepare for later sessions. Before this time of sharing remind the class that it is OK to "pass" on sharing their expectations.

Scripture and prayer

Read the following verse and prayer, or ask a volunteer to do so.

. . . so shall my word be that goes out from my mouth; it shall not return to me empty, but it shall accomplish that which I purpose, and succeed in the thing for which I sent it. (Isaiah 55:11)

O God of power and purpose, as we begin our study of your greatest story may your Holy Spirit open our hearts and minds to be transformed by your word. Guide us in discovering how we, too, are part of this story of your continuing love. In Jesus' name we pray. Amen.

TELLING THE STORY (15 MINUTES)

You or your designated storyteller should now turn to telling the portion of the story that is highlighted in session 1. Incorporate any or all of the Background File notes in the participant book (p. 15) as part of the telling. Use one of the following three options for telling the story, or devise your own.

See the storytelling tips on p. 10 of this guide.

1. Read through, summarize, and comment on the story as provided in the participant book.
2. Ask for volunteers to tell portions of the story.
3. Read the story script provided below.

At the end of the storytelling time, summarize the Story Keys for this session.

The Story Script for Session 1

"Let me tell you a story." These six words can silence any size crowd. Why? Because each listener knows that what follows will ignite curiosity and illuminate imaginations. Family stories, fictional stories, even historical stories immediately grab our attention and help us explore and make sense of the world as it once was, as it is, and as it might become.

Each one of us has a story that is interwoven with the stories of others, both past and present. Our shared stories reveal who we are and what is true about ourselves. Our stories are intersected by the greatest story of all, the Bible, which gives us profound new truth about our own stories and about how we can live our lives in relationship with God and with one another.

The Story Script for Session 1 (continued)

The Bible was not simply dropped from the sky. Imagine sitting around a fire hearing a story about a young shepherd boy (David) taking down a towering giant (Goliath) with a slingshot! The stories and other writings of the Bible first circulated verbally long before they were written down. These stories were written down much later on scrolls of papyrus and reed by many different people over a span of about one thousand years.

The Bible is like a library with books expressing God's experiences with the Jewish community (Old Testament) and God's experiences with the Christian community (New Testament). No one recorded an account of Jesus' life, death, and resurrection while these events were occurring, so even these stories were passed along by word of mouth. The letters of the Apostle Paul were the first to be written in the New Testament in the 50s C.E., or about twenty to thirty years after Jesus lived. The Gospels came even later and probably were written somewhere between the years 70 and 90 C.E.

Eventually, both the Hebrew Scriptures and the books and letters being used by various Christian communities were gathered together into a single canon. *Canon* is the word used to describe the list of accepted writings that became authoritative for the life and teachings of the church. It took nearly three hundred years for a final canon to be agreed upon. In 367 C.E., the bishop Athanasius offered a list of 27 books he thought had the proper authority to be included in the New Testament. This is the New Testament we know today.

Bibles, however, may vary in their content. Protestant Bibles contain 39 Old Testament books and 27 New Testament books. Roman Catholic and Orthodox Bibles include additional books known as the Apocrypha.

The Bible is God's story, the powerful Word of God, and it centers around Jesus Christ. The Bible inspires trust and faith in Christ, even as it demands and judges, forgives and hopes. In the Old Testament the focus is on the people of Israel, the promises God made to them, and how these chosen people lived between the tension and hope of salvation.

The New Testament continues this story of God's loving relationship with humanity. God's love and fullness are seen in the life, ministry, death, and resurrection of Jesus. Jesus is God come in the flesh to overcome sin and death and restore our relationship with God, with other people, with ourselves, and with the whole creation.

The Story Script for Session 1 (continued)

When Jesus left this earth, he sent the Holy Spirit to empower the early Christians to tell the good news and to perform signs and wonders. Passionate followers like Paul wrote down what they felt inspired to preach and teach about Jesus. So powerful were these words that they have continued to come alive for generation upon generation ever since. God is still speaking to us!

In the book of Genesis we hear that human beings are created "in the image of God." This means that from the beginning of creation the Bible tells the story of God's relationship with us. We all come from God and share in God's life-giving concern for creation and for one another.

However, from the story of Adam and Eve on, we learn that God is perfect, but we are not. The people we meet in the Bible are both heroically faithful and painfully unfaithful. This unfaithfulness we call sin.

The Bible tells the story of God's people who are challenged and who struggle; who are self-absorbed and self-giving; who worship God and then forget God while going their own way. This is the way the world really is as communities of faith struggle to be faithful in becoming the people of God.

As a very human book, the Bible calls us to pick up the story, live it, and pass it on. As we respond to God's Spirit, the voices of the mentors and teachers of the Bible become our voices, living and relevant to life in the twenty-first century. In God becoming human in Jesus Christ we gain a picture of what this might look like for us.

Are you ready to enter the story and meet the living God? Absolutely no qualifications are needed, except the desire to discover your life all over again. Who are we? Who do we belong to? What is the purpose of life? These are the kinds of questions you will engage in as the greatest story comes alive for you.

Here are the stories of people like us who yearn for the presence of God who loves us, no matter what. God's Spirit is awaiting your encounter with this story and will help you to set aside your fears and hear the story of awe and wonder, of healing and peace. This is God's story. It is also our story starting with "In the beginning . . ."

PICTURING THE STORY (20 MINUTES)

Briefly introduce the reflection questions listed in this section in the participant book (p. 15). Then play the segment called The Story (session 1) on the course DVD. Encourage the participants to watch the story unfold as artist Joe Castillo depicts the scenes of the story. Participants may be invited to write down their own questions.

When the segment is done, address the questions together as a large group, or ask the participants to discuss in smaller teams. Invite participants to share their own questions or observations. What difference did it make to see the story in this way?

SINGING AND PRAYING THE STORY (10 MINUTES)

Use one or both of the psalms provided in the participant book to help address the story and its themes. Psalms are best read aloud. You may have one volunteer read the entire psalm or portion of a psalm. Or you may wish to have the psalm read responsively, verse by verse or line by line. Use a solo reader with the group responding, or read responsively using different groups.

As time allows, discuss the observations and questions provided.

Psalm 119:73-80, 105-112 is an instructional psalm celebrating God's laws and commandments. It is also an acrostic psalm. (The lines in an acrostic psalm begin with consecutive letters in the Hebrew alphabet.) Here the psalmist thanks God for the ability to know and understand God's commandments and to live within their precepts. Even when struggling and afflicted, the writer clings to God's word as a light to illumine the darkness.

Psalm 29 is a hymn of praise celebrating God's glory and power over nature. God's voice can shake the wilderness and transform creation. The psalm ends with a request that God bless the people with strength and peace.

LOOKING AHEAD (5 MINUTES)

You are encouraged to do the "Mark it" exercise as well.

Mark it

Encourage participants to read and mark one or more of the passages listed in this section during the week ahead. Let the group know that at the start of next week's session you will ask volunteers to share any insights they have from this exercise.

You may find it helpful to take some notes or highlight items in the readings to share next week as part of Telling the Story.

Next time

Briefly introduce the next chapter of the story that appears in session 2. In the next session you will begin to explore the greatest story from the beginning with the stories in Genesis. To review this week's story and to help prepare for the next session, you and your group are encouraged to read introductions to the following in a study Bible:

- The Old Testament
- Pentateuch
- Genesis

OUR STORY

WELCOME

Whether done consecutively along with the Core Session Plan or planned for a separate time or location, consider providing hospitality in the form of refreshments.

- Arrange the room comfortably for small group discussion.
- Introduce newcomers in the group.
- Begin with prayer, using the session prayer on p. 25 or another prayer of your choice. Ask volunteers to provide prayers, if they feel comfortable doing so.
- You may wish to begin by asking if anyone has a particular question or thought to share from the large group session. As an alternative to discussing those questions, simply note them or write them down on newsprint. Small groups may decide to discuss further.

Ideas for optional settings and schedules for this time are provided in the introduction on page 13 of this leader guide.

CONVERSATION

The reflection questions are intended to help participants connect their own stories to the key themes of the greatest story. These questions can be used for personal reflection while reading or used to guide group discussion. It is unlikely a group could discuss all the questions in one discussion period. Don't be concerned about this. Here are some options for approaching the questions:

1. As leader, you may choose to focus on certain questions from the list.
2. Ask participants to suggest questions to discuss.
3. Divide the groups into smaller teams, assign the teams a designated number of questions to discuss, and then have each group report back to the large group.
4. If you have a group that has the time and interest, you could assign each participant a question or two to think about and prepare a response during the week. These responses could be shared as discussion starters when the group meets for Our Story discussion time.

See the tips for leading and participating in small group discussion on page 17 of this guide. Make available to all participants copies of the reproducible Guidelines for Small Group Discussion.

Questions and Responses

The questions below are designed with personal reflection and response in mind. They do not require a certain amount of prior knowledge in order to respond. Responses may vary according to individual insights and context. Even so, a few guiding thoughts are provided for some of the questions.

- *What is one of your favorite stories to tell?*

- *What is a favorite family story? Who first told you that story?*

- *How much do you feel you know about the Bible, the greatest story? (Don't worry if the answer is "little" or "nothing." We are here to discover it together.)*

Many people can feel insecure studying the Bible because it was written for and during times quite different than our own. Some parts of the Bible also tell stories and use imagery that are foreign to us. Reassure the class that together you'll be learning about some of the background that will help them have a better grasp of God's greatest story. But the important part is listening to the story and being open to how the Holy Spirit uses it to transform each hearer. It's not about how much you know or can remember; it's all about how God works through God's Living Word.

- *What, if anything, were you taught about how the Bible came to be?*

- *Early in your life, were you told stories from the Bible? If so, which ones? Who told these stories to you?*

- *Who is the best storyteller you know?*

Ask about the characteristics that make a good storyteller. What are some of the things people generally include? Encourage participants to think of all the many places they've heard stories told. These might include television, radio, and Internet, but can also include all the places their daily lives intersect with stories. Even places like work or church may be the source of the best storyteller someone knows.

- *How do writings or public documents become authoritative? Why do you think some books made it into the Bible and others did not?*

Ask the group to think about the other writings or documents that they think of as having authority in life. What are they and how did they become authoritative? Authority often comes from accepted practice or norms. This is one criterion for a book making it into the Bible. People used the book in worship and teaching. Authority also comes from reputation and experience. Books associated with Jesus' first apostles had authority. Authority derives from message. Books that focused on the true message about Jesus were considered authoritative. Those that did not have this central focus or seemed at odds with the accepted writings were not considered as authoritative.

Questions and Responses (continued)

- *What book or story has been powerful, even life-changing, for you? Why?*

- *How do you imagine God? Is God "out there"? Is God "here"? What difference does it make?*

Working through this course will give participants a big-picture view of God that may transform their current thoughts and feelings about how they imagine God. Give them an opportunity to discuss these questions now and consider returning to these same questions at the conclusion of the course. How have their thoughts changed as a result of their participation?

- *How would you describe the power of words? Can you think of a time when spoken or written words really affected you?*

- *Who is one of the most interesting people you have ever met? Why?*

- *What are some human behaviors that illustrate that we are complicated beings?*

Brainstorm with your group to produce a list. When you brainstorm, call out the first thing that comes to mind. After you're done, review the list for further discussion.

- *What are some of the biggest barriers preventing God's story from continuing into the next generation?*

As you reflect upon some of the barriers, think also about the possibilities open for your congregation to share the greatest story in ways that may be attractive to an Internet generation. How might you use social media tools to share God's story and how it intersects with ours?

- *What is your biggest question about God? What is your biggest question about life?*

- *What do you think is the biggest barrier for you in reading and understanding the Bible?*

- *Have you ever thought that you have a faith story worth telling? What would help you to tell your faith story?*

Provide colored markers, paper, construction paper, poster board, magazines, scissors, or other materials that may be used to complete this creative assignment.

Creative Corner

Depending on how your schedule is organized, you may wish to assign this activity for individuals or small groups.

Working individually or in pairs, ask participants to design/create their ideal Bible cover. Ask them to consider what colors seem most appropriate. What materials might the cover be made of? Would the cover have any images on it or not? How would their cover encourage readers to pick up the Bible and actually read it? Have them "pitch" their cover to the class, explaining their design decisions.

BEGINNINGS
Genesis

2

A God-created world . . . a God-formed people . . . two beginnings

SESSION PREPARATION

OVERVIEW

With an introduction to the Bible complete, it's time to dive into the story. Session 2 focuses on Genesis, the first chapter of the greatest story. Genesis is the first book of the section known as the Pentateuch, or the first five books of the Hebrew Scriptures. Genesis is filled with many great stories that set the stage for all that is to come.

Materials for this session available on the Leader Reference CD:

- Bible History Timeline (CHART)
- The Ancient Near East and Key Locations in Genesis (MAP)

Scenes in this Session

Creation! (Genesis 1)
Falling Up (Genesis 2–4)
Do Over! (Genesis 6–9)
A Promising Start (Genesis 12:1—25:18)
Family Feud (Genesis 25:19—36:43)
God's Dreamer (Genesis 37–50)

What's the Story?

The Bible begins at the beginnings. The dawn of creation when God's breath blew across the face of the darkness and spoke the universe into being. But that's not all the breathing God did. God breathed life, human life, into the dust of the newly formed earth and created people. That was the big beginning. But Genesis tells of a second beginning when God called and blessed a people, the family of Abram and Sarai. Why? So all the nations of the world might be blessed.

So, Genesis is really divided into two primary sections: Genesis 1–11 portrays the beginnings of the world, including creation, the fall into sin, and the flood and its aftermath. Genesis 12–50 tells the story of Israel's ancestors and is especially concerned to speak of God's promises to this family.

STORY KEYS

- God created the world and people, and called them good.
- God continues to call us to care for the earth.
- God called and blessed a people, the family of Abraham and Sarah, so they might be a blessing to the world.
- God works for good through the lives of real people who are both faithful and flawed.

Because this course will focus on the story as it is told, questions of Genesis authorship and dating will not be emphasized. If such questions arise, you will want to address them, but don't dwell on these issues. Keep the focus on the story itself.

Traditionally, Genesis and other books of the Pentateuch have been called the Books of Moses because Moses was the primary figure and suggested author. Moses does not appear in Genesis. Bible scholars today have a number of theories about who wrote Genesis and the other books of the Pentateuch. It is most likely that the stories and laws and genealogies we have in the Pentateuch were written and compiled much later than the time of Moses.

What's the Message?

Genesis provides a framework for understanding the great story of God and God's people. But it does not start with the chosen people. Rather it starts with creation. God's purposes—at work among the people of Israel and in Jesus Christ—have to do with all of God's good creation. "For God so loved the world . . ." (John 3:16).

God created the world and people, and called them good. In God's world sin and evil did not exist. Tragically, human beings did not trust God, and sin disrupted the life of God's good world. Relationships between God and people, between people and people, between people and their very selves, and even between people and the created world fell apart. Sin and evil became powerful forces at work in the life of the world.

God did not abandon the world, but promised to continue to shower blessings at every turn. Genesis continues by describing God's strategy to save a world broken by sin and evil. God chose to bless the family of Abraham and Sarah, so that all the families of the world would be blessed (Genesis 12:1-3). God chose one family as a means to save all families. This exclusive move (choosing one family) had an inclusive goal: salvation of the entire creation, both human and nonhuman.

In his book *The Gates of the Forest*, author Elie Weisel makes the statement: "God created [people] because [God] loves stories." This is what makes the story begun in Genesis and continued throughout the Bible so amazing. God's strategy to save the world and its people includes us. God works through real people who are both flawed and faithful. We see this clearly in the stories of the first family in Genesis. Abraham and Sarah and their descendants are not perfect. In fact, they are downright devious once in a while. But they display great faith as well.

God also continues to work though circumstances that appear to put God's strategy and God's promises at risk. Even though Joseph's brothers nearly killed him and thought they had gotten rid of him for good, God was at work in his life. And because God was with him, Joseph was able to help his family and the whole land of Egypt in its hour of need.

Focus on the Story Keys as you tell the story and help your group reflect on the meaning of the story in their lives. They are part of the story, and now that they have heard the beginning, they are in it for good!

PREPARE

1. Review chapter 2 in the participant book.
2. Review the Overview and Session Plan for session 2 in the leader guide.
3. Watch the DVD segment for session 2.
4. Have extra Bibles available for those who did not bring one.
5. Have equipment for projecting or viewing the DVD set up and ready to go.
6. Consider distributing handouts or projecting images of reference materials (see list on p. 33) in the session. You might want to do this during Telling the Story or while discussing the Background Files.
7. If you are having the class do the Creative Corner activity, gather any materials suggested.
8. Pray for your class members and for God's presence and guidance as you gather in God's Word.

MATERIALS NEEDED

- Extra copies of the Bible
- Participant books
- Computer or DVD player; projector or TV monitor
- Course DVD
- Reference Materials
- Creative Corner materials (optional)
- Name tags
- Refreshments (optional)

LEADER PRAYER

Gracious God, creator of the universe, thank you for your story, and thank you for including us in it. Be present with me in my preparation and be present with each participant as we come together to hear the greatest story and reflect on what it means in our lives. In Jesus' name. Amen.

CORE SESSION PLAN

The Core Session Plan is designed for use in one 60-minute period. The Core Session Plan can be extended 45-60 minutes by incorporating the group reflection time called Our Story, found at the end of the Core Session Plan. Suggestions for alternative settings and schedules are provided on page 13 of this guide.

GATHERING (10 MINUTES)

Welcome and check-in

Provide name tags again as you welcome participants to the session. If you are serving refreshments, have them set out ahead of time. Spend a few minutes asking if anyone wants to share any thoughts or insights from their personal "Mark it" reading for the week. You won't be able to spend much time on this, but hearing a couple of testimonials will encourage more in the group to make this weekly reading and devotional reflection a part of their routine.

Scripture and prayer

Read the following verse and prayer, or ask a volunteer to do so.

God saw everything that he had made, and indeed, it was very good. (Genesis 1:31)

Dear God, we give thanks that you have created us and the world we live in. We humbly pray that you would continue to shower your blessings on the land and seas. Help us to be wise caretakers of creation. We thank you also for choosing the family of Abraham and Sarah to bring your blessings to the world. Thank you for blessing us through them, and give us faith to be your people of promise today. Amen.

See the storytelling tips on p. 10 of this guide.

TELLING THE STORY (15 MINUTES)

You or your designated storyteller should now turn to telling the portion of the story that is highlighted in session 2. Incorporate any or all of the Background File notes in the participant book (p. 23) as part of the telling. Use one of the following three options for telling the story, or devise your own.

1. Read through, summarize, and comment on the story as provided in the participant book.
2. Ask for volunteers to tell portions of the story.
3. Read the story script provided below.

At the end of the storytelling time, summarize the Story Keys for this session.

The Story Script for Session 2

In the beginning God created the world, the universe, and everything therein. What God created was VERY GOOD. Wind and sea, sky and earth, human beings and animals, plants and fish, planets and stars were all created with holy precision and intricacy working together to provide the cycles of life. This was the perfect gift of God to human creatures, whom God made in his own image with the responsibility to care for this creation and to live wisely within it.

However, it seems that having been made "in God's image," human beings were tempted by another creature, the serpent, into wanting to be like God. This first sin led to consequences both bad and good. These first human beings were sent out of the special garden that God had given them to tend.

But there was good news too. God, who gave them the sacred gift of creation also continued to care for them outside the garden. God gave them clothing and provided the tools for growing their own food and caring for the earth and its creatures. The perfection of the Creator's gift remained while human beings learned how to live obediently as mortal creatures before the immortal and almighty Creator.

And what a learning experience it was. Murder, incest, and meddling with the "sons of God" made for a world God could no longer stomach. Still, the Creator could not give up on humanity. God drowned this world of sin in a great and mighty flood while saving Noah and his family. By raising this family up from the flood, all life could begin again. Along with the sign of the rainbow, God promised never to send a destroying flood again.

Generations upon generations of humans populated this fertile earth until God selected two people for a promising new chapter in the life of the world. God chose Abraham and Sarah in their old age to begin a family of blessing. God blessed them with generations upon generations of descendants carrying the blessing into the future.

By sheer miracle, at an age far past that for normal childbearing, Sarah and Abraham had a son named Isaac. And Isaac and his wife Rebekah had two sons, Esau and Jacob. Jacob, though the younger son, tricked his older brother and his father into giving him the blessing and the birthright of the firstborn son. Jacob then received that blessing first given to Abraham and Sarah.

Each bearer of the blessing was confronted by many challenges. Abraham was called to the brink of sacrificing his one and only son. Isaac was deceived by his wife Rebekah and son Jacob into favoring his secondborn son over his firstborn. Jacob was tricked by his father-in-law into marrying both his daughters. He had to restore his broken relationship with his brother Esau, and ultimately had to wrestle all night long with an angel of the Lord who broke Jacob's hip.

Jacob was renamed Israel, and his descendants would eventually be part of tribes named after his twelve sons. Jacob's sons got into a feud with their youngest brother, Joseph, whom Jacob adored, and who made no bones about sharing his dreams of wielding authority over his highly jealous older brothers. They were so jealous that they faked Joseph's death while actually selling him to traders who took him to Egypt, where they sold Joseph as a slave to an official named Potiphar, who served the Pharaoh of Egypt.

Joseph's life in Egypt took a nasty turn when Potiphar's wife accused Joseph of trying to seduce her. Though he was innocent, the episode landed Joseph in prison. But prison brought good fortune to Joseph as he became known as a fine interpreter of dreams. Based on his reputation he was summoned to interpret a dream of the Pharaoh, which Joseph correctly interpreted as the coming cycle of seven years of fruitful plenty followed by seven years of devastating drought.

With the skill of interpreting dreams Joseph landed the job of overseeing Egypt's entire food storage program. He was highly successful in storing an abundance of food that would feed the people throughout the drought. This success brought his deceitful brothers from distant drought-stricken Canaan to Egypt and right smack into the presence of Joseph. Joseph eventually revealed himself to his brothers who then brought their father Jacob to live with them under Joseph's care.

After Jacob's death, Joseph's brothers feared that he would retaliate for what they did to him many years earlier. Instead, Joseph told them how God worked through their bad behavior in order to bring a blessing to the whole family of Israel. God's promises continued alive and well through the lives of real human beings, both faithful and flawed.

PICTURING THE STORY (20 MINUTES)

Go through the reflection questions listed in this section in the participant book (p. 23). Then play the segment called Beginnings (session 2) on the course DVD. Encourage the participants to watch the story unfold as artist Joe Castillo depicts the scenes of the story. Participants may be invited to write down their own questions.

When the segment is done, address the questions together as a large group or ask the participants to discuss in smaller teams. Invite participants to share their own questions or observations. What difference did it make to see the story in this way?

SINGING AND PRAYING THE STORY (10 MINUTES)

Use one or both of the psalms provided in the participant book to help address the story and its themes. Psalms are best read aloud. You may have one volunteer read the entire psalm or portion of a psalm. Or you may wish to have the psalm read responsively, verse by verse or line by line. Use a solo reader with the group responding, or read responsively using different groups.

As time allows, discuss the observations and questions provided.

Psalm 8 is a psalm of creation. The psalmist is amazed by God's creation and wonders why God would care for human beings enough to give them a meaningful role within God's mission—to care for creation. God makes human beings the royalty of creation and gives them dominion over the works of God's hands. This dominion does not mean "dominate" creation in the sense of shaping it for our own selfish purposes. We can see the negative effects of that kind of dominion. Rather, we live in harmony with creation and use it wisely, so the gifts of creation can benefit all for today and future generations.

Psalm 32 is a prayer confessing sin and asking for forgiveness. It connects with both the story of the fall when sin entered the world and the story of the flood when God acted to give the earth and people a fresh start. Because "all have sinned and fall short of the glory of God" (Romans 3:23), God sent Jesus to justify us (make us right in God's eyes) by grace as a gift. The law reminds us that we sin, just as Adam and Eve first sinned. We confess our sins and seek forgiveness, knowing that we need God's grace and mercy.

LOOKING AHEAD (5 MINUTES)

Mark it

Encourage participants to read and mark one or more of the passages listed in this section during the week ahead. Let the group know that at the start of next week's session you will ask volunteers to share any insights they have from this exercise.

You may find it helpful to take some notes or highlight items in the readings to share next week as part of Telling the Story.

Next time

You are encouraged to do the readings as well.

In the next session we will see and hear about God's people on the move. To review this week's story and to help prepare for the next session, you and your group are encouraged to read introductions to the following in a study Bible:

- Pentateuch
- Exodus
- Leviticus
- Numbers
- Deuteronomy

OUR STORY

WELCOME

Ideas for optional settings and schedules for this time are provided in the introduction on page 13 of this leader guide.

Whether done consecutively along with the Core Session Plan or planned for a separate time or location, consider providing hospitality in the form of refreshments.

- Arrange the room comfortably for small group discussion.
- Introduce newcomers in the group.
- Begin with prayer, using the session prayer on p. 36 or another prayer of your choice. Ask volunteers to provide prayers, if they feel comfortable doing so.
- You may wish to begin by asking if anyone has a particular question or thought to share from the large group session. As an alternative to discussing those questions, simply note them or write them down on newsprint. Small groups may decide to discuss further.

CONVERSATION

See the tips for leading and participating in small group discussion on page 17 of this guide. Make copies of the reproducible Guidelines for Small Group Discussion available to all participants.

The reflection questions in the participant book are intended to help participants connect their own stories to the key themes of the greatest story. These questions can be used for personal reflection while reading or used to guide group discussion. It is unlikely a group could discuss all the questions in one discussion period. Don't be concerned about this. Here are some options for approaching the questions:

1. As leader, you may choose to focus on certain questions from the list.
2. Ask participants to suggest questions to discuss.
3. Divide the groups into smaller teams, assigning the teams a designated number of questions to discuss, and then have each group report back to the large group.

4. If you have a group that has the time and interest, you could assign each participant a question or two to think about and prepare a response during the week. These responses could be shared as discussion starters when the group meets for Our Story discussion time.

Questions and Responses

The questions below are designed with personal reflection and response in mind. They do not require a certain amount of prior knowledge in order to respond. Responses may vary according to individual insights and context. Even so, a few guiding thoughts are provided for some of the questions.

- *How do you see the stories of creation fitting with modern scientific theories about how the world was created?*

The key question about creation in Genesis is "Who created?" The key question about creation in modern scientific theories is "How?"

- *What's the most amazing thing to you about the world we live in?*

- *What do you think it means that people were called to "keep" the earth (2:15)?*

- *Describe your understanding of the relationship between Creator and creation (including human beings).*

Genesis makes it clear that God is the creator and we are the created ones. Sometimes we forget our place. Sometimes we view creation and human beings as utterly fallen and evil. Only when this evil is gone will God's vision of perfection return. But God's creation is good, and that includes human beings. In spite of sin and evil, God's creation has the capacity to bear great good and blessing.

- *Where do you see signs of the "upward fall" in the world? How can you stay "grounded" in your relationship with God? With others?*

The concept of "falling up," of trying to be like God, may be a new way of describing sin for many. It is a useful image when thinking also about God's purpose to redeem and bring salvation. We don't have to try to climb the ladder of salvation up to God. God in Christ comes down to us and by grace saves us. Living in this promise grounds us. Our relationships are strengthened and grounded also by prayer, worship, and treating others with kindness and mercy.

- *What do you think of God's "do-over"?*

Some may question how God could bring such a disaster on the world. Answering that question is not easy. God was clearly not pleased and exercised power as judge.

However, God did save humanity and creation from total destruction and promised not to do this again.

Questions and Responses (continued)

- *What does God's commitment to all nonhuman creatures mean for us?*

We share God's commitment. It's part of the caring for creation theme begun in Genesis 1.

- *How do you think we are doing caring for the gift of the earth?*

- *What do you think it means to be "called" by God?*

- *What promises affect or shape your life?*

- *What do you think the phrase "Blessed to be a blessing" meant to Abram and Sarai and their family? What does it mean for you?*

- *Name the ways Abram's and Sarai's faith was tested. How would you define "faith"?*

Their faith was tested in many ways. They were asked to leave home and family and travel to a strange land. They were asked to have faith in the promise of many descendants, even though they had no children and were beyond the normal age of childbearing. They were challenged by their own actions, including Abram allowing the Egyptian pharaoh to bring Sarai into his household as a potential mistress. God tested Abram by asking him to sacrifice his son Isaac.

- *Does it surprise you that God's promises got worked out through family members who feuded, tricked one another, and even lied to get what they wanted? Why or why not?*

Answers may vary. It is good news for us, because we know that God can work through us in spite of our weaknesses and faults.

- *God promised Jacob: "I am with you and will keep you wherever you go . . ." (28:15). How might this promise relate to your life?*

- *How would you describe the way God was at work in Joseph?*

Clearly God gave Joseph a unique gift of discernment. Joseph's relationship with God opened him to envisioning the present and the future in new ways.

- *How would you say God is at work in you?*

- *In what ways can bad circumstances be used for good? Have you ever experienced something like that?*

While we do not say that God causes bad things to happen, we acknowledge that God can work in the midst of these bad things.

Creative Corner

Depending on how your schedule is organized, you may wish to assign this activity for individuals or small groups.

How might you retell one or all of the "Beginnings" stories in Genesis in a creative way? You might consider drawing, sculpting, creating a photo gallery, silent movie video, scrapbook, cartoon, commercial ad, song, board game, contest, TV script, etc. Do this individually or work with one or more partners.

Provide colored markers, paper, construction paper, poster board, magazines, scissors, or other materials that may be used to complete this creative assignment.

3 GOD'S PEOPLE ON THE MOVE
Exodus-Deuteronomy

A freedom leader . . . a gift of law . . . and a long journey home

Materials for this session available on the Leader Reference CD:

- The Ten Plagues on Egypt (CHART)
- Jewish Festivals and Feasts (CHART)
- Numbering the Ten Commandments (CHART)
- Bible History Timeline (CHART)
- Exodus and Sinai Wilderness Wanderings (MAP)
- Ark of the Covenant (ILLUSTRATION)
- The Tabernacle (ILLUSTRATION)
- Sacred Vestments of the High Priest (ILLUSTRATION)
- The Israelites' Wilderness Encampment (DIAGRAM)
- Offerings in Israel (CHART)

STORY KEYS

- God is faithful to the Israelites in the Exodus and wilderness.
- God gives the Israelites teachings on living the lives God desires of them.
- God expects the Israelites to honor the covenant.

SESSION PREPARATION

OVERVIEW

The end of the last session introduced us to God's dreamer, Joseph, who correctly interpreted the dreams of the pharaoh of Egypt and was promoted to a position of honor, eventually bringing his clan to Egypt. These next books of the Pentateuch continue the story of the Israelites who are living as slaves in a foreign land, but then become wanderers on a journey to their promised land.

Scenes in this Session

Basket Baby (Exodus 1–2)
Burning Bush (Exodus 3–4)
Let Go, Pharaoh! (Exodus 5–13)
Through the Sea and Beyond (Exodus 14–18)
I Am the LORD Your God (Exodus 19–40)
God in the Center (Leviticus and Numbers)
Keep These Words (Deuteronomy)

What's the Story?

Movement abounds in the stories told in Exodus, Leviticus, Numbers, and Deuteronomy. These books portray the unfolding tale of God's love for, and rocky relationship with, the Israelites. Exodus 1–18 describes the plight of the people in Egypt under the reign of an unidentified pharaoh and how God leads the Israelites out of slavery. Exodus 19–24 focuses on God's covenant relationship with Israel through the Torah or "teachings" God gives to Moses on Mount Sinai. The remainder of Exodus describes the construction of a new, movable, sacred tent to use to worship God as the people journey on the road to the promised land.

Leviticus further details God's laws, which the Israelites are expected to follow as they live out their part of the covenant relationship. Leviticus 1–16; 27–34 has laws on everything from offerings to ordination of priests. Leviticus 17–26 introduces a group of laws, known as the Holiness Code, to help the people keep God at the very center of their lives. These laws include both rules for daily living and for special celebrations, concluding with penalties for disobedience.

Numbers contains a variety of Israelite "on-the-road stories." We see and hear the people mumble and grumble to God about their living conditions, in spite of the fact that God holds up God's part of the covenant. Numbers is a continuation of God's efforts to bring order to this disorderly people, even to the point of creating a census to count the tribes of Israel.

Deuteronomy was written in the seventh century B.C.E. when many people began to play fast and loose with some of God's laws because they feared the Assyrian Empire would destroy them. So while Moses's speech about God's faithfulness and laws was a reminder to the Israelites, it was also quite relevant to the people living at the time Deuteronomy was written. This book ends with the death of Moses and his burial just outside the promised land.

What's the Message?

The books of Exodus through Deuteronomy portray the development of God's covenant relationship with Israel, the chosen people. This relationship is initiated in the book of Exodus when God hears the lament of the people and delivers them from slavery under Pharaoh through the intervention of God's chosen prophet, Moses, and Moses's brother, Aaron. The actual event of the Israelites' exodus out of Egypt is a foundational faith story that the Jewish people remember and celebrate each year at Passover. This story also has great significance for Christians as it was at a celebration of the Passover that Jesus instituted the Lord's Supper, another meal of salvation (see Luke 22:7-23).

God's faithfulness continues in the wilderness journey of the Israelites, in spite of the fact that the people continually fall into their sinful ways and become impatient and rebellious with God. They act out their sinfulness by their constant complaining and distrust of God—even to the point of creating a new god of their own making, a golden calf. Through all the rebelliousness God proves to be a God of second, third, and even more chances. Though the Israelites are undeserving of God's love, God's faithfulness is steadfast.

God seeks to bring order to the rebelliousness of the Israelites by giving to them laws and rituals to help them more clearly live out their identity as God's holy people. While the laws did have legal and ritual significance, the most important thing the laws established was the relationship between God and the people, as well as the relationship of justice and peace that would guide their communal relationship. Relationships require attention and nurturing. The Ten Commandments, Torah, and Holiness Code provided a framework for the relationship between God and the people to flourish. They also served as a witness to other peoples and nations around them. As others saw how the people of Israel worshiped God and lived out God's sense of justice, they would be attracted to worshiping God as well. Even the law was part of the original promise that through the descendants of Abraham and Sarah, all nations would be blessed.

But these stories also remind us that there are consequences to pay when the people fail to trust and love God above all else. Even Moses discovered that. Moses himself had disobeyed God during the time in the wilderness, so—like the others in his generation—he did not set foot in Canaan. Instead, he died and was buried in Moab (Deuteronomy 34:5-6) as Joshua took over full command. With a new leader in place, the people were ready to head into the land God had promised to give them. The story of God's continued blessing in the face of Israel's rebellion was about to take a new turn.

PREPARE

1. Review chapter 3 in the participant book.
2. Review the overview and session plan for session 3 in the leader guide.
3. Watch the DVD segment for session 3.
4. Have extra Bibles available for those who did not bring one.
5. Have equipment for projecting or viewing the DVD set up and ready to go.
6. Consider distributing handouts or projecting images of reference materials (see list on p. 44) in the session.You might want to do this during Telling the Story or while discussing the Background Files.
7. If you are having the class do the Creative Corner activity, gather any materials suggested.
8. Pray for your class members and for God's presence and guidance as you gather in God's Word.

MATERIALS NEEDED

- Extra copies of the Bible
- Participant books
- Computer or DVD player; projector or TV monitor
- Course DVD
- Reference Materials
- Creative Corner materials (optional)
- Name tags
- Refreshments (optional)

LEADER PRAYER

God of salvation, we give you thanks for leading your people, Israel, from slavery into a promised land and into a deeper relationship with you. Empower me as study leader and the participants to come to a fuller understanding of the depth of your love for your people—both then and now. Amen.

CORE SESSION PLAN

GATHERING (10 MINUTES)

The Core Session Plan is designed for use in one 60-minute period. The Core Session Plan can be extended 45-60 minutes by incorporating the group reflection time called Our Story, found at the end of the Core Session Plan. Suggestions for alternative settings and schedules are provided on page 13 of this guide.

Welcome and check-in

Provide name tags again as you welcome participants to the session. If you are serving refreshments, have them set out ahead of time. Spend a few minutes asking if anyone wants to share any thoughts or insights from their personal "Mark it" reading for the week. You won't be able to spend much time on this, but hearing a couple of testimonials will encourage more in the group to make this weekly reading and devotional reflection a part of their routine.

Scripture and prayer

Read the following verse and prayer, or ask a volunteer to do so.

I am the LORD your God, who brought you out of the land of Egypt, out of the house of slavery; you shall have no other gods before me. (Exodus 20:2-3)

Dear God, we thank you for your faithfulness to the Israelites and to your followers throughout all generations. We know that you desire our hearts and devotion to you in return. We confess that we are often caught up in the distractions of life, finding ourselves in bondage to things, and our desires. Free us from our self-imposed slavery so that we might love and honor you as you deserve. Amen.

TELLING THE STORY (15 MINUTES)

You or your designated storyteller should now turn to telling the portion of the story that is highlighted in session 3. Incorporate any or all of the Background File notes in the participant book (p. 32) as part of the telling. Use one of the following three options for telling the story, or devise your own.

See the storytelling tips on p. 10 of this guide.

1. Read through, summarize, and comment on the story as provided in the participant book.

2. Ask for volunteers to tell portions of the story.
3. Read the story script provided below.

At the end of the storytelling time, summarize the Story Keys for this session.

The Story Script for Session 3

As the greatest story continues in Exodus, a new Egyptian pharaoh has come on the scene, and he is threatened by the growing number of Hebrew people living in Egypt. To keep them in line, he orders them into oppressive slavery and tries to thin the Hebrew population by killing all of their firstborn sons.

Israel's next leader, Moses, was saved from this early death when his mother hid him in a basket amid the reeds in the river. Discovered by Pharaoh's daughter and raised by Pharaoh's own mother within Pharaoh's house, Moses was forced to flee to Midian after he killed an Egyptian who he saw beating a Hebrew. Far away from the bitter labor of his Hebrew brothers and sisters, God called Moses (through a burning bush!) to go back to mighty Pharaoh and negotiate the release of the Israelites.

This negotiation was no easy task, as Moses was not gifted with persuasive speech. God appointed Moses's brother Aaron to go with him to Egypt to negotiate with Pharaoh. Because of these negotiations, conditions grew worse for both the Hebrews and the Egyptians. Ten plagues were sent by God to force Pharaoh to allow the Hebrews to leave their tortured life in Egypt. Bloody rivers, gnats, frogs, boils, and locusts were among the gruesome tactics, but Pharaoh's heart was not moved. (See the chart called "The Ten Plagues on Egypt.")

It was the last plague that turned the tide. God sent an angel of death to strike dead Egypt's firstborn males. The homes of the Hebrew people were protected by the blood of a slaughtered lamb. The celebration of Passover began that very night, and is still celebrated by Jewish families today. (See the chart called "Jewish Festivals and Feasts.")

The Israelites poured out of Egypt and were headed for a promised new future until they came up against the sea. Caught between drowning in the sea and brutal capture by the armies of Pharaoh, God came to the rescue again by parting the waters of the sea so that they could cross on dry land. As the people watched from shore, God unleashed the waters upon the pursuing Pharaoh and his armies.

The Israelites were now free and Moses led them on a vast wilderness journey. Soon, the people began to complain bitterly. They wondered how life in the wilderness was better than life in Egypt. At least they had food and water there! God demonstrated a remarkable patience with these whining Israelites, providing them with water from a rock, quail for meat, and a new culinary treat called *manna*.

The Story Script for Session 3 (continued)

Even so, God's gifts just never satisfied the people, who continued to test Moses and God. Eventually, Moses brought the people to Mount Sinai where God provided the first of many sets of laws. These laws would enable the Israelites to better live together as God's holy people. These first laws were called the Ten Commandments. (See the chart called "Numbering the Ten Commandments.")

Unfortunately, while Moses was far up on the mountain receiving these laws the people grew impatient and convinced Aaron to craft a golden calf to worship. When Moses returned down the mountain he was so angry that he trashed the first copy of the Ten Commandments. The very first law written on these tablets of stone was, "You shall have no other gods before me"!

Once again, God chose to move forward with the chosen people. The people were taught how to nurture a deepening relationship with God through the establishment of a portable tent, or tabernacle, where they could worship God. Priests were appointed to oversee the worship and sacrifices to God. They also developed a very special and ornate box called an *ark*, which was used to carry the Ten Commandments from place to place. While the people were in camp, the ark was placed inside the tabernacle.

The book of Leviticus contains the introduction of countless laws directing everything from sacrifices and offerings to the behavior of priests and the purity of the people. The purpose of these laws, just like the Ten Commandments, was to maintain the identity of the people as God's "holy people."

When the people finally approached their promised destination, Canaan, they grew skeptical of God's promise after hearing the report of spies who had been sent ahead of them. The people lost their nerve when they heard about dangerous people living in this land. Their lack of faith led to nearly forty more years of wandering and learning a very clear lesson: ALWAYS FOLLOW GOD! The book of Numbers focuses on this part of the story. We hear of internal rebellions within the tribes of Israel as well as battles against other peoples.

The saga of Moses draws to a conclusion as we enter the book of Deuteronomy. We hear several speeches of Moses recounting the wandering years and encouraging the people to obey God's law and teach it to each and every generation. He warns of the consequences that will come to those who do not keep God's commands. Moses knew God's punishment firsthand, as he handed leadership over to Joshua who would lead the Israelites into Canaan. Moses was forbidden to enter the land he had worked so hard to reach because he had doubted and disobeyed God. Before he died, he got a mountaintop view of the land that he would not get to enter.

PICTURING THE STORY (20 MINUTES)

Go through the reflection questions listed in this section in the participant book (p. 32). Then play the segment called God's People on the Move (session 3) on the course DVD. Encourage the participants to watch the story unfold as artist Joe Castillo depicts the scenes of the story. Participants may be invited to write down their own questions.

When the segment is done, address the questions together as a large group or ask the participants to discuss in smaller teams. Invite participants to share their own questions or observations. What difference did it make to see the story in this way?

SINGING AND PRAYING THE STORY (10 MINUTES)

Use one or both of the psalms provided in the participant book to help address the story and its themes. Psalms are best read aloud. You may have one volunteer read the entire psalm or portion of a psalm. Or you may wish to have the psalm read responsively, verse by verse or line by line. Use a solo reader with the group responding, or read responsively using different groups.

As time allows, discuss the observations and questions provided.

Psalm 1 is an instructional psalm, also known as a Wisdom psalm because it was intended to impart wisdom to the community. The psalmist compares two ways of living in relationship to God and God's law. The first way is followed by those who find great pleasure in reflecting upon God's instructions for living. These people will prosper and yield fruit in their lives. The second is the exact opposite way of living. These are the wicked who will not abide by God's instructions for living. At times they will even intentionally oppose God because they feel no desire to be subject to anyone or be held in judgment of their actions in any way.

Psalm 105:23-45 is both a hymn of praise and a historical psalm that recounts how God rescued the Israelites, leading them from slavery into freedom in a glorious promised land. The psalmist gives a summary of God's faithfulness to Israel. Although Israel found itself in slavery in a foreign land, God sent prophets, Moses and Aaron, as messengers to perform signs and miracles so Pharaoh would release God's people. Once freed, God provided for them in the desert and brought them to the promised land to live according to God's laws.

LOOKING AHEAD (5 MINUTES)

Mark it

Encourage participants to read and mark one or more of the passages listed in this section during the week ahead. Let the group know that at the start of next week's session you will ask volunteers to share any insights they have from this exercise.

You are encouraged to do the "Mark it" exercise as well.

Next time

In the next session we will see and hear God's people resettle in the promised land. To review this week's story and to help prepare for the next session, you and your group are encouraged to read introductions to the following in a study Bible:

- Historical Books
- Joshua
- Judges
- Ruth

You may find it helpful to take some notes or highlight items in the readings to share next week as part of Telling the Story.

OUR STORY

WELCOME

Whether done consecutively along with the Core Session Plan or planned for a separate time or location, consider providing hospitality in the form of refreshments.

- Arrange the room comfortably for small group discussion.
- Introduce newcomers in the group.
- Begin with prayer, using the session prayer on p. 47 or another prayer of your choice. Ask volunteers to provide prayers, if they feel comfortable doing so.
- You may wish to begin by asking if anyone has a particular question or thought to share from the large group session. As an alternative to discussing those questions, simply note them or write them down on newsprint. Small groups may decide to discuss further.

Ideas for optional settings and schedules for this time are provided in the introduction on page 13 of this leader guide.

CONVERSATION

See the tips for leading and participating in small group discussion on page 17 of this guide. Make available to all participants copies of the reproducible Guidelines for Small Group Discussion.

The reflection questions are intended to help participants connect their own stories to the key themes of the greatest story. These questions can be used for personal reflection while reading or used to guide group discussion. It is unlikely a group could discuss all the questions in one discussion period. Don't be concerned about this. Here are some options for approaching the questions:

1. As leader, you may choose to focus on certain questions from the list.
2. Ask participants to suggest questions to discuss.
3. Divide the groups into smaller teams, assign the teams a designated number of questions to discuss, and then have each group report back to the large group.
4. If you have a group that has the time and interest, you could assign each participant a question or two to think about and prepare a response during the week. These responses could be shared as discussion starters when the group meets for Our Story discussion time.

Questions and Responses

The questions below are designed with personal reflection and response in mind. They do not require a certain amount of prior knowledge in order to respond. Responses may vary according to individual insights and context. Even so, a few guiding thoughts are provided for some of the questions.

- *Moses survived because of the bravery and compassion of his mother, his sister Miriam, and Pharaoh's own daughter. Who helps you "survive"?*

- *Imagine you were Moses and heard God calling you to go back to Egypt. What questions would you have for God? What would convince you to go?*

Many of God's prophets weren't exactly thrilled to learn that God was asking them to speak on God's behalf. Very often the first question they asked was: Why me? But after a little conversation with God each was able to hear and actually fulfill the call. God always empowers those who are called into God's service—including us!

- *Have you ever experienced God's presence? If so, what was it like? Where did it happen?*

- *Who has been your "Aaron" when you really needed him or her?*

Questions and Responses (continued)

- *The plagues are described in Exodus 7—12. Why do you think it took so much to get Pharaoh to change his mind?*

Some people might wonder why God would choose to use plagues to wear Pharaoh down. However, the plagues, which become successively more severe as time goes on, reveal God's power over all creation. God made all that exists, and God alone has mastery over it. Participants may also wonder about God "hardening Pharaoh's heart" (4:21; 7:3). This, too, has to do with God's complete control over the events in the story. Later, Pharaoh hardens his own heart (8:15; 8:23), so human freedom and responsibility also play a part.

- *Why do you think the night the angel of death passed over is remembered in a special meal?*

Take the opportunity to explore the significance of the Passover meal, both the original meal and in New Testament times. In the Gospels of Matthew, Mark, and Luke, Jesus' Last Supper is said to have occurred during the Passover meal. Jesus and his followers continued in this tradition of remembrance, as do modern day Jews.

- *What events do we tend to celebrate or remember regularly?*

- *What thoughts or questions do you have about what happened at the Red Sea?*

- *The manna God provided was to be eaten each day and not stored. There was always enough. How does this vision of everyone having enough compare to or contrast with our eating habits and distribution of food?*

- *How do you keep going when things are not going right?*

- *The Ten Commandments are listed in Exodus 20:1-17. Why do you think they are sometimes called a "gift" from God?*

Laws often bring to mind limits and punishment. And God certainly did warn that disobedience would bring consequences. But, more importantly, God's laws defined the relationship between God and the people and provided guidance for living together in peace and justice. Life lived in relationship with God is a life of blessing. This blessed life can be a gift to all.

- *What's the most important thing you have ever been taught? Why?*

- *How would you describe what it means to be a holy person, or part of God's holy people?*

It's important to note that we, like the Israelites, are not the ones calling the shots to make ourselves holy. Only God can do that.

Questions and Responses (continued)

- *How do you keep God at the center of your life?*
- *What is the most difficult thing you have ever faced? How did you face it?*
- *What, in your opinion, is hard about waiting for God to lead?*
- *Why do you think Moses needed to remind the people how they had come so far?*
- *How do we keep God's words on our hearts and minds? Why do you think that is important?*

Provide colored markers, paper, construction paper, poster board, magazines, scissors, or other materials that may be used to complete this creative assignment.

Creative Corner

Depending on how your schedule is organized, you may wish to assign this activity for individuals or small groups.

Working on your own or with a partner, choose one image, scene, or concept from the "Moses chapter" of Israel's history. Use your imagination to bring it to life. Think 3-D. How can the story become an object, an advertisement, a living drama, or something else?

GETTING SETTLED
Joshua–Ruth

4

Holy land, holy war . . . unsettling times . . . and a love story

SESSION PREPARATION

OVERVIEW

The last session ended with God commanding Moses to turn over leadership of the Israelites to Joshua. Under Joshua, the people end their wilderness wandering and cross over into the promised land. These next three books begin a section in the Bible known as the Historical Books because they tell the story of Israel in this new land. It becomes clear very quickly that things will go well for the people when they follow God's laws, but watch out if they don't!

Materials for this session available on the Leader Reference CD:

- Bible History Timeline (CHART)
- Palestine and Key Locations in Joshua and Judges (MAP)
- Judges in Israel (CHART)

Scenes in this Session

Joshua, Jordan, and Jericho (Joshua 1–6)
Holy War (Joshua 7–12)
A Land Divided but Unsettled (Joshua 13:1—Judges 3:6)
You Be the Judge! (Judges 3:7—21:25)
Where You Go, I Will Go (Ruth)

What's the Story?

The Israelites soon learn that getting settled in the promised land is actually pretty unsettling because other people already live there. That means they have to invade the land that God has given them to take control of it. Joshua 1–12 describes their invasion and eventual occupation of the land promised to their ancestor Abraham and his family. Things tend to go well when the Israelites are faithful to God and follow God's lead, but not so well when they don't. And they soon discover even the unfaithfulness of just one person can affect everybody! The importance of the blessings and curses that come from obedience and disobedience winds throughout the Historical Books. Because this is also a predominant theme in Deuteronomy, these books are known as part of a longer work known as the Deuteronomistic History that runs all the way through

STORY KEYS

- With God leading, the Israelites fight to obtain the land God promised them.
- Unsettling times continue, and the Israelites break their promise to keep God central in their lives.
- God appoints judges to help guide the people through tough times.
- Ruth, a non-Jew, is an example of love and faithfulness and finds herself in Jesus' family tree.

2 Kings. The book of Joshua ends with Joshua's parting words prior to his death. He reminds the Israelites their mantra should be: Remember the covenant!

The book of Judges speaks about the Israelites' life in Canaan without a king, or central leader, to unite them. Without a ruler the people get themselves into big trouble and begin worshiping local gods, violating their commitment to the God who has been faithful to them. So, God lifts up and empowers people called *judges* to assist the people when they need it. You might think of them as the superheroes of the Old Testament who performed impossible feats, because they were blessed by God to protect and save God's people.

Ruth is a story of love and faithfulness that appears like a glimmer of sunshine amid all the turmoil of the previous two books. It begins with the decision of Ruth's mother-in-law, Naomi, to return to her native Bethlehem after the death of her husband and two sons. Even though Ruth will be a foreigner, she sticks by Naomi, refusing to let her go it alone. Ruth finds love with Boaz, a relative of Naomi, who recognizes Ruth's traits of faithfulness and devotion. They marry and from their family line rise both King David and Jesus of Nazareth.

What's the Message?

While dreadfully violent at times, the book of Joshua is a reminder to Israel that God is their ultimate leader. Their role is to follow. When they don't, bad things happen. It is only with God's help that God's chosen people can secure the land of Canaan. Some may struggle with this part of the story, in which the land's indigenous people had to be defeated, and sometimes massacred, in order for Israel to live in the land promised to them. The ongoing struggle over this land continues even today. Clearly, the stories reported in Joshua and other Old Testament books are written from the perspective of the Jewish people. The struggle for this land is described from their particular point of view. Christians receive the Hebrew Scriptures as part of this complete faith story. At the same time, we can also see many examples in the Old Testament of God calling all God's people to do justice and seek the best for the neighbor.

We also are reminded of the continuing theme of rebellion. Even though the people promised Joshua that they would renew and uphold their part of God's covenant, they continued their stubborn and self-serving ways. They turned away from God's laws and teachings even to the point of worshiping other gods. The book of Judges shows again how God stands by the people through tough times by lifting up the judges to assist them.

Both Joshua and Judges were likely written during a later time when the people were facing the threat of invasion by foreign powers. The prophets would interpret this threat as God's just punishment for acts of faithlessness. But the books also provided messages of hope that their circumstances could be reversed if they only got their act together and once again began to uphold their part of God's covenant. God listens to the prayers of God's people, both then and now. God desires faithfulness, both then and now.

All three of these books remind us to expect the unexpected when God is at work in the world. Samson, a wisecracking smart aleck, becomes a judge to help God's people. Ruth is a beautiful story of love and devotion that explains how a faithful non-Jewish woman became the great-grandmother of King David, a beloved king of Israel. In Matthew's Gospel (1:1-17), we discover that Jesus comes from David's family line, and so he is connected to Ruth as well. This story shows that God loves and works through the Gentiles, too, and that ordinary people can have extraordinary places in God's story of salvation.

Use the Story Keys to help your group explore how God might be active in their lives in unexpected ways, especially during tough times.

PREPARE

1. Review chapter 4 in the participant book.
2. Review the overview and session plan for session 4 in the leader guide.
3. Watch the DVD segment for session 4.
4. Have extra Bibles available for those who did not bring one.
5. Have equipment for projecting or viewing the DVD set up and ready to go.
6. Consider distributing handouts or projecting images of reference materials (see list on p. 55) in the session. You might want to do this during Telling the Story or while discussing the Background Files.
7. If you are having the class do the Creative Corner activity, gather any materials suggested.
8. Pray for your class members and for God's presence and guidance as you gather in God's Word.

MATERIALS NEEDED

- Extra copies of the Bible
- Participant books
- Computer or DVD player; projector or TV monitor
- Course DVD
- Reference materials
- Creative Corner materials (optional)
- Name tags
- Refreshments (optional)

LEADER PRAYER

Faithful God, there are times when we are like the faithless people we read about in Joshua and Judges. And yet, you continue to stand by us. Guide me as I lead participants through this session. Help them come to a deeper understanding of the true meaning of your faithfulness so that it might empower them during tough and uncertain times. Amen.

CORE SESSION PLAN

The Core Session Plan is designed for use in one 60-minute period. The Core Session Plan can be extended 45-60 minutes by incorporating the group reflection time called Our Story, found at the end of the Core Session Plan.

GATHERING (10 MINUTES)

Welcome and check-in

Provide name tags again as you welcome participants to the session. If you are serving refreshments, have them set out ahead of time. Spend a few minutes asking if anyone wants to share any thoughts or insights from their personal "Mark it" reading for the week. You won't be able to spend much time on this, but hearing a couple of testimonials will encourage more in the group to make this weekly reading and devotional reflection a part of their routine.

Scripture and prayer

Read the following verse and prayer, or ask a volunteer to do so.

May the LORD reward you for your deeds, and may you have a full reward from the LORD, the God of Israel, under whose wings you have come for refuge! (Ruth 2:12)

Faithful God, it's easy for us to turn to you when we are going through tough and uncertain times. Still, we know you desire our devotion no matter what our circumstances may be. Empower us to stick by you the way you faithfully stick by us, even when we get rebellious and turn from you as the Israelites did. Help us to know that you are our refuge throughout all the days of our lives. Amen.

TELLING THE STORY (15 MINUTES)

See the storytelling tips on p. 10 of this guide.

You or your designated storyteller should now turn to telling the portion of the story that is highlighted in session 4. Incorporate any or all of the Background File notes in the participant book (p. 40) as part of the telling. Use one of the following three options for telling the story, or devise your own.

1. Read through, summarize, and comment on the story as provided in the participant book.
2. Ask for volunteers to tell portions of the story.
3. Read the story script provided below.

At the end of the storytelling time, summarize the Story Keys for this session.

The Story Script for Session 4

The death of Moses ends one major chapter in the story of the Israelite people, but a new chapter is about to begin. With God's mighty strength showing the way, it is now up to a man named Joshua to lead Israel across the Jordan River and into the promised land. God continues to be faithful to God's promise!

Entering the land was not going to be a piece of cake. Israelites would have to fight their way into a land already occupied. The entry into Canaan began with a spy mission to Jericho. There, a prostitute named Rahab saved the spies, who were able to return to Joshua with good news about a land that was Israel's for the taking.

Now all that had to be done was to get *all* the Israelites across the river safely! And just as God had done at the Red Sea earlier, God parted the waters of the Jordan River so the people could cross on dry ground. After marking their crossing with an altar, the people headed straight to Jericho. Here the priests took the lead blowing trumpets and circling around the city walls. With the loudest shouting and commotion the people could muster, the walls fell on the seventh day. Only Rahab and her family were spared.

As Israel moved forward it was critical that the people obeyed everything that God told them. If even one of them did not obey, the punishment was brought upon them all. This was the situation when Israel failed at their first attempt to take the city of Ai. Israel's next swipe at Ai was a bloody and destructive one that left the city in a heap of ruins. Joshua led the people to conquer a large territory from Goshen in Egypt to northern Canaan, taking many kings and their lands. Despite the failures of Joshua and the people, God was determined to lead them forward.

Now began a complicated process of dividing land among the twelve tribes. The priestly tribes of Levi had responsibilities throughout the entire nation and so they were not given a specific geographical place. Refugee cities were set up for any Israelite who accidentally caused the death of someone to preserve their safety until a fair trial could be held before the community of faith. (See the division of land and the cities of refuge on the map "The Twelve Tribes of Israel, 1200-1030 B.C.E.")

At the death of Joshua, Israel entered a new era of governance when God did not appoint a new leader for the nation but left the tribes to fend for themselves. Even though they had confidently promised to serve God prior to Joshua's death, without the leadership of a Joshua or Moses, the situation among the Israelites became very unsettled. Some tribes managed well, while others did not. Some of the people began to worship the Baals, the gods of the Canaanites. An extreme survival test had begun as the people living in the land made life very difficult for the Israelites.

The Story Script for Session 4 (continued)

God remained faithful, however, despite the many problems the Israelites brought on themselves. To help them face numerous threats, God raised up a cadre of leaders called judges. These were cult heroes who organized the people to defend themselves against their foes. Deborah, Gideon, and Samson were among the string of heroic leaders who saved the people from defeat. Their stories are filled with all kinds of interesting and unusual battle techniques. Regardless of how successful a particular judge might be, when each one died the people lapsed into even greater sins than before.

And just when we are about to tire of the shenanigans of the people of Israel, the story takes a pleasant diversion into the realm of love. The book of Ruth engages us in an intimate and delightful story about a Moabite woman named Ruth who marries one of the sons of Naomi, an Israelite from Bethlehem. Tragedy falls upon this family as Naomi's husband and two sons die. As Naomi plans to return home to Bethlehem, Ruth binds herself to her mother-in-law in a unique act of love and faithfulness.

By making such a choice Ruth has taken the more difficult route. Not only is she leaving her Moabite family behind, but she is also going to Israel where she will be a foreigner and a widow with no one to look out for her survival. Fortunately, Boaz, one of Naomi's husband's relatives, raised grain. Israelite law allowed for the poor to collect any leftovers from the newly harvested fields.

And so, it was there that Boaz took notice of Ruth and made a deal to marry her. Ruth and Boaz had a son named Obed, who had a son named Jesse, who had a son named David, who became the most famous king of Israel. From David's family line came a man named Joseph, who married a young girl named Mary. And they had a son whose name was Jesus.

PICTURING THE STORY (20 MINUTES)

Go through the reflection questions listed in this section in the participant book (p. 40). Then play the segment called Getting Settled (session 4) on the course DVD. Encourage the participants to watch the story unfold as artist Joe Castillo depicts the scenes of the story. Participants may be invited to write down their own questions.

When the segment is done, address the questions together as a large group or ask the participants to discuss in smaller teams. Invite participants to share their own questions or observations. What difference did it make to see the story in this way?

SINGING AND PRAYING THE STORY (10 MINUTES)

Use one or both of the psalms provided in the participant book to help address the story and its themes. Psalms are best read aloud. You may have one volunteer read the entire psalm or portion of a psalm. Or you may wish to have the psalm read responsively, verse by verse or line by line. Use a solo reader with the group responding, or read responsively using different groups.

As time allows, discuss the observations and questions provided.

Psalm 47 is a hymn of praise and an enthronement psalm celebrating God's rule over all nations. The psalmist praises God who has subdued the nations for the sake of Israel and their inheritance of a promised land. The people are encouraged to sing praises to the God of all creation, a God who has kept the promises made to Abraham (see Genesis 17:1-8).

Psalm 46 is a hymn of praise celebrating God's sure and steady presence through all turmoil. The psalmist describes both cosmic and political threats that God's people face and how God is present and immovable throughout all dangers. God will bring peace to the nations and to the hearts of the people. God is indeed their refuge.

LOOKING AHEAD (5 MINUTES)

Mark it

Encourage participants to read and mark one or more of the passages listed in this section during the week ahead. Let the group know that at the start of next week's session you will ask volunteers to share any insights they have from this exercise.

You are encouraged to do the "Mark it" exercise as well.

Next Time

In the next session we see the settled, but divided, tribes temporarily come together under the rule of one king, only to discover that old rivalries will split the kingdom into two. To review this week's story and to help prepare for the next session, you and your group are encouraged to read introductions to the following in a study Bible:

- Historical Books
- 1 Samuel
- 2 Samuel
- 1 Kings

You may find it helpful to take some notes or highlight items in the readings to share next week as part of Telling the Story.

- 2 Kings
- 1 Chronicles

OUR STORY

Ideas for optional settings and schedules for this time are provided in the introduction on page 13 of this leader guide.

WELCOME

Whether done consecutively along with the Core Session Plan or planned for a separate time or location, consider providing hospitality in the form of refreshments.

- Arrange the room comfortably for small group discussion.
- Introduce newcomers in the group.
- Begin with prayer, using the session prayer on p. 58 or another prayer of your choice. Ask volunteers to provide prayers, if they feel comfortable doing so.
- You may wish to begin by asking if anyone has a particular question or thought to share from the large group session. As an alternative to discussing those questions, simply note them or write them down on newsprint. Small groups may decide to discuss further.

See the tips for leading and participating in small group discussion on page 17 of this guide. Make available to all participants copies of the reproducible Guidelines for Small Group Discussion.

CONVERSATION

The reflection questions are intended to help participants connect their own stories to the key themes of the greatest story. These questions can be used for personal reflection while reading or used to guide group discussion. It is unlikely a group could discuss all the questions in one discussion period. Don't be concerned about this. Here are some options for approaching the questions:

1. As leader, you may choose to focus on certain questions from the list.
2. Ask participants to suggest questions to discuss.
3. Divide the groups into smaller teams, assign the teams a designated number of questions to discuss, and then have each group report back to the large group.
4. If you have a group that has the time and interest, you could assign each participant a question or two to think about and prepare a response during the week. These responses could be shared as discussion starters when the group meets for Our Story discussion time.

Questions and Responses

The questions below are designed with personal reflection and response in mind. They do not require a certain amount of prior knowledge in order to respond. Responses may vary according to individual insights and context. Even so, a few guiding thoughts are provided for some of the questions.

- *In the New Testament, Rahab is described as a person of faith in Hebrews 11:31. In the book of James, she is said to be justified (made right with God) by her works, namely helping the spies (James 2:25). How is faith joined with works in your life?*

Doing good works should be a natural manifestation of our life of faith lived out in response to all that God has done for us. We don't do good works to achieve God's favor, but instead we do them as a thankful outpouring of love and respect for God's action on our behalf. Good works are our gift of thanksgiving to God.

- *The Israelites put up stones to remember God's hand in helping them cross the Jordan River. What symbols help you remember God's involvement in your life?*

- *What do you think of the idea that God takes sides in wars or conflicts?*

- *What do you think of the idea that the sin or broken faith of one or a few can affect the lives—or even the faith—of all? Can you think of an example of this?*

As Christians we live our lives and faith in community so it's more than reasonable to reflect upon how the actions of one person, or a few, will affect others within that body of faith. Holding a discussion in light of 1 Corinthians 12:12-26 sheds a different and more positive light on how the actions of one can affect the well-being of the whole. Together, we are the body of Christ and are therefore closely connected.

- *In your opinion, can war ever be holy? Why or why not?*

The concept of "holy war" has been adopted by many in the Christian Church as being justified in order to repel evil or put an end to the unjust suffering caused by those who impose power. Others would argue that war cannot be justified for any reason.

- *How do you react to this statement: "Joshua and the people were simply reclaiming the land God had promised to give to their ancestors Abraham and Sarah." In what ways do you see this statement continuing to affect this land today?*

- *What do you think it would be like to live in a town or city or country where everyone had exactly the same religious beliefs?*

Questions and Responses (continued)

- *Why do you think it is hard to serve God only?*

Explore the meaning of what it means to serve God. The word *serve* often means to honor or respect someone or something. Our actions and the way we live our lives are an indication of the things that we serve in life. Do we spend as much time focusing on our relationship with God as we do surfing the Internet or even watching TV? Taking this perspective, it can be eye-opening to look at what it means to serve and what our actions really say.

- *Are you surprised the people of Israel went back on their promise to worship and serve God only? Why or why not?*

- *Imagine what it would be like to live in a time and place as wild and unsettled as Canaan in the time of the judges. What is your reaction to the violence of these times?*

- *Many parts of the Bible are just plain hard to understand. Sometimes it's just best to say, "I don't get it." From what you know about the Bible, what parts are pretty clear to you? What parts are particularly hard to understand?*

- *What do you think of the idea that God uses people the way they are, not the way they ought to be?*

- *Though she was a foreigner, Ruth eventually is named right along with earliest matriarchs and patriarchs of Israel's family. Who do you think of as matriarch or patriarch in your own church or community of faith?*

- *How have you seen or experienced newcomers and people from other countries shaping your community or your community of faith?*

Provide items needed to create a resume large enough for others to see. This might include poster board or newsprint, markers, stencil materials, or pictures.

Creative Corner

Depending on how your schedule is organized, you may wish to assign this activity for individuals or small groups.

Create a resume and brief cover letter for one of the people featured in this part of the story. Include a pictorial form of identification. Imagine what kind of job this person may be applying for. How would he or she describe his or her qualifications for the job?

KINGS AND KINGDOMS

Samuel–Chronicles

5

Israel's tribes unite under one king . . . the temple is built . . . the kingdom splits in two

SESSION PREPARATION

OVERVIEW

In the previous session, the Israelites put down roots in the promised land. God appointed judges to assist them when they began to get themselves in trouble. We also met Ruth and Boaz, the great-grandparents of King David, one of Israel's kings. As the story continues, the kingdom unites, only to break apart again after the death of Solomon.

Materials for this session available on the Leader Reference CD:

- Kings of Judah and Israel (CHART)
- United Kingdom of Israel, 1000-924 B.C.E. (MAP)
- Ancient Jerusalem (MAP)
- The Kingdoms of Israel and Judah, 924-722 B.C.E. (MAP)
- Solomon's Temple (DIAGRAM and ILLUSTRATION)
- The Tabernacle (ILLUSTRATION)

Scenes in this Session

Here I Am! (1 Samuel 1–7)
To King or Not To King (1 Samuel 8–15)
On a Sling and a Prayer (1 Samuel 16–30)
A King with So Much Promise (2 Samuel)
Temple Builder (1 Kings 1–11)
The Great Divide (1 Kings 12:1—16:28)
Foul Baals (1 Kings 16:29—22:53)

What's the Story?

Changes are once again in the works for God's people. They go from living in the wild and unruly times we learned about in Judges to desiring a sovereign ruler and king who will unite them as one. 1 Samuel focuses on several important characters, including Samuel, Saul, and David. Samuel has an important role serving as one of God's judges (1 Samuel 1–7) and naming Saul as Israel's first king (1 Samuel 8–15). David enters the story when Samuel anoints him as the next king. He begins his rise to power after beating Goliath, a giant Philistine, in a dramatic battle.

STORY KEYS

- God raises up leaders and prophets for the good of the people.
- God creates an earthly monarchy when the people ask for unity under a king.
- God creates a covenant with the house of David.
- Solomon builds God's temple in Jerusalem.

2 Samuel focuses on David's reign as king of Israel, with all of its ups and downs. Because of his devotion to God and his prowess in battle, David has been called Israel's greatest king. However, David also makes some poor personal decisions and engages in adultery with Bathsheba, eventually ensuring that her husband, Uriah, dies in battle. When Nathan, God's prophet, reveals David's sins, David repents. In spite of David's shortcomings, God is faithful to the people and makes a timeless covenant with David and his lineage, which includes Jesus. (See Matthew1:1-17.)

1 Kings continues with a selective history of Israel's monarchy that is difficult to date. 1 Kings 1–11 focuses on Solomon and the building of the temple to serve as God's dwelling place in Jerusalem. This is followed by the description of the eventual division of the kingdom into Israel in the north and Judah in the south (1 Kings 12:1—16:28).

What's the Message?

This session focuses on some significant characters in the Old Testament. God is at work through them and through some of the secondary characters who interact with them. The intertwined stories act as a reminder to Israel to remember the covenant with God and to walk in God's ways. At the same time, they show God's constant love and faithfulness toward the people.

The Israelites struggled to live lives more grounded in faith and devotion to God and God's covenant rather than in fear. Fear typically caused the people to make choices that led to alienation from God. Saul is a good example of someone who initially was a great king, but whose trust in God began to falter and fail. So, God anointed a new king, David. Session 4 pointed out the thread of the Deuteronomistic History that runs throughout all these Historical Books: Israel will be blessed when the people uphold God's covenant. God is faithful, no matter what, and expects our devotion in return.

In 2 Samuel, David is recognized as a strong and devoted king in his service to God and the Israelites. God made a covenant with the house of David and, although the earthly kingdom would be divided, God stood by this promise to David. This assurance is an important thread that continues in the New Testament, where we learn that Jesus is a descendant of David through Joseph's line. Through Jesus, God fulfills the promise to "establish the throne of his kingdom forever" (2 Samuel 7:13).

The construction of the temple in Jerusalem is an important part of 1 Kings. The ark of the covenant, which traveled with the Israelites throughout their wilderness journey and into the promised land, was placed in the innermost part of the temple, known as the Holy of Holies. Now, God had a home and the people had a place to go and offer sacrifices as specified in God's laws. With the building of the temple, Jerusalem was established as the center of all religious activity.

PREPARE

1. Review chapter 5 in the participant book.
2. Review the overview and session plan for session 5 in the leader guide.
3. Watch the DVD segment for session 5.
4. Have extra Bibles available for those who did not bring one.
5. Have equipment for projecting or viewing the DVD set up and ready to go.
6. Consider distributing handouts or projecting images of reference materials (see list on p. 65) in the session. You might want to do this during Telling the Story or while discussing the Background Files.
7. If you are having the group do the Creative Corner activity, gather any materials suggested.
8. Pray for the participants and for God's presence and guidance as you gather in God's Word.

MATERIALS NEEDED

- Extra copies of the Bible
- Participant books
- Computer or DVD player; projector or TV monitor
- Course DVD
- Reference materials
- Creative Corner materials (optional)
- Name tags
- Refreshments (optional)

LEADER PRAYER

Steadfast God, like the Israelites, we often live lives that are steeped more in fear than in faith. Empower me and the participants to explore together what it means to live in faith and rely on you for everything in our daily lives. Amen.

CORE SESSION PLAN

GATHERING (10 MINUTES)

Welcome and check-in

Provide name tags again as you welcome participants to the session. If you are serving refreshments, have them set out ahead of time. Spend a few minutes asking if anyone wants to share any thoughts or insights from their personal "Mark it" reading for the week. You won't be able to spend much time on this, but hearing a couple of testimonials will encourage more in the group to make this weekly reading and devotional reflection a part of their routine.

The Core Session Plan is designed for use in one 60-minute period. The Core Session Plan can be extended 45-60 minutes by incorporating the group reflection time called Our Story, found at the end of the Core Session Plan.

Scripture and prayer

Read the following verse and prayer, or ask a volunteer to do so.

"The Lord! His adversaries shall be shattered; the Most High will thunder in heaven. The Lord will judge the ends of the earth; he will give strength to his king, and exalt the power of his anointed." (1 Samuel 2:10)

God, throughout history you have stood by your people. You have raised up and blessed faithful leaders like Samuel, Nathan, David, and Solomon. Help us to learn from them what it means to live a godly life that serves you. When we falter, strengthen us. When we are afraid, stir up faith within us. Thank you for your devotion to your people throughout the ages, and for your steadfast promise that we will never be alone. Amen.

TELLING THE STORY (15 MINUTES)

See the storytelling tips on p. 10 of this guide.

You or your designated storyteller should now turn to telling the portion of the story that is highlighted in session 5. Incorporate any or all of the Background File notes in the participant book (p. 49) as part of the telling. Use one of the following three options for telling the story, or devise your own.

1. Read through, summarize, and comment on the story as provided in the participant book.
2. Ask for volunteers to tell portions of the story.
3. Read the story script provided below.

At the end of the storytelling time, summarize the Story Keys for this session.

The Story Script for Session 5

A new age for Israel followed the chaotic period of the judges. This new age began with a woman named Hannah. Hannah had no children, but she vowed that if God gave her a son, she would dedicate him to serve God. God heard Hannah's prayer, and Hannah kept her word. She gave birth to Samuel, gave him to serve God with a priest named Eli, and sang a song of praise.

The boy Samuel lived with Eli and assisted him. Now Eli's sons were scoundrels who cut corners and stole offerings. Things were so bad that God's Word was rarely heard during that time. But one night, with Eli's help, Samuel recognized God's voice and God spoke to him. He committed himself to God with the words "Here I am." Samuel excelled as a priest, so God appointed him to be a judge to lead the Israelites in war against their enemies, the Philistines.

The Story Script for Session 5 (continued)

Like Eli, as Samuel grew older he relied on his sons, who abused their positions as judges. Eventually the tribal leaders demanded to have a king like other nations. Although Samuel felt strongly that God was Israel's king, God instructed Samuel to go ahead and let Israel have a king.

Samuel poured oil over the head of a man named Saul. This pouring of oil was called anointing, and it set Saul apart to be Israel's first king. Saul's reign began well, with many victories in battle, but then it started to unwind as he became less and less obedient to God. Then God told Samuel to anoint a new king, even while Saul was still king. The next king was revealed to be David, the youngest son of Jesse and the great-grandson of Ruth. David quickly proved himself the ideal candidate to follow Saul when David killed the Philistine giant Goliath with just a slingshot and a stone.

As strange as it sounds, Saul liked David and made him his armor-bearer. But as David struck up a close friendship with Saul's son, Jonathan, his relationship with Saul deteriorated. Saul attempted to kill David, but God spared David's life. Saul's twenty-year reign ended when he died in battle against the mighty Philistines.

David, who earlier had been privately anointed to be the next king, was now publicly chosen as king by the people. God made a covenant with him, promising that David's kingdom would last forever. David promised to build God a temple.

As time went on, David's sins became as great as his victories. He greatly expanded the kingdom of Israel, but also committed adultery with a woman named Bathsheba and ordered her husband to the front lines of battle so he would be killed. David's sins had consequences, and David was forbidden to build a temple for God. His son with Bathsheba and another son, Absalom, both died.

After reigning as king for forty years, David made it clear that his son Solomon would succeed him. Solomon, like his father, offered prayers and sacrifices to God. He prayed for wisdom, which served him well in governing the kingdom and distinguishing between good and evil. He even decided a dramatic case between two women who both claimed to be the mother of the same child!

Solomon's greatest achievement was building God's temple in Jerusalem. Five hundred years after the people left Egypt the temple was begun. Solomon obtained cedar wood from Lebanon and huge stones cut from quarries, all by forced labor. Once the temple was built, he capped off this great accomplishment by furnishing it elaborately and constructing a lavish palace for himself. Solomon dedicated the temple, which represented God's presence with the people, in memory of his father and of God's enduring faithfulness.

The Story Script for Session 5 (continued)

Solomon, like David, didn't always follow God's ways. He married women from foreign nations and built altars to their gods. And so, rebellion set in against Solomon.

When Solomon died, rebellion broke out against the line of David. The ten northernmost tribes of Israel formed a northern kingdom, called Israel. Jeroboam, who had tried to take the throne from Solomon, ruled Israel. The tribes of Judah and Simeon formed the southern kingdom, Judah. Rehoboam, Solomon's son and chosen successor, ruled Judah.

Both kings indulged themselves in building shrines to foreign gods, and God's judgment came down on them. Their reigns were severely affected by civil war, political infighting, and idol worship. Kings who followed them tried to restore the worship of God alone, but did not prevail.

King Ahab would become known as one of the worst kings. He married Jezebel, the daughter of the King of Sidon, and together they created disaster. They introduced the worship of the Canaanite gods Baal and Asherah. They abused innocent people. One of these was Naboth, who was murdered so that Ahab and Jezebel could steal his vineyard.

Into this terrible situation, God sent the prophet Elijah. He stood up to Ahab and put the prophets of the false god Baal to a mighty test, which they lost in embarrassing fashion. This infuriated Queen Jezebel and Elijah fled into the wilderness for his own safety. But God sought him out and in a small, quiet voice instructed Elijah to anoint Elisha, the prophet who would follow him, and to anoint a new king in Israel.

PICTURING THE STORY (20 MINUTES)

Go through the reflection questions listed in this section in the participant book (p. 49). Then play the segment called Kings and Kingdoms (session 5) on the course DVD. Encourage participants to watch the story unfold as artist Joe Castillo depicts the scenes of the story. Participants may be invited to write down their own questions.

When the segment is done, address the questions together as a large group or ask the participants to discuss them in smaller groups. Invite participants to share their own questions or observations. What difference did it make to see the story in this way?

SINGING AND PRAYING THE STORY (10 MINUTES)

Use one or both of the psalms provided in the participant book to help address the story and its themes. Psalms are best read aloud. You may have one volunteer read the entire psalm or portion of a psalm. Or you may wish to have the psalm read responsively, verse by verse or line by line. Use a solo reader with the group responding, or read responsively using different groups.

As time allows, discuss the observations and questions provided.

Psalm 72 is a royal psalm, attributed to Solomon, that asks God to bless and assist the king. The psalmist asks God to empower the king to judge with righteousness so the needy are uplifted, oppressors are dealt with justly, and his foes pay him homage. The psalm also includes prayers for the king's good health and for a plentiful harvest. Through the king the people would be blessed.

Psalm 101 is another royal psalm in which the king pledges to be loyal to God, rule with integrity, and live an honorable life that promotes justice and turns away evil and perversity. This psalm is attributed to David.

LOOKING AHEAD (5 MINUTES)

Mark it

Encourage participants to read and mark one or more of the passages listed in this section during the week ahead. Let the group know that at the start of next week's session you will ask volunteers to share any insights they have from this exercise.

You are encouraged to do the "Mark it" exercise as well.

Next Time

Briefly introduce the next chapter of the story that appears in session 6. In the next session, the story of the divided kingdom continues on to a tragic end, but God leads some of the people back home to start over. To review this week's story and to help prepare for the next session, you and your group are encouraged to read introductions to the following in a study Bible:

- Historical Books
- 2 Kings
- 2 Chronicles
- Ezra
- Nehemiah

You may find it helpful to take some notes or highlight items in the readings to share next week as part of Telling the Story.

- Esther
- Lamentations
- Daniel

OUR STORY

Ideas for optional settings and schedules for this time are provided in the introduction on page 13 of this leader guide.

WELCOME

Whether done consecutively along with the Core Session Plan or planned for a separate time or location, consider providing hospitality in the form of refreshments.

- Arrange the room comfortably for small group discussion.
- Introduce newcomers in the group.
- Begin with prayer, using the session prayer on p. 68 or another prayer of your choice. Ask volunteers to provide prayers, if they feel comfortable doing so.
- You may wish to begin by asking if anyone has a particular question or thought to share from the large group session. As an alternative to discussing those questions, simply note them or write them down on newsprint. Small groups may decide to discuss further.

See the tips for leading and participating in small group discussion on page 17 of this guide. Make available to all participants copies of the reproducible Guidelines for Small Group Discussion.

CONVERSATION

The reflection questions are intended to help participants connect their own stories to the key themes of the greatest story. These questions can be used for personal reflection while reading or used to guide group discussion. It is unlikely a group could discuss all the questions in one discussion period. Don't be concerned about this. Here are some options for approaching the questions:

1. As leader, you may choose to focus on certain questions from the list.
2. Ask participants to suggest questions to discuss.
3. Divide the groups into smaller teams, assign the teams a designated number of questions to discuss, and then have each group report back to the large group.
4. If you have a group that has the time and interest, you could assign each participant a question or two to think about and prepare a response during the week. These responses could be shared as discussion starters when the group meets for Our Story discussion time.

Questions and Responses

The questions below are designed with personal reflection and response in mind. They do not require a certain amount of prior knowledge in order to respond. Responses may vary according to individual insights and context. Even so, a few guiding thoughts are provided for some of the questions.

○ *What would it be like to dedicate a child to God?*

○ *How are promises made at Baptism like this kind of dedication?*

During a baptismal service the parents and/or sponsors promise to ensure that the child being baptized is raised in the faith. This means making sure they grow up in a Christian community, own a Bible, and learn important faith basics such as the Lord's Prayer and Apostles' Creed.

○ *How can we hear God's voice?*

Reflect with your group on the ways that we hear God's voice today, for example, through reading the Bible, hearing a sermon, and praying. God also speaks to us through the sacraments of Baptism and Holy Communion, when we both hear and see the power of God's love for us, and receive the gifts of faith and eternal life.

○ *What makes the appointing of a king such a turning point for the tribes of Israel?*

○ *What would you say is the ideal role of a government leader?*

○ *Do you think faith (not religion) and politics ought to mix? If so, how? If not, why not?*

Faith is a gift that draws us into a deep, all-encompassing relationship with God. Religion is a system of beliefs.

○ *How would you describe God's role in choosing leaders, especially leaders in communities of faith?*

○ *Can you think of any modern David vs. Goliath stories? What role, if any, does faith play in these stories?*

○ *Prophets in Israel would later talk about a messiah who would come from the family of David (Isaiah 11:1-3). Where have you heard the word* messiah *before? What do you think of when you hear the word?*

The Hebrew word *messiah* means "anointed one."

○ *David was known as one of Israel's greatest leaders and a man of God. He also made some huge mistakes. What might this tell you about those through whom God does great things, including you?*

○ *How would you define godly wisdom?*

Questions and Responses (continued)

- *The temple was said to be God's house, a place where God was present and could be worshiped. How is that similar to or different from our churches? Where is God?*

Solomon, in his prayer blessing the temple, acknowledges that God is present in all places and cannot be contained, even within a holy space dedicated to God (1 Kings 8:27-30).

- *What is your reaction to finding out that Solomon worshiped other gods?*

- *The split in the united kingdom of Israel led to a number of dangerous problems. What do you think some of those problems might have been?*

- *Moses had warned the people over 300 years earlier that they would only be able to keep the land promised to them if they obeyed and worshiped God alone. How do you suppose they forgot this so easily?*

- *What "idols" do we turn to?*

- *Christians believe in one God, who is creator of all, who chose to bless the people of Israel, who became flesh in Jesus Christ, and who is present as Holy Spirit. What do you think sets God apart from other gods?*

- *What about people of other religions who believe in other gods? Do you think we should be tolerant of them? Work to destroy them? Try to convert them? Not sure? Why?*

Provide colored markers, paper, construction paper, poster board, magazines, scissors, or other materials that may be used to complete this creative assignment.

Creative Corner

Depending on how your schedule is organized, you may wish to assign this activity to individuals or small groups.

Create a job description for the perfect king or queen or political leader. Illustrate it if you wish.

TRAILS OF TEARS AND JOY

6

2 Kings—Esther, Lamentations, Daniel

Israel falls to Assyria . . . Judah falls to Babylon . . . into exile and back again

SESSION PREPARATION

OVERVIEW

In the previous session, the Israelites began to put down roots and unite under a king. God made a covenant with the house of King David. Solomon built a temple in Jerusalem to honor God. However, the kingdom split in two after Solomon's death. Further adventures now ensue when the people fail to worship God alone and are conquered by Babylon and sent into exile, temporarily losing their land. Hope is restored when they return home and rebuild the temple.

Materials for this session available on the Leader Reference CD:

- Bible History Timeline (CHART)
- Kings of Judah and Israel (CHART)
- Jerusalem in Nehemiah's Time (MAP)
- Ancient Assyrian Empire (MAP)
- Ancient Babylonian Empire (MAP)
- Ancient Persian Kingdom (MAP)

Scenes in this Session

One Down! (2 Kings 1–17)
All Is Lost (2 Kings 18–25; 2 Chronicles 36:11-21)
How Can We Sing the Lord's Song in a Foreign Land? (Lamentations; Daniel 1–6)
Going Home (2 Chronicles 36:22-23; Ezra 1–2; Isaiah 40–43)
Reconstruction and Reclaimed Identity (Ezra, Nehemiah)
Queen in Persia (Esther)

What's the Story?

Collectively, these books narrate the downfall of the divided kingdoms, the people's time in exile, and the eventual return to Jerusalem.

STORY KEYS

- God wants steadfast love and devotion from the people.
- Both Israel and Judah fall to foreign nations, and Jerusalem is destroyed.
- The Babylonian exile is a time of great lament and learning from the past.
- God's people return home to recover their identity as God's people.
- Esther saves her people from persecution in Persia.

2 Kings picks up where 1 Kings left off, telling stories associated with the kings of the divided kingdoms, Israel (north) and Judah (south). The prophet Elisha becomes Elijah's successor and plays a significant role as the story unfolds. Israel is the first kingdom to fall, followed by Judah. As noted in the previous session, the author of both 1 and 2 Kings told selected stories to make a theological point. That makes it difficult to assign actual dates to the events recorded here.

2 Chronicles retells the story of Solomon and the formation of the divided kingdoms, and goes on to describe how the Babylonians capture Jerusalem, destroy the temple, and force the people into exile. But God stirs up a foreign leader, King Cyrus of Persia, who declares an end to the exile.

Lamentations is a collection of poems that lament the fall of Jerusalem. Tradition attributes these poems to the prophet, Jeremiah, but we really don't know who wrote them. A Hebrew acrostic pattern is used in four of the poems, utilizing the letters of the alphabet in order.

Ezra and Nehemiah originally made up one book. They tell us about the release of the people from exile, their return to Jerusalem, and the rebuilding of the city and the temple. Nehemiah also highlights the return of God's laws as central to the identity of the people. Additional laws are passed to make sure the people really stick with it this time.

The book of Esther reveals another angle of the exile—that of a Jewish family residing in the Persian Empire after many people returned home. Esther, a Jew, becomes Queen of Persia and saves the day when an evil member of the king's court seeks to condemn the Jews still residing in Persia. Purim, a Jewish festival, was created to celebrate the rescue of the people from this persecution.

What's the Message?

The Historical Books convey a very specific type of history—a theological history of God's chosen people. Part of their message is that God requires steadfast devotion and faithfulness in adhering to God's laws. We've seen this demonstrated over and over again. When Israel and Judah don't hold up their part of the covenant by worshiping only God and following God's laws, things go poorly for the people—very poorly. God's rebellious people never anticipated losing their land to foreigners and then being forced to live in exile. But it happened. First Israel fell and then Judah followed. And God's temple, God's holy habitation in the midst of the people, was destroyed.

But there is more to the message in these books. We also see that God offers second chances. God will never desert God's people.

Ezra and Nehemiah describe a time of repentance and renewal in which God's people not only rebuild the temple and the city of Jerusalem, but rebuild their lives around the law. This is a time when focusing on worship of God alone and adhering to God's law are critical. The people have already learned what can happen if they don't tend to their part of the covenant. Additional strict laws are established to make sure that the people are separated from foreigners to help prevent them from backsliding into worshiping foreign gods and idols again. Marriage outside the faith is no longer permitted.

The book of Esther is written, in part, to explain the origin of the festival of Purim. But it also gives us a look at what persecution in a foreign land looks like and how a brave woman participates in saving her people. It's a book that highlights leadership during troubled times, with both the good and bad that it can bring. The scoundrel Haman is clearly out to do evil, while Esther and Mordecai save the day for their people. But the rejoicing at the end of the book is also tempered by Esther's order encouraging her people to take revenge on Haman's family. And the revenge does not end there, as Esther's people killed thousands more thoughout the Persian Empire.

PREPARE

1. Review chapter 6 in the participant book.
2. Review the overview and session plan for session 6 in the leader guide.
3. Watch the DVD segment for session 6.
4. Have extra Bibles available for those who did not bring one.
5. Have equipment for projecting or viewing the DVD set up and ready to go.
6. Consider distributing handouts or projecting images of reference materials (see list on p. 75) in the session. You might want to do this during Telling the Story or while discussing the Background Files.
7. If you are having the class do the Creative Corner activity, gather any materials suggested.
8. Pray for your class members and for God's presence and guidance as you gather in God's Word.

MATERIALS NEEDED

- Extra copies of the Bible
- Participant books
- Computer or DVD player; projector or TV monitor
- Course DVD
- Reference materials
- Creative Corner materials (optional)
- Name tags
- Refreshments (optional)

LEADER PRAYER

Dear God, thank you for demonstrating your faithfulness to your people throughout the ages. Help me to experience your faithful presence as I prepare for this session. Make me a reflection of your love during the group's time together. I pray in Jesus' name. Amen.

CORE SESSION PLAN

The Core Session Plan is designed for use in one 60-minute period. The Core Session Plan can be extended 45-60 minutes by incorporating the group reflection time called Our Story, found at the end of the Core Session Plan.

GATHERING (10 MINUTES)

Welcome and check-in

Provide name tags again as you welcome participants to the session. If you are serving refreshments, have them set out ahead of time. Spend a few minutes asking if anyone wants to share any thoughts or insights from their personal "Mark It" reading for the week. You won't be able to spend much time on this, but hearing a couple of testimonials will encourage more in the group to make this weekly reading and devotional reflection a part of their routine.

Scripture and prayer

Read the following verse and prayer, or ask a volunteer to do so.

But many of the priests and Levites and heads of families, old people who had seen the first house on its foundations, wept with a loud voice when they saw this house, though many shouted aloud for joy, so that the people could not distinguish the sound of the joyful shout from the sound of the people's weeping, for the people shouted so loudly that the sound was heard far away. (Ezra 3:12-13)

Dear God, we are like your rebellious people, who sometimes turned from you to follow tempting and unfaithful ways of living. Like them, we often bring trials and tears upon ourselves. We thank you for your steadfast love that renews us, offering repentance and second chances. You turn our tears into joy and restore us as your blessed children. Amen.

TELLING THE STORY (15 MINUTES)

You or your designated storyteller should now turn to telling the portion of the story that is highlighted in session 6. Incorporate any or all of the Background File notes in the participant book (p. 57) as part of the telling. Use one of the following three options for telling the story, or devise your own.

See the storytelling tips on p. 10 of this guide.

1. Read through, summarize, and comment on the story as provided in the participant book.
2. Ask for volunteers to tell portions of the story.
3. Read the story script provided below.

At the end of the storytelling time, summarize the Story Keys for this session.

The Story Script for Session 6

After Elijah anointed him to be the next prophet, Elisha quickly became a miracle worker, raising a boy from the dead and curing an enemy Aramean of leprosy. He also anointed a man named Jehu to be king of Israel, the northern kingdom. Jehu wiped out Queen Jezebel and many members of King Ahab's family. He killed many who worshiped the false god Baal, too, but failed God by not tearing down idols that had been built by King Jeroboam.

In the southern kingdom of Judah, Jehoash, a seven-year-old king, repaired parts of the temple that had been destroyed, but did not destroy shrines built to other gods.

The eventual destruction of Israel and Judah started with a threat from Aram (Syria). Then, the devastation of the kingdoms and deportation of the people began. Assyria captured Samaria in Israel in 722 B.C.E., ending the northern kingdom and replacing the people of Israel with peoples from many lands.

Meanwhile, King Hezekiah of Judah worked hard to please God by destroying many places of idol worship. God protected the southern kingdom by sending an angel to end the Assyrian threat, striking down thousands, including King Sennacherib. Hezekiah, however, ignored the prophetic warnings of Isaiah. His short-sightedness caused the eventual unraveling of Judah.

King Manasseh undid Hezekiah's work by rebuilding altars to foreign gods. Josiah became king of Judah in 640 B.C.E., and reformed the kingdom based on the book of laws that was rediscovered in the temple. Josiah tore down altars and shrines to foreign gods, killed many of the priests that served these gods, and brought back the celebration of the Passover. He died at the hands of King Neco of Egypt.

The Story Script for Session 6 (continued)

Under Babylon's Nebuchadnezzar, Jerusalem was captured in 597 B.C.E. The temple treasures were deported to Babylon, along with many of Judah's skilled leaders. Judah's puppet king Zedekiah tried to fight back against Babylon, but this rebellion was crushed and both the temple and the city walls were burned to the ground. In 586 B.C.E. the southern kingdom also fell to Babylon.

The kingdoms of Israel and Judah had been sorely punished for failing to give their sole loyalty to God. A period of sorrowful prayers, called laments, followed as the people cried out from exile in Babylon. This is captured in the book of Lamentations and in Psalm 137.

The story of Daniel is about a man and his friends who refused to reject God and worship a statue of King Nebuchadnezzar of Babylon that the king had set up himself! The friends were saved from a fiery furnace, and Daniel survived a night in a lions' den, because they all remained faithful to God.

Finally, Babylon fell to the Persians led by King Cyrus. God used Cyrus to free the people to return home and rebuild God's house in Jerusalem. Long ago, God had led the Israelites out of slavery in Egypt to the promised land. Now God freed the people from captivity in Babylon and led them home.

The people immediately began to worship at the old temple site when they arrived home. Opposition to the rebuilding delayed the reconstruction, yet the prophets Haggai and Zechariah encouraged the people to keep at it. In 515 B.C.E. the second temple was completed and dedicated in Jerusalem.

Some years later, a Jewish man serving as a wine server to the king of Persia heard that Jerusalem's city walls had not been rebuilt. At his request, Nehemiah was given permission to return to Jerusalem and he had three-foot-thick city walls built in less than two months.

For the people, returning home meant hard work in rebuilding the temple and their true identity as God's people. Long-forgotten laws were reinstated, covering everything from the Sabbath or holy day to restrictions on marriage to foreigners. But now the people were back, the temple was rebuilt, and the city walls were secured.

The Persian Empire continued to grow, extending as far east as India and as far west as Greece. A story is told about a young Jewish woman named Esther who lived in Susa, the capital of Persia. This dramatic story gives a sense of life inside Persia for Jews still living there under the rule of King Xerxes (486-465 B.C.E.).

Haman, the king's highest official, plotted to have all of the Jewish people killed. Esther outwitted Haman, becoming the new queen and saving the day. Esther and her Uncle Mordecai turned the tables on Haman, having him hanged on the same gallows he had built to kill Mordecai. Mordecai became the king's highest official, in place of Haman. Still today, the Jewish festival of Purim celebrates the day the people were saved.

PICTURING THE STORY (20 MINUTES)

Go through the reflection questions listed in this section in the participant book (p. 57). Then play the segment called Trails of Tears and Joy (session 6) on the course DVD. Encourage the participants to watch the story unfold as artist Joe Castillo depicts the scenes of the story. Participants may be invited to write down their own questions.

When the segment is done, address the questions together as a large group or ask the participants to discuss them in smaller groups. Invite participants to share their own questions or observations. What difference did it make to see the story in this way?

SINGING AND PRAYING THE STORY (10 MINUTES)

Use one or both of the psalms provided in the participant book to help address the story and its themes. Psalms are best read aloud. You may have one volunteer read the entire psalm or portion of a psalm. Or you may wish to have the psalm read responsively, verse by verse or line by line. Use a solo reader with the group responding, or read responsively using different groups.

As time allows, discuss the observations and questions provided.

Psalm 137 is a lament, or community prayer for help, written during the people's exile in Babylon. The psalmist is tormented by captors who say they want to hear a song of Zion (Jerusalem). The psalmist laments Jerusalem's fall, vows not to forget God's holy city and habitation, and looks to the day when Jerusalem will receive its due retribution.

Psalm 85 is another lament or community prayer, that asks for God to once again show favor to the descendants of Jacob. The psalmist reminds God of previous times when God pardoned the people. Together, people of the community ask for God's anger to be put aside so that God might establish a renewed intimate relationship with the people.

LOOKING AHEAD (5 MINUTES)

Briefly introduce the next chapter of the story that appears in session 7.

Mark it

You are encouraged to do the "Mark it" exercise as well.

Encourage participants to read and mark one or more of the passages listed in this section during the week ahead. Let the group know that at the start of next week's session you will ask volunteers to share any insights they have from this exercise.

Next time

You may find it helpful to take some notes or highlight items in the readings to share next week as part of Telling the Story.

In the next session we will take a look at the story of God's people through the lenses of the Old Testament prophets who lived and worked during the time of the kings and kingdoms and into the time after the exile. To review this week's story and to help prepare for the next session, you and your group are encouraged to read introductions to the following in a study Bible. It's a long list, so if you can't get to all the reading, focus on the first five items.

- Prophets
- Isaiah
- Jeremiah
- Lamentations
- Ezekiel
- Daniel
- Hosea
- Joel
- Amos
- Obadiah
- Jonah
- Micah
- Nahum
- Habakkuk
- Zephaniah
- Haggai
- Zechariah
- Malachi

OUR STORY

WELCOME

Ideas for optional settings and schedules for this time are provided in the introduction on page 13 of this leader guide. .

Whether Our Story is done consecutively along with the Core Session Plan, or planned for a separate time or location, consider providing hospitality in the form of refreshments.

- Arrange the room comfortably for small group discussion.

- Introduce newcomers in the group.
- Begin with prayer, using the session prayer on p. 78 or another prayer of your choice. Ask volunteers to provide prayers, if they feel comfortable doing so.
- You may wish to begin by asking if anyone has a particular question or thought to share from the large group session. As an alternative to discussing those questions, simply note them or write them down on newsprint. Small groups may decide to discuss further.

CONVERSATION

The reflection questions are intended to help participants connect their own stories to the key themes of the greatest story. These questions can be used for personal reflection while reading or used to guide group discussion. It is unlikely that a group could discuss all the questions in one discussion period. Don't be concerned about this. Here are some options for approaching the questions:

See the tips for leading and participating in small group discussion on page 17 of this guide. Make available to all participants copies of the reproducible Guidelines for Small Group Discussion.

1. As leader, you may choose to focus on certain questions from the list.
2. Ask participants to suggest questions to discuss.
3. Have participants form smaller groups, assign the groups a designated number of questions to discuss, and then have each group report back to the large group.
4. If participants have the time and interest, you could assign each person a question or two to think about and prepare a response during the week. These responses could be shared as discussion starters when the group meets for Our Story discussion time.

Questions and Responses

The questions below are designed with personal reflection and response in mind. They do not require a certain amount of prior knowledge in order to respond. Responses may vary according to individual insights and context. Even so, a few guiding thoughts are provided for some of the questions.

○ *The First Commandment says, "You shall have no other gods." Why do you think it was so hard for the people and their rulers to live out this commandment? What makes it so difficult for us today?*

Any time something gets in the way of our relationship with God, it becomes a "god" in our lives. Sometimes money or other material wealth takes God's place in our lives. Other times emotions like fear or arrogance rule our lives. Ask your group to list various things that get in the way of our relationship with God.

Questions and Responses (continued)

- *How predictable was Israel's bad ending that came in 722 B.C.E.? Why?*

Despite many warnings and second chances from God, the people failed to worship God alone and follow God's laws.

- *How was Hezekiah short-sighted? How do actions in the present affect the future?*

- *Why do you think the discovery of the book of the law was so surprising and so important? Imagine living in a world without laws or rituals. What would it be like?*

The fact that the people didn't even know where the book of God's law was located is an indication of how far they had strayed from God's laws. The rediscovery of the law offered an opportunity to begin to abide by God's law again.

- *God's people cried out to God using prayers of deepest grief called laments. Why do you think this was important? What laments have you cried?*

- *How can we support those who face the testing of their faith in God?*

- *In the book of Isaiah, Persian King Cyrus is referred to as God's shepherd (44:28). Do you think it is surprising that a non-Israelite is described this way? Why or why not?*

These questions offer an opportunity for your group to discuss who God does and doesn't use to serve God's mission and purpose in the world. If God is the God of all of creation, does any part of humanity or creation fall outside of serving God's intentions?

- *What do you think of the idea that the exile was God's way of penalizing the people of Israel?*

- *What, if anything, enslaves you?*

- *What issues or projects are worth completing, no matter what opponents or circumstances arise?*

- *What influences, both inside and outside of our communities of faith, threaten our relationship with God?*

- *Ezra and Nehemiah were considered reformers. What do you think needs reform or rebuilding in the church today?*

Ezra was instrumental in leading the people back to Jerusalem and in beginning to institute new laws to protect the Jewish people from straying again. Nehemiah began the repair of the city walls and demanded that the people follow the laws given by God, including keeping the Sabbath.

Questions and Responses (continued)

- *The Jewish people have often been the target of unjust persecution. What can we do to help those who are treated unjustly, especially those who suffer persecution?*
- *Who would you identify as a hero? Why?*

Creative Corner

Imagine that you are one of the people of Israel or Judah forced to go into exile in a foreign land far away. You can only take whatever you can fit into a small duffle bag. Make a list of the things you will bring with you. How did you decide what to put on your list?

Provide colored markers, paper, construction paper, poster board, magazines, scissors, or other materials that may be used to complete this creative assignment.

7

WHEN GOD SPEAKS
The Prophets

God speaks . . . through the prophets . . . to God's people

SESSION PREPARATION

OVERVIEW

Materials for this session available on the Leader Reference CD:
- Bible History Timeline (CHART)
- Prophets (CHART)
- Ezekiel's Vision of the Restored Temple (DIAGRAM)

Last time we learned more about the downs and then ups of the people of God whose divided kingdom fell and suffered the destruction of the temple and Jerusalem. Their Babylonian Exile lasted nearly seventy years before they returned to make a fresh start. Session 7 gives an overview of the messages of the prophets which forewarn the kingdoms of the impending threat of foreign domination and give hope for promised restoration of Jerusalem.

Scenes in this Session

Who Were the Prophets?
Early Warning (Amos, Hosea, Isaiah, Micah)
Storm Clouds Gather (Zephaniah, Jeremiah, Habakkuk, Nahum)
Hope Restored (Ezekiel, Isaiah II, Haggai, Zechariah)
It's God's Future (Obadiah, Joel, Malachi, Daniel)
God's Surprising Grace (Jonah)

STORY KEYS
- God is an active participant in history.
- God holds every nation accountable for its actions.
- God uses prophets to bring messages of judgment and hope.
- The messages of the prophets unite the past, present, and future.

What's the Story?

The seventeen prophets listed in this session lived and preached their messages from God from the eighth century all the way to the fifth century B.C.E. and beyond. They cover a vast time period and variety of conditions in the Middle East region. And each carried a message specific to the situation of his time.

The prophets who arose in the eighth century (Amos, Hosea, Isaiah, Micah) carried the early warnings regarding what the people and leaders of both Israel and Judah were doing to undermine their covenant relationship with God. They warned of judgment that would fall upon the people if they did not begin to live faithful and just lives. These messages were spoken using imagery from everything from nature to military life. However, in Hosea's case, his personal life became part of his prophecy, too. His marriages to two unfaithful women symbolized the unfaithfulness of both Israel and Judah to God.

Things really got stormy during the period in which the next group of prophets appeared on the scene (Zephaniah, Jeremiah, Habakkuk, Nahum). The warnings of the earlier prophets had unfolded and Israel fell to foreign domination. These prophets turned their attention to Judah during a time of political instability. They warned that Judah faced the same fate as Israel if the people didn't return to God. Nahum had harsh words for Nineveh, the capital city of Israel's enemy Assyria.

While Ezekiel began prophesying before Judah was conquered and Jerusalem fell, the prophets of this third group preached during the exile (Ezekiel, Isaiah II). God's threats of destruction had already been fulfilled and the downtrodden people needed to hear a message of hope and restoration.

This last group (Haggai, Zechariah, Obadiah, Joel, Malachi, Daniel) rose on the scene after the people returned to Jerusalem and the temple was rebuilt. Out of these, Daniel stands out as a very different book revealing a series of wild and often violent apocalyptic visions.

The last book, Jonah, is actually more of a short story than a traditional prophetic book, because it tells the story of God's decision to withdraw judgment upon Nineveh after the city repents. This book may have been written between 722 B.C.E. and 612 B.C.E., when Nineveh actually fell, or it may have been written later during a time when intolerance of foreigners was running high in Judah after the return from exile.

What's the Message?

While the prophets speak to God's people over a long period of time there are certain themes that run through their time-specific messages. One of the predominant themes is that God wants the people to be faithful to God alone and to the laws associated with Moses at Mount Sinai. This theme was prevalent throughout the Historical Books, too. In Jeremiah 2:8-13, the prophet reminds the people that even the priests have forgotten God's laws and have "forsaken" God. Amos 2:4-5 clearly calls for Judah's punishment because "they have rejected the law of the LORD, and have not kept his statutes."

The people are also called to repent both for their worship of foreign deities and their abuse of the poor. Sexual imagery is used throughout the prophets referring to the people's relationship with other gods as being adulterous (Jeremiah 3:6), demonstrating faithlessness in their relationship with God. This is especially true in Hosea where his marriages mirror his message. Ezekiel speaks of the death and destruction that will result from worshiping idols (Ezekiel 6:11-14). The message of abuse of power and unfair treatment of the poor is predominant in the books of Amos and Micah. Micah 2:1-2 denounces those who are already wealthy and seize land and property to "oppress householder and house, people and their inheritance."

Another theme that runs through the prophets is the call to trust God alone for all things and not to engage in foreign alliances. Isaiah 39:1-8 gives an example of Judah's king Hezekiah welcoming Babylonian envoys and showing them everything, including his treasure house and armory. Hezekiah, because of his brazen stupidity, brings God's promise of wrath upon the people.

But judgment is not the only message the prophets bring. They also bring beautiful words of promise and hope. Isaiah 40:1-8 carries a message of the promise of new beginnings to God's people: "Comfort, O comfort my people, says your God," foretelling the coming end of the exile in Babylon. Ezekiel 28:25 promises that God will "gather the house of Israel from the peoples among whom they are scattered, and manifest my holiness in them in the sight of the nations."

Throughout the books of the prophets it is clear that God is at work in and through the history of all nations, and the future is in God's hands. The book of Jonah also reminds the people that God is willing and able to forgive any who repent, even their worst enemies.

PREPARE

1. Review chapter 7 in the participant book.
2. Review the overview and plan for session 7 in the leader guide.
3. Watch the DVD segment for session 7.
4. Have extra Bibles available for those who did not bring one.
5. Have equipment for projecting or viewing the DVD set up and ready to go.
6. Consider distributing handouts or projecting images of reference materials (see list on p. 86) in the session. You might want to do this during Telling the Story or while discussing the Background Files.
7. If you are having the class do the Creative Corner activity, gather any materials suggested.
8. Pray for your class members and for God's presence and guidance as you gather in God's Word.

MATERIALS NEEDED

- Extra copies of the Bible
- Participant books
- Computer or DVD player; projector or TV monitor
- Course DVD
- Reference materials
- Creative Corner materials (optional)
- Name tags
- Refreshments (optional)

LEADER PRAYER

Loving God, you seek deep and committed relationships with your people of all time and ages, so much so that you send prophets to speak your word when we falter and go astray. Be with me as I prepare and lead this session so that all who participate may come to understand the power of your Word more fully. Amen.

CORE SESSION PLAN

The Core Session Plan is designed for use in one 60-minute period. The Core Session Plan can be extended 45-60 minutes by incorporating the group reflection time called Our Story, found at the end of the Core Session Plan.

GATHERING (10 MINUTES)

Welcome and check-in

Provide name tags again as you welcome participants to the session. If you are serving refreshments, have them set out ahead of time. Spend a few minutes asking if anyone wants to share any thoughts or insights from their personal "Mark It" reading for the week. You won't be able to spend much time on this, but hearing a couple of testimonials will encourage more in the group to make this weekly reading and devotional reflection a part of their routine.

Scripture and prayer

Read the following verse and prayer, or ask a volunteer to do so.

He has told you, O mortal, what is good; and what does the LORD require of you but to do justice, and to love kindness, and to walk humbly with your God? (Micah 6:8)

O God, throughout all of history you have made it clear that you desire your people to love and honor you not only directly, but also by living just lives that respect and honor all of your creation. Empower us to live as the good stewards of the earth and to treat all its inhabitants with the justice you desire. Help us to fulfill the calling to walk humbly in the light of your love. Amen.

TELLING THE STORY (15 MINUTES)

See the storytelling tips on p. 10 of this guide.

You or your designated storyteller should now turn to telling the portion of the story that is highlighted in session 7. Incorporate any or all of the Background File notes in the participant book (p. 67) as part of the telling. Use one of the following three options for telling the story, or devise your own.

1. Read through, summarize, and comment on the story as provided in the participant book.
2. Ask for volunteers to tell portions of the story.

3. Read the story script provided below.

At the end of the storytelling time, summarize the Story Keys for this session.

The Story Script for Session 7

Call them what you want—messengers, preachers, rabble-rousers, truth-tellers, pot-stirrers—the prophets of the Bible played a big role in the greatest story. They were an inspired group. Inspired and recruited by God to speak for God. We think of prophets as being people who make predictions about the future. But God's prophets were about much more than forecasting the future. Their messages were timely, meaning they reminded Israel and Judah of God's faithfulness in the past, of the critical need for them to be faithful in the present, and the future consequences of their unfaithfulness.

They were in tune with what was happening in their time and place. They filtered their observations through God's laws and sense of justice. They called the people to open their eyes and look around at what was happening. Were they and their leaders being faithful to God alone and living according to the covenant promises they and their ancestors had made with God? Did they need to repent and return to God? Were they treating one another, and especially the poor among them, with justice, as the law required? Were they trusting in God or making alliances with foreign powers to ensure their political future?

Each prophet had his own story, though some who have studied Isaiah carefully think that this book contains the messages of more than one prophet, each living at different times in Israel's history and bringing messages that spoke to different situations.

Amos, a shepherd and tree farmer, spoke against King Jeroboam and the wealthy of Israel for growing wealthy on the backs of the poor. He pointed to a coming day of judgment that was fulfilled when Assyria defeated Israel in 722 B.C.E.

During the reign of five kings, **Hosea** demonstrated in his own marriage the unfaithfulness of the people's worship of Canaanite fertility gods and their forging of alliances with Assyria and Egypt. He warned that punishment as severe as exile might be the result of such religious and political prostitution.

Isaiah emerged as Assyria threatened and destroyed Samaria, the capital of Israel. Similar to Amos and Hosea, he warned Judah and its capital Jerusalem of their abuse of the poor, making alliances with foreign powers, and following other gods. A second and perhaps a third prophet found in the writings of Isaiah offered hope of return from exile and the promise of a messiah, or savior of the people.

The Story Script for Session 7 (continued)

Micah spoke against the powerful priests, politicians, and traders, and on behalf of the poor. He called for a return to faithfulness to God, saying "What does the Lord require of you but to do justice, and to love kindness, and to walk humbly with your God" (6:8).

Zephaniah appeared on the scene after the northern kingdom had been captured by Assyria while the southern kingdom stood on its own. He delivered a harsh message against idolatry, injustice, and crooked deals, but he also pointed toward a time when God would forgive and restore the fortunes of Judah.

Jeremiah suffered personally for his stern warnings against Judah's kings who turned to foreign powers rather than to God for help. Although the people didn't think that Jerusalem could be defeated, Babylon consumed Egypt, Assyria, and then Judah in its hunger to increase its empire. Poor, battered Jeremiah wrote of hope and promise to come from his existence among the exiles in Babylon.

Habakkuk complained against the corruption, arrogance, and idolatry going on in Jerusalem even as the situation with Babylon grew worse. As disaster approached, he prayed for the people with complete trust in God.

Nahum focused his message on the horrible evils of Nineveh, the capital of Assyria. He called on Judah to celebrate the destruction of Nineveh by God, the divine warrior, who sets the oppressed free while holding oppressors accountable!

Speaking in Judah's darkest hour, **Ezekiel** used bizarre images to speak words of judgment against the disgusting worship of idols right in the heart of God's temple. For these and other sins, Ezekiel declared that God would abandon Jerusalem. His message also lifted up hope through the image of God breathing new life into dry bones, which represented God's people in exile.

The words of an unknown prophet are presented in Isaiah 40–56. His words sing with hope in a future for God's people as their exile ends and they return home to rebuild Jerusalem. His words included the promise of drawing all nations to worship at Jerusalem. Sections of this prophecy called Servant Songs are often used to describe a suffering servant who would suffer and even die for the sake of the people, just as Jesus' suffering and death saves humanity from sin.

Haggai encouraged the people to get the temple completed after they returned from exile so that God could be fully present again with the chosen people.

The Story Script for Session 7 (continued)

Zechariah also preached during the time of the restoration of the temple as he envisioned a restored temple with priests rededicated to God. A second section of this prophecy, perhaps written later by Zechariah II, described a triumphant king riding humbly into Jerusalem, as Jesus did in the Gospels, and a vision of God's victory over all enemies later echoed in the book of Revelation.

As we enter the period of **Obadiah,** Jerusalem had been resettled, the temple rebuilt, but the people were under the control of a larger empire. Obadiah directed his message against the people of Edom, descendants of Jacob's brother Esau, who had celebrated the destruction of Jerusalem as they looted the fallen city.

Joel prophesied after the people had returned from exile and before 348 B.C.E., threatening a swarm of destructive locusts as a way to urge a return to God who would be "gracious and merciful, slow to anger, and abounding in steadfast love" (2:13).

Malachi spoke of a time when the unfaithful would be destroyed and the faithful would see the "sun of righteousness" rise, "with healing in its wings" (4:2). Malachi appeared sometime after the return from exile and the rebuilding of both the temple and Jerusalem. Sadly, it didn't take long before the people relapsed into the old ways of injustice against the poor and improper worship.

Although listed among the prophets in our Christian version of the Old Testament, **Daniel** is listed among the Writings in the Hebrew Scriptures. In the first six chapters we read of the drama of Daniel and his friends living in Babylon. In the second half of the book we encounter what is called apocalyptic literature. This includes images of the end times when God will battle evil, and win the ultimate victory, raising the faithful to everlasting life.

Even though the prophet **Jonah** addressed the city of Nineveh before its destruction, this book of prophecy probably comes from a much later time. In contrast to the prophet Nahum's celebration of Nineveh's destruction, God sent the reluctant Jonah to warn Nineveh to repent and thus be spared. It's a remarkable story about God's mercy, even though it's the big fish that often gets all the attention.

PICTURING THE STORY (20 MINUTES)

Briefly review the reflection questions listed in this section in the participant book (p. 67). Then play the segment called When God Speaks (session 7) on the course DVD. Encourage the participants to watch the story unfold as artist Joe Castillo depicts the scenes of the story. Participants may be invited to write down their own questions.

When the segment is done, address the questions together as a large group or ask the participants to discuss in smaller teams. Invite participants to share their own questions or observations. What difference did it make to see the story in this way?

SINGING AND PRAYING THE STORY (10 MINUTES)

Use one or both of the psalms provided in the participant book to help address the story and its themes. Psalms are best read aloud. You may have one volunteer read the entire psalm or portion of a psalm. Or you may wish to have the psalm read responsively, verse by verse or line by line. Use a solo reader with the group responding, or read responsively using different groups.

As time allows, discuss the observations and questions provided.

Psalm 14 is an instructional, or Wisdom, psalm. Here the psalmist talks about fools who don't believe in God and engage in horrid behavior. God searches for a wise man, but is unable to find one because humanity has been caught up in evil. We are reminded that God is a God of the poor and righteous and will ultimately prevail.

Psalm 68:1-20 is a hymn of thanksgiving and praise celebrating the fact that God elevates the righteous, but casts down the wicked. The psalmist describes God as one "who rides upon the clouds" as king and protects the most lowly people of society while all God's enemies flee in defeat.

LOOKING AHEAD (5 MINUTES)

Mark it

Encourage participants to read and mark one or more of the passages listed in this section during the week ahead. Let the group know that at the start of next week's session you will ask volunteers to share any insights they have from this exercise.

You are encouraged to do the "Mark it" exercise as well.

Next Time

You may find it helpful to take some notes or highlight items in the readings to share next week as part of Telling the Story.

In the next session we will explore the final group of books in the Old Testament. We will call them Wisdom and Poetry books, but they are also known as the Writings. They help fill in the story of God's people by giving us a clearer picture of how people thought about God and how to live as God's people in the world. To review this week's story and to help prepare for the next session, you and your group are encouraged to read introductions to the following in a study Bible:

- Wisdom and Poetry Books
- Job
- Psalms
- Proverbs
- Ecclesiastes
- Song of Solomon

OUR STORY

WELCOME

Ideas for optional settings and schedules for this time are provided in the introduction on page 13 of this leader guide.

Whether done consecutively along with the Core Session Plan or planned for a separate time or location, consider providing hospitality in the form of refreshments.

- Arrange the room comfortably for small group discussion.
- Introduce newcomers in the group.
- Begin with prayer, using the session prayer on p. 89 or another prayer of your choice. Ask volunteers to provide prayers, if they feel comfortable doing so.
- You may wish to begin by asking if anyone has a particular question or thought to share from the large group session. As an alternative to discussing those questions, simply note them or write them down on newsprint. Small groups may decide to discuss further.

CONVERSATION

See the tips for leading and participating in small group discussion on page 17 of this guide. Make available to all participants copies of the reproducible Guidelines for Small Group Discussion.

The reflection questions are intended to help participants connect their own stories to the key themes of the greatest story. These questions can be used for personal reflection while reading or used to guide group discussion. It is unlikely a group could discuss all the questions in one discussion period. Don't be concerned about this. Here are some options for approaching the questions:

1. As leader, you may choose to focus on certain questions from the list.

2. Ask participants to suggest questions to discuss.
3. Divide the groups into smaller teams, assign the teams a designated number of questions to discuss, and then have each group report back to the large group.
4. If you have a group that has the time and interest, you could assign each participant a question or two to think about and prepare a response during the week. These responses could be shared as discussion starters when the group meets for Our Story discussion time.

Questions and Responses

The questions below are designed with personal reflection and response in mind. They do not require a certain amount of prior knowledge in order to respond. Responses may vary according to individual insights and context. Even so, a few guiding thoughts are provided for some of the questions.

○ *Who comes to mind when you think of a modern-day prophet? Why?*

In the Old Testament God raised up prophets to speak God's message to the people. They came from many walks of life and often are portrayed as somewhat reluctant to serve in this capacity (see Jeremiah, for example). Participants may think of people who predict the future, but encourage them to think more broadly of those who speak messages of deep truth within their current context. Would that make people such as Martin Luther King, Jr. or Ghandi prophets?

○ *How would you say the future is based on the past and present? How do you see this relating to the message of the prophets?*

○ *If you could get the world to listen to one message from God, what would it be?*

Encourage participants to think of the one message from the Bible that speaks to each of them most clearly and strongly.

○ *Does it surprise you that the prophets delivered so many messages about justice and caring for the poor? Why or why not?*

○ *Another key message the prophets brought was about trust in God. How is trust broken? How do we break trust with God?*

God's chosen people have a clear biblical history of placing their faith in everything from idols to foreign nations.

○ *Prophets brought God's words of warning and words of promise to the people. How do we hear God's warnings and promises today?*

Questions and Responses (continued)

- *What are some ways for you or your congregation to do justice, love kindness, and walk humbly with God?*

- *It's clear that the prophets believed that politics and religion were supposed to mix. God was the ultimate ruler. How do we translate this kind of message to our own situation, where religion and government are said to be separate?*

Not only in the books of the prophets, but throughout the Bible God is clearly demonstrated as an active participant in history and the lives of all people.

- *Do you agree or disagree with this statement: "People don't usually like to hear the truth." Why or why not?*

Determining "truth" is often rather subjective. What is truth to one person might not be truth to another. Synonyms of truth are: reality, fact, and honesty. Using these words in the discussion might be helpful.

- *What does it mean to pray even in the face of disaster?*

- *What do you think about the idea of celebrating the destruction of an enemy?*

- *Some people talked about how beautiful Ezekiel's words were, but they didn't take his words to heart and act on them. How do we hear God's words and take them to heart?*

- *What words of God give you hope?*

- *How do we balance personal needs with the needs of a faith community?*

- *How might we share our vision of worshiping God with those who don't believe in our God?*

- *What would it be like to hear that your city and place of worship, which had been destroyed, would be restored?*

- *How does a description of God as judge seem to fit with Joel's description of God as gracious, loving, and slow to anger? How have you experienced both sides of God?*

- *Do you think there is a proper way to live out your faith? If not, why not? If so, what does this look like?*

Questions and Responses (continued)

- *Daniel's visions have been linked to the apocalyptic visions in Revelation in the New Testament. Some interpret these visions as predictions of current world events. What do you think about this? Do you think Daniel was meant to be read this way?*

Apocalyptic writings usually present a picture of the battle between the cosmic forces of good and evil, often portraying God and Satan going head-to-head. In both Daniel and Revelation this is done through wild metaphoric visions. But apocalyptic writings in the Bible actually are often code language that people living at the time of the writing would have understood. They were often living in times of persecution and challenge. Images of God gaining victory over the forces of evil offered hope and promise for the future. Apocalyptic writings speak to each generation that faces these challenges to faith, but they were not written to predict specific historical events 2000 years in the future.

- *What do you know or remember about the story of Jonah? Why didn't Jonah want to go to Nineveh and deliver God's message? (If you aren't sure, read the story. It's short.)*

The big fish and Jonah's attempt to run away from God usually get all the attention in the book of Jonah. But this is what makes the message of the book all the more surprising. Jonah didn't want to go to Nineveh because he knew that if he delivered God's message there was a good chance the people of Nineveh, Israel's sworn enemies, would repent and be forgiven by God. Jonah had a hard time with the wideness of God's mercy. The story is really one that demonstrates that no one is outside of the realm of God's forgiveness, not even enemies of God's chosen people.

Creative Corner

Depending on how your schedule is organized, you may wish to assign this activity for individuals or small groups.

Create a full-page newspaper ad that captures the message of a modern prophet. Using as few words as necessary, what message from God would you like to deliver to your local community, or to a national audience in a newspaper like *USA Today*? Would you need any pictures to go with the words? Remember, you are trying to get people to notice and talk about the newspaper ad.

Provide colored markers, paper, construction paper, poster board, magazines, scissors, or other materials that may be used to complete this creative assignment.

8

FOR EVERY MATTER UNDER HEAVEN

Wisdom and Poetry Books

Poetry and songs, proverbs and prayers . . . for worship . . . for all of life

SESSION PREPARATION

OVERVIEW

Materials for this session available on the Leader Reference CD:

- Types of Psalms (CHART)
- Types of Proverbs (CHART)

In the previous session we learned about God's prophets and their messages of warning when the people did not abide by God's laws and their later messages of hope and restoration for a people in exile. This session offers an opportunity to look at some books of wisdom and poetry in the Bible.

Scenes in this Session

Why Do the Innocent Suffer? (Job)
Songs for All Times (Psalms)
Woman Wisdom Calls (Proverbs)
Search for Meaning (Ecclesiastes)
Set Me as a Seal upon Your Heart (Song of Solomon)

STORY KEYS

- Rely upon God and strive to be content, no matter what life brings.
- The foundation of wisdom is to fear (meaning respect) God.
- Sometimes suffering cannot be explained.
- Proverbs describes the differences between the wise, who will prosper, and the foolish, who will suffer and fail.
- God has a deep love for all of creation.

What's the Story?

Job, Proverbs, and Ecclesiastes vary in their content and theological approaches, but they are all made up of wisdom literature. This type of literature, which dates back to ancient times, seeks to educate readers on how life is to be lived in relation to God and to neighbors.

Job is the story of a faithful and good, yet beleaguered, man whose fortune goes from bad to worse after God permits Satan to test him. As a result, Job loses all that he holds dear in life: his property, his children, and finally his health. Three friends come to comfort him, but end up arguing that he must deserve his suffering.

God finally responds to Job in chapters 38–41,and gives him a cosmic view of the universe that is far greater than just humanity. While Job's initial response to God is one of silence, he finally declares his repentance and God restores his life and fortune.

Proverbs, written in the fourth century B.C.E., is a collection of maxims that together serve as an instruction manual to daily living. While this book tends to deal mostly with secular living, it opens with the reminder that "the fear of the LORD is the beginning of knowledge" (1:7) and the admonition to keep God's commandments (3:1).

Ecclesiastes also includes these two admonitions, but it is written from a very different perspective. It is a record of a "Teacher," believed to be a person named Oohelet, which is actually the Hebrew translation of the name of the book. The Teacher writes of his life and experience and speaks frequently of how unreliable life really is.

The book of Psalms is a collection of poetry and songs written by a variety of authors to address different needs. See the chart "Types of Psalms" on the Leader Reference CD.

The Song of Solomon is a poetic conversation that celebrates the power of human love, which some believe is a metaphorical description of the love of God.

What's the Message?

Suffering is the focus of the book of Job. Why do bad things happen to good people and what is the response, born out of faith, when it does hit? When faced with trite responses from his friends, Job remains skeptical and turns out to be the only one who actually engages God in conversation through prayer. This is lifted up as a faithful response to the presence of suffering in one's life, even though God gives Job no direct response to his questions about why suffering exists. However, God's long and detailed response to Job makes it very clear that God has an intimate relationship with all of creation and deeply loves all of it.

Ecclesiastes carries a similar theme to the one found in Job: the world is not fair and sometimes bad things do happen to good people. The Teacher talks about elements of a meaningful life as one lives with this knowledge and the knowledge that all people will die. Ultimately, you need to rely upon God for meaning and simply go on with living your life.

Proverbs lays out the dichotomy between the lifestyles of the wise and the foolish, and shares practical insights about living a life of wisdom. The foundation for a well-lived life is grounded in living in fear of (respect for) God. Proverbs would disagree with Ecclesiastes that death levels the playing field. Instead, the message here is that the wise will prosper, while the foolish will suffer and fail.

The book of Psalms explores the fullness of life and living with depth and emotion. No matter where you are in life, or what you are feeling, you can find it echoed in the poems of the Psalms. This book is an excellent handbook and companion for daily living.

While the Song of Solomon doesn't really talk about God, it does go into great depth and detail to affirm human sexuality and the gift of love. When you read this book, come at it from two different levels. Read it as a book that celebrates human sexuality and love, but also as one that celebrates God's love for us.

PREPARE

1. Review chapter 8 in the participant book.
2. Review the overview and plan for session 8 in the leader guide.
3. Watch the DVD segment for session 8.
4. Have extra Bibles available for those who did not bring one.
5. Have equipment for projecting or viewing the DVD set up and ready to go.
6. Consider distributing handouts or projecting images of reference materials (see list on p. 98) in the session. You might want to do this during Telling the Story or while discussing the Background Files.
7. If you are having the class do the Creative Corner activity, gather any materials suggested.
8. Pray for your class members and for God's presence and guidance as you gather in God's Word.

MATERIALS NEEDED

- Extra copies of the Bible
- Participant books
- Computer or DVD player; projector or TV monitor
- Course DVD
- Reference materials
- Creative Corner materials (optional)
- Name tags
- Refreshments (optional)

LEADER PRAYER

Loving God, you care deeply for all of creation and you desire that your people live meaningful lives in relationship with you. Guide me as I prepare for this session. Be at work in me and in the group to bring us into deeper relationship with you. Amen.

CORE SESSION PLAN

GATHERING (10 MINUTES)

The Core Session Plan is designed for use in one 60-minute period. The Core Session Plan can be extended 45-60 minutes by incorporating the group reflection time called Our Story, found at the end of the Core Session Plan.

Welcome and check-in

Provide name tags again as you welcome participants to the session. If you are serving refreshments, have them set out ahead of time. Spend a few minutes asking if anyone wants to share any thoughts or insights from their personal "Mark it" reading for the week. You won't be able to spend much time on this, but hearing a couple of testimonials will encourage more in the group to make this weekly reading and devotional reflection a part of their routine.

Scripture and prayer

Read the following verse and prayer, or ask a volunteer to do so.

The human mind plans the way, but the Lord directs the steps. (Proverbs 16:9)

O God, we humans often walk through life with the illusion that we are in control. Free us from this burden that leads us into thinking we live solely on our own. Strengthen our relationship with you and help us to rely on you during all the times of our lives, especially when things become difficult and stressed. Teach us to live meaningful lives fully grounded in you. Amen.

TELLING THE STORY (15 MINUTES)

See the storytelling tips on p. 10 of this guide.

You or your designated storyteller should now turn to telling the portion of the story that is highlighted in session 8. Incorporate any or all of the Background File notes in the participant book (p. 75) as part of the telling. Use one of the following three options for telling the story, or devise your own.

1. Read through, summarize, and comment on the story as provided in the participant book.
2. Ask for volunteers to tell portions of the story.
3. Read the story script provided below.

At the end of the storytelling time, summarize the Story Keys for this session.

The Story Script for Session 8

The book of Job asks, "Why is there suffering in the world? Why do bad things happen to good people?" The story is about Job, a good man and model citizen, who believes in God. A character named Satan comes along and persuades God to offer up Job as a test case in faithfulness. Job then loses his wealth, health, and children.

Job's friends come by to visit. They explain that he is suffering because of some sin—he must have done something wrong. But this explanation is not true (Job is "blameless before God"), and it doesn't help Job at all.

The mystery of Job's suffering isn't solved or fully explained, but the story does have some important things to say. Sin and evil do cause suffering, but not all suffering. When suffering comes, we aren't alone. We can cry out to God, who is with us in all the ups and downs of life. God takes delight in creation, and invites us to take delight in creation, too.

The book of Psalms is like a treasury of 150 of Israel's prayers, songs, liturgies, and poems. Many different people wrote psalms for a variety of purposes—the coronation of kings, personal laments, confession, praise, and community prayers. They remembered and celebrated God's mighty deeds in history and revealed the suffering and distress of the people. Taken all together, the psalms reflect the highs and lows of a life of faith for individuals and communities.

In the life of faith, sometimes practical, down-to-earth advice is helpful. That's what the book of Proverbs gives us. Proverbs is filled with bits and pieces of knowledge for living wisely with God and with one another, and living according to God's laws. As Christians, we know that what we do cannot make us right with God, but we are made right by God's grace through faith in Christ Jesus. Still, wisdom for daily living is seen as a gift from God. Proverbs even pictures wisdom as a woman inviting people into a banquet!

The book of Ecclesiastes contains wise sayings or proverbs written by someone called "the Teacher." One of the most well-known passages, Ecclesiastes 3:1-8, describes life on earth. It begins like this: "For everything there is a season, and a time for every matter under heaven: a time to be born, and a time to die . . . ." The writer says the world is not fair, and the meaning of life isn't found in riches, smarts, or having fun all the time. But once we realize that we can't find meaning in life on our own, we can leave it to God and find pleasure in simple living.

Song of Solomon is a book of poetry named for King Solomon. The poetry celebrates human love—the mutual respect, intimate conversation, fidelity, and physical love shared between two lovers. It also celebrates God's love, as a reflection of God's deep embrace for God's people.

PICTURING THE STORY (20 MINUTES)

Go through the reflection questions listed in this section in the participant book (p. 75). Then play the segment called For Every Matter under Heaven (session 8) on the course DVD. Encourage the participants to watch the story unfold as artist Joe Castillo depicts the scenes of the story. Participants may be invited to write down their own questions.

When the segment is done, address the questions together as a large group or ask the participants to discuss in smaller teams. Invite participants to share their own questions or observations. What difference did it make to see the story in this way?

SINGING AND PRAYING THE STORY (10 MINUTES)

Use one or both of the psalms provided in the participant book to help address the story and its themes. Psalms are best read aloud. You may have one volunteer read the entire psalm or portion of a psalm. Or you may wish to have the psalm read responsively, verse by verse or line by line. Use a solo reader with the group responding, or read responsively using different groups.

As time allows, discuss the observations and questions provided.

Psalm 23 is a trust psalm that gives an example of how God's people can respond when they are struggling through difficult times. The psalmist uses the metaphor of a shepherd to talk about God's loving relationship with the faithful. Even in the presence of enemies, the shepherd is with the sheep, uplifting and defending them.

Psalm 13 is a prayer for help and deliverance from enemies. The psalm begins with the pain of feeling distanced from God and pleas for assistance, and closes with trust and hope for the future.

LOOKING AHEAD (5 MINUTES)

Briefly introduce the next chapter of the story that appears in session 9.

Mark it

Encourage participants to read and mark one or more of the passages listed in this section during the week ahead. Let the group know that at the start of next week's session you will ask volunteers to share any insights they have from this exercise.

You are encouraged to do the "Mark it" exercise as well.

Next time

You may find it helpful to take some notes or highlight items in the readings to share next week as part of Telling the Story.

In the next session we will review the meaning and message of the Old Testament and take a brief look at the time in between the Old and New Testaments. To review this week's story and to help prepare for the next session, you and your group are encouraged to read an introduction to the following in a study Bible:

- The Old Testament

OUR STORY

WELCOME

Ideas for optional settings and schedules for this time are provided in the introduction on page 13 of this leader guide.

Whether Our Story is done consecutively along with the Core Session Plan, or planned for a separate time or location, consider providing hospitality in the form of refreshments.

- Arrange the room comfortably for small group discussion.
- Introduce newcomers in the group.
- Begin with prayer, using the session prayer on p. 101 or another prayer of your choice. Ask volunteers to provide prayers, if they feel comfortable doing so.
- You may wish to begin by asking if anyone has a particular question or thought to share from the large group session. As an alternative to discussing those questions, simply note them or write them down on newsprint. Small groups may decide to discuss further.

CONVERSATION

See the tips for leading and participating in small group discussion on page 17 of this guide. Make available to all participants copies of the reproducible Guidelines for Small Group Discussion.

The reflection questions are intended to help participants connect their own stories to the key themes of the greatest story. These questions can be used for personal reflection while reading or used to guide group discussion. It is unlikely that a group could discuss all the questions in one discussion period. Don't be concerned about this. Here are some options for approaching the questions:

1. As leader, you may choose to focus on certain questions from the list.
2. Ask participants to suggest questions to discuss.
3. Have participants form smaller groups, assign the groups a designated number of questions to discuss, and then have each group report back to the large group.
4. If participants have the time and interest, you could assign each person a question or two to think about and prepare a response during the week.

These responses could be shared as discussion starters when the group meets for Our Story discussion time.

Questions and Responses

The questions below are designed with personal reflection and response in mind. They do not require a certain amount of prior knowledge in order to respond. Responses may vary according to individual insights and context. Even so, a few guiding thoughts are provided for some of the questions.

- *Can you think of examples of bad things happening to good people? How do you or others deal with "why" this suffering happens?*

Job received a lot of unhelpful advice and guidance from his friends in dealing with the immensity of his suffering. They basically blamed him for all that had happened to him, even when he said he was innocent. People often look for reasons why a calamity happened, and seek to attach either a reason or blame to the situation. But the book of Job clearly tells us that not all suffering is the direct result of someone's sin or misdoing. Sometimes bad things just happen.

- *What do you think is the best way to help someone who is suffering? What can be said? What kinds of things might you choose* not *to say?*

Job's friends weren't really present with him to listen and empathize. They didn't care how he felt about what he had gone through, but they were all too willing to lecture and cast blame. This was not helpful.

- *How can times of suffering be times of deeper connections with God and others? How have you experienced this?*

The book of Job makes it clear that one very appropriate response to suffering is prayer. It's an acknowledgment that God is still working for good, even in the midst of pain. And it indicates a willingness to deepen your relationship with God even when you are the most vulnerable.

- *How can prayers written so long ago still speak to us and help us speak to God?*

Although we live in very different times, the joys and challenges of faith are still very similar to what people experienced long ago. In the prayers, songs, liturgies, and poems contained in the book of Psalms, we see and learn about the highs and lows in the life of faith. The psalms can help us speak to God and confess our sins, ask for forgiveness, cry out in times of suffering and distress, sing for joy, and praise God.

- *What part does prayer play in your life?*

Questions and Responses (continued)

- *How does God's wisdom become our wisdom?*

- *Who is the wisest person you know? What makes that person wise?*

- *Why do you think wise sayings alone can't make a person right with God?*

Job and Ecclesiastes make it clear that meaningful lives rely upon God alone. We are made right with God only by God's grace through faith in Jesus Christ.

- *Do you agree that life can sometimes seem meaningless? How does a person deal with those kinds of feelings?*

- *What do you think of the idea of leaving hard questions and matters to God, and finding pleasure in living life?*

- *If you could ask the Teacher a question, what would it be?*

- *Are you surprised that a book of the Bible is a series of poems about human love? Why or why not?*

In reality the Bible is one continuous love story! It's the story of God's love for a rebellious humanity. Poems about human love probably look a bit different when seen from this angle.

- *What makes human love so powerful?*

- *How is human love like God's love? How do you think it is different?*

Provide colored markers, paper, construction paper, poster board, magazines, scissors, or other materials that may be used to complete this creative assignment.

Creative Corner

Depending on how your schedule is organized, you may wish to assign this activity for individuals or small groups.

Pick one of the major themes introduced in this session (love, suffering, meaning of life, wisdom, or another). Write a poem or psalm about it. Or illustrate one of the psalms, proverbs or poems from these books that fits one of these themes. If you are musical, consider setting one of the psalms, proverbs, or poems to music.

PEOPLE OF PROMISE
The Old Testament Story for Us

9

Ancient promises speak in new ways for a new day

SESSION PREPARATION

OVERVIEW

Our last session looked at the literature of the Old Testament. The Wisdom books, Job, Proverbs, and Ecclesiastes showed us some wisdom for daily living and varied approaches to what it means to rely upon God in tough times. Psalms and Song of Solomon introduced us to songs and poetry on topics from God's love to human love. In this session, we'll take a wide-angle view of what we've already learned about the Old Testament, and lay the foundation for our journey into the New Testament. Take time to celebrate with your group as you review how much of the Bible you've already covered!

Materials for this session available on the Leader Reference CD:

- Bible History Timeline (CHART)
- Different Canons of the Hebrew Bible (Old Testament) (CHART)
- Thirty Key Old Testament Stories (CHART)

Scenes in this Session

Created and Blessed
Called and Claimed
Loved and Challenged
Remember the Future
The Time Between the Testaments

What's the Story?

The Old Testament begins with the creation story in Genesis and moves to the origin of sin. God's intent for a good and holy world is polluted by evil and separation, and God now has to deal with a rebellious humanity. But throughout it all, God demonstrates love and faithfulness to the people in a variety of ways, most notably through the promise of an everlasting relationship with Israel. God doesn't break this promise, even though Israel can't seem to stay focused on God alone and constantly turns to worshiping idols and foreign gods.

STORY KEYS

- The Bible's story of faith continues even today.
- The Bible is God's love story for humanity.
- The Old Testament promises the coming of God's messiah, or chosen one, to carry out God's vision for the world.
- Different versions of the Bible include different books.

When the people maintain their part of the covenant and follow God's laws, things go well for them. When they don't, God uses the prophets to warn them to repent or pay the consequences, which include foreign domination and the loss of their land. Eventually the temple at Jerusalem falls, and the people are forced to live in exile. And still, God remains faithful and eventually restores the people's hope and their land. They return home, rediscover the law, and rebuild the temple.

The Old Testament also gives us a preview of things to come. The story isn't over yet, because creation is still not what God intended it to be. God's prophets foretell the coming of a chosen one, or Messiah, who will come from the house of David. We've already come a long way, but stay tuned! There's more to come!

What's the Message?

The Old Testament is really a dance between God and God's rebellious people. Sometimes they are in step with each other, and sometimes not. God wants to be in a deep and constant relationship with humanity, but when the people face tough times they lose faith and have difficulty trusting God. Then they turn to other gods and idols for help. Throughout it all, we learn a lot about how God interacts with the world. Primarily we learn about the depth of God's love for all of creation, but especially for God's chosen people. And since we see from the very beginning that God is a God for whom "relationship" is central, God desires that all people reciprocate with their love and devotion. All of God's actions in the Bible are a result of this intense desire for a two-way relationship with humanity.

God makes promises and keeps those promises. Early on, God sends a rainbow-shaped promise to Noah after the flood (Genesis 9:13). But most importantly, God promises Abraham that his descendants will be "as numerous as the stars of heaven" (Genesis 22:17). God gives Israel laws to guide the people's behavior and sends prophets to remind them that there will be consequences when they don't follow the laws. God remembers the covenant with Israel and proves to be steadfast—even when the people rebel. This theme dominates the entire Old Testament.

God often calls the most unlikely, unexpected people into service. In fact, even the individuals themselves are sometimes surprised! When God called prophets to speak messages to the people, it wasn't unusual for God to hear "Why me?" in response. God even used people outside Israel to serve God's cause. King

Cyrus of Persia called an end to the Babylonian Exile and Ruth, a non-Jew, became an ancestor of both David and Jesus.

PREPARE

1. Review chapter 9 in the participant book.
2. Review the overview and plan for session 9 in the leader guide.
3. Watch the DVD segment for session 9.
4. Have extra Bibles available for those who did not bring one.
5. Have equipment for projecting or viewing the DVD set up and ready to go.
6. Consider distributing handouts or projecting images of reference materials (see list on p. 107) in the session. You might want to do this during Telling the Story or while discussing the Background Files.
7. If you are having the class do the Creative Corner activity, gather any materials suggested.
8. Pray for your class members and for God's presence and guidance as you gather in God's Word.

MATERIALS NEEDED

- Extra copies of the Bible
- Participant books
- Computer or DVD player; projector or TV monitor
- Course DVD
- Reference materials
- Creative Corner materials (optional)
- Name tags
- Refreshments (optional)

LEADER PRAYER

God of Abraham and Sarah and of promises made and kept, I thank you for the honor of learning your holy Word as we've explored these sessions on the Old Testament. Be with me and members of the group as we further explore how these stories of old speak to our lives today. Amen.

CORE SESSION PLAN

GATHERING (10 MINUTES)

Welcome and check-in

Provide name tags again as you welcome participants to the session. If you are serving refreshments, have them set out ahead of time. Spend a few minutes asking if anyone wants to share any thoughts or insights from their personal "Mark it" reading for the week. You won't be able to spend much time on this, but hearing a couple of testimonials will encourage more in the group to make this weekly reading and devotional reflection a part of their routine.

The Core Session Plan is designed for use in one 60-minute period. The Core Session Plan can be extended 45-60 minutes by incorporating the group reflection time called Our Story, found at the end of the Core Session Plan.

Scripture and prayer

Read the following verse and prayer, or ask a volunteer to do so.

Tell your children of it, and let your children tell their children, and their children another generation. (Joel 1:3)

O God, help us to see the Old Testament part of the greatest story as our story. Through this story, invigorate our faith in the here and now. Empower us to share what we have heard with others, especially with those who need to hear stories of hope and promise. We thank and praise you for the love and steadfastness you show to us throughout all of the greatest story. Amen.

TELLING THE STORY (15 MINUTES)

See the storytelling tips on p. 10 of this guide.

You or your designated storyteller should now turn to telling the portion of the story that is highlighted in session 9. Incorporate any or all of the Background File notes in the participant book (p. 82) as part of the telling. Use one of the following three options for telling the story, or devise your own.

1. Read through, summarize, and comment on the story as provided in the participant book.
2. Ask for volunteers to tell portions of the story.
3. Read the story script provided below.

At the end of the storytelling time, summarize the Story Keys for this session.

The Story Script for Session 9

We are part of a really BIG story of faith that began "in the beginning," continued as a story of blessing through Abraham and Sarah, and was handed down through the ages to us. The story of God and God's people is now our story. And this story tells us a lot about God and about ourselves.

The Old Testament part of the story tells us that God creates us and blesses us. The same God who created everything created us and continues to give us food and every good thing. The same God who blessed Abraham and Sarah and their descendants blesses us also.

The Old Testament tells us that God calls us and claims us, too. The same God who called people in ancient times—Abraham, Sarah, Jacob, Joseph, Moses, Miriam, Hannah, Deborah, Samuel, Isaiah,

The Story Script for Session 9 (continued)

Esther, and others—calls us also to love and serve. The same God who claimed Israel and said, "I am your God and you are my people," claims us, too, in baptism.

The story of the Old Testament also tells us that God loves and challenges us. The same God who loved the people of Israel—even when they disobeyed, rebelled, and ran after other gods—loves us also. The same God who challenged the Israelites to bless others as "a light to the nations" challenges us also to be blessings in the world.

And God does more than create and bless, call and claim, love and challenge. God gives us the power to do what we are called to do. And when we fall short, God shows mercy, like the mercy the people of Israel experienced over and over when they fell away. As Christians, the mercy of God is made real for us in the grace and forgiveness of Jesus, God's own son.

The prophets speak of a long-awaited Messiah or "chosen one" in the Old Testament, and tell of one who will be called "Wonderful Counselor, Mighty God, Everlasting Father, Prince of Peace" (Isaiah 9:6). Writers of the New Testament would later see God's promises to Israel fulfilled in Jesus, God's Son. We will turn to his story in the New Testament in the next session. There is more to come in the greatest story, and we are a part of it!

Let's go back to the story of the people of Israel for a few moments now. More than 500 years separates the time between the people's return from exile and the birth of Jesus. But, except for the book of Daniel, the Bible says very little about these years. We do know that during this time Israel was ruled by the Persian Empire. Then, during the Greek or Hellenistic period, Egypt and Syria took turns dominating the Jews.

In 165 B.C.E. the Jews rebelled, regained control of their land, and rededicated the temple. The story of the Jewish revolt is told in the books of 1 and 2 Maccabees. These books are listed in the Apocrypha or Deuterocanonical Books.

Although the Jews regained control for a time, eventually the Roman Empire conquered the land. Rome was still in charge when Jesus was born.

PICTURING THE STORY (20 MINUTES)

Go through the reflection questions listed in this section in the participant book (p. 82). Then play the segment called People of Promise (session 9) on the course DVD. Encourage the participants to watch the story unfold as artist Joe Castillo depicts the scenes of the story. Participants may be invited to write down their own questions.

When the segment is done, address the questions together as a large group or ask the participants to discuss in smaller teams. Invite participants to share their own questions or observations. What difference did it make to see the story in this way?

SINGING AND PRAYING THE STORY (10 MINUTES)

Use one or both of the psalms provided in the participant book to help address the story and its themes. Psalms are best read aloud. You may have one volunteer read the entire psalm or portion of a psalm. Or you may wish to have the psalm read responsively, verse by verse or line by line. Use a solo reader with the group responding, or read responsively using different groups.

As time allows, discuss the observations and questions provided.

Psalm 22 is an individual prayer for help often used as part of the Maundy Thursday liturgy. (Maundy Thursday is observed the day before Good Friday.) The psalmist speaks of suffering while remembering God's past faithfulness to Israel and to him, even while he was in the womb. He calls for God's saving help in the midst of a dire situation. In anticipation of his salvation, he celebrates God's goodness and faithfulness.

Psalm 103 is a hymn of praise for God's overwhelming goodness. The psalmist honors God as one who cares for individuals, gives laws to the people, and rescues the oppressed. God's steadfast love endures throughout time for those who are faithful to God's covenant.

LOOKING AHEAD (5 MINUTES)

Briefly introduce the next chapter of the story that appears in session 10.

Mark it

Encourage participants to read and mark one or more of the passages listed in this section during the week ahead. Let the group know that at the start of next week's session you will ask volunteers to share any insights they have from this exercise.

You are encouraged to do the "Mark it" exercise as well.

Next time

In the next session we will turn to the New Testament portion of the greatest story. In the Gospels we will meet Jesus, the One who is at the center of the story.

You may find it helpful to take some notes or highlight items in the readings to share next week as part of Telling the Story.

To review and help you prepare for the next session, you and your group are encouraged to read introductions to the following in a study Bible:

- The New Testament
- The Gospels
- Matthew
- Mark
- Luke
- John

OUR STORY

WELCOME

Whether Our Story is done consecutively along with the Core Session Plan, or planned for a separate time or location, consider providing hospitality in the form of refreshments.

Ideas for optional settings and schedules for this time are provided in the introduction on page 13 of this leader guide.

- Arrange the room comfortably for small group discussion.
- Introduce newcomers in the group.
- Begin with prayer, using the session prayer on p. 110 or another prayer of your choice. Ask volunteers to provide prayers, if they feel comfortable doing so.
- You may wish to begin by asking if anyone has a particular question or thought to share from the large group session. As an alternative to discussing those questions, simply note them or write them down on newsprint. Small groups may decide to discuss further.

CONVERSATION

See the tips for leading and participating in small group discussion on page 17 of this guide. Make available to all participants copies of the reproducible Guidelines for Small Group Discussion.

The reflection questions are intended to help participants connect their own stories to the key themes of the greatest story. These questions can be used for personal reflection while reading or used to guide group discussion. It is unlikely that a group could discuss all the questions in one discussion period. Don't be concerned about this. Here are some options for approaching the questions:

1. As leader, you may choose to focus on certain questions from the list.
2. Ask participants to suggest questions to discuss.
3. Have participants form smaller groups, assign the groups a designated number of questions to discuss, and then have each group report back to the large group.
4. If participants have the time and interest, you could assign each person a question or two to think about and prepare a response during the week. These responses could be shared as discussion starters when the group meets for Our Story discussion time.

Questions and Responses

The questions below are designed with personal reflection and response in mind. They do not require a certain amount of prior knowledge in order to respond. Responses may vary according to individual insights and context. Even so, a few guiding thoughts are provided for some of the questions.

- *How can the story of faith be both old and new at the same time?*

The fact that the story of God's love has unfolded and continued through many generations is what makes it old. But when we engage in conversations with the Bible, we are part of a continuing faith story that unfolds in our daily living. That makes the story new through us! We're in the line of Abraham and Sarah, David, and Jesus, too.

- *Describe a person or people who have been a "light" in your life, or light for the world.*
- *For what blessings are you especially grateful? What blessings are you willing to share?*
- *What message do you wish God would give you? How are you listening?*

Questions and Responses (continued)

God speaks to us through the Bible (as we read it, study it, and hear it read and preached in worship), through Baptism and Holy Communion, and through Jesus (God's Word made flesh).

○ *How do you feel about God knowing you so well?*

○ *What do you think about being called a holy priest, or being part of the priesthood of all believers?*

○ *How does love start with God?*
Consider using 1 John 4:7-19 in your discussion.

○ *How are we doing, living out God's vision of love?*

○ *How are the past and the future linked in both the Old and New Testaments?*
Throughout the Old Testament we encounter God's promise to send a chosen one or messiah to carry out God's vision of peace in the world. This promise is made directly to David and through the prophets. The New Testament is then the story of God's promise fulfilled through Jesus Christ. This links the God and promise of the past with the God and hope of the future.

○ *Why do you think the promise of a messiah is such a powerful promise?*

○ *How would you describe your purpose in life? What would your "purpose statement" be?*

○ *What do you imagine life might have been like for Jewish people living in Judah and Jerusalem during the many years leading up to the birth of Jesus?*

○ *What more would you like to know about the different lists of books found in different versions of the Bible?*

Creative Corner

Depending on how your schedule is organized, you may wish to assign this activity for individuals or small groups.

Look back over this session, or any other sessions studied so far. Choose a favorite verse or passage to illustrate or treat in an artistic way. For example, you could add the verse to a meaningful photograph. Be prepared to show your creation to the group and tell why you chose this verse.

Provide colored markers, paper, construction paper, poster board, magazines, scissors, or other materials that may be used to complete this creative assignment.

10 THE WORD BECAME FLESH

The Gospels, Part 1

The main character in the greatest story hits the stage

SESSION PREPARATION

Materials for this session available on the Leader Reference CD:

- Bible History Timeline (CHART)
- Jesus' Ministry: Miracles, Parables, and Teachings (CHART)

OVERVIEW

In the previous session we reviewed some of the major themes of the Old Testament and reflected upon the promise of a coming messiah revealed through some major texts. In this session we'll begin to look at the Gospels of the New Testament. They tell us about the good news of Jesus Christ, whom Christians believe is indeed the promised one.

Scenes in this Session

The Word Became Flesh (John 1:1-14; Matthew 1:1-17)
Jesus Is Born (Luke 1-2; Matthew 1)
Jesus Is Baptized by John (Luke 3; Matthew 3)
Jesus Faces Temptation (Matthew 4:1-11; Luke 4:1-13; Mark 1:12-13)
Jesus Calls the First Disciples (Luke 5:1-11, 27-32; Mark 3:13-19)
Jesus Heals (Mark 5:1-43)
Jesus Feeds the 5000 (Mark 6:30-44; John 6:1-51)

STORY KEYS

- The Gospels tell the "good news" about Jesus.
- Jesus is the Messiah, or promised one, born in David's line.
- Jesus is Emmanuel, "God with us."
- Jesus trusted God and was without sin.
- Jesus healed many people through the power of God.

What's the Story?

The New Testament opens with the four Gospels: Matthew, Mark, Luke and John. The word *gospel* means "good news." The main purpose of these books is to tell the good news about Jesus Christ, whom Christians believe is the Messiah promised in the Old Testament. These Gospels contain frequent references to Old Testament passages that point to this being true.

Matthew, Mark, and Luke take a similar approach to talking about the life of Jesus, so they have come to be known as the *Synoptics*, a word formed from two Greek words meaning "seeing together." These Gospels include stories like the parables, Jesus' transfiguration, and the Last Supper, which don't appear in the Gospel of John. Some have said that the Synoptics tell stories of the outward life of Jesus, while John takes a more spiritual approach.

It is believed that Mark was the first Gospel to be written, most likely around 70 C.E. Matthew and Luke were probably written between 80 and 90 C.E. While they draw upon parts of Mark in their retelling of the life of Jesus, they also have another common source known simply as "Q." John, which has its own sources, was probably written at the end of the first century.

Each Gospel was written with a somewhat different emphasis, so although they all talk about the life of Jesus, they each do it in a unique way. Mark, the shortest Gospel, has a theme known as the "messianic secret." Jesus performs a lot of amazing miracles in Mark, but he tells his followers to keep silent about them until his death and resurrection. Only then will it all make sense. Matthew contains many teachings, like the Beatitudes, while Luke has a strong theme of Jesus ministering to those considered poor and outcast. John portrays Jesus, the Word made flesh, from a more cosmic approach.

What's the Message?

One of the central messages in the Gospels is that Jesus is the son of God who has come to dwell among humanity. Each of the Gospels talks about this in different ways. In describing Jesus' birth, Matthew refers back to Isaiah, who prophesied that the promised one would be born of a virgin and be named Emmanuel, or "God is with us." The Gospel of John refers to Jesus as the Word who was with God at creation and became flesh only at an appointed time. But not only has Jesus become human, he's done so for a definite purpose. The Gospel of Mark opens by stating that it is: "The beginning of the good news of Jesus Christ, the Son of God" (Mark 1:1). The word *Christ* is Greek for the Hebrew word "Messiah," which means that Jesus is clearly identified as the promised or anointed one prophesied in the Old Testament. And Matthew, in particular, gives us an actual genealogy that clearly places the Messiah in the line of the house of David. God was faithful to the Israelites in the past and God's faithfulness continues as God fulfills this most important promise.

The Gospels portray Jesus as one who, like God, is faithful and without sin. He's baptized by his cousin, John, not because he needs forgiveness, but in order to fulfill a prophecy. This act also identifies him with sinful humanity. Jesus trusts God through all things and remains faithful, even when he is tempted by Satan in the wilderness. In fact, Jesus' trust in God is so powerful that he is even willing to face death on a cross.

The Gospels also show us that Jesus Christ, the Messiah, is very active in the lives of the people whom he encounters. He is present with them as he teaches them, and he also releases many from their pain and suffering. In fact, his power is so great that even by touching the hem of his garment a hemorrhaging woman is healed (Mark 5:24-34). His compassion for humanity runs deep. He demonstrates the power of God through his many healings and, in dramatic fashion, when he raises a little girl and Lazarus from the dead (Mark 5:35-43; John 11:1-44).

MATERIALS NEEDED

- Extra copies of the Bible
- Participant books
- Computer or DVD player; projector or TV monitor
- Course DVD
- Reference materials
- Creative Corner materials (optional)
- Name tags
- Refreshments (optional)

PREPARE

1. Review chapter 10 in the participant book.
2. Review the overview and plan for session 10 in the leader guide.
3. Watch the DVD segment for session 10.
4. Have extra Bibles available for those who did not bring one.
5. Have equipment for projecting or viewing the DVD set up and ready to go.
6. Consider distributing handouts or projecting images of reference materials (see list on p. 116) in the session. You might want to do this during Telling the Story or while discussing the Background Files.
7. If you are having the class do the Creative Corner activity, gather any materials suggested.
8. Pray for your class members and for God's presence and guidance as you gather in God's Word.

LEADER PRAYER

O God, thank you for sending your Son, Jesus Christ, to embody the great love which you have for all your children. Be with me as I prepare and lead this session, that I might mirror the depth of your love to those in my group. May your love fuel us for service and mission in Jesus' name. Amen.

CORE SESSION PLAN

The Core Session Plan is designed for use in one 60-minute period. The Core Session Plan can be extended 45-60 minutes by incorporating the group reflection time called Our Story, found at the end of the Core Session Plan.

GATHERING (10 MINUTES)

Welcome and check-in

Provide name tags again as you welcome participants to the session. If you are serving refreshments, have them set out ahead of time. Spend a few minutes asking if anyone wants to share any thoughts or insights from their personal "Mark it" reading for the week. You won't be able to spend much time on this, but hearing a couple of testimonials will encourage more in the group to make this weekly reading and devotional reflection a part of their routine.

Scripture and prayer

Read the following verse and prayer, or ask a volunteer to do so.

And a voice from heaven said, "This is my Son, the Beloved, with whom I am well pleased." (Matthew 3:17)

O God, you fulfilled the promise made to your servant David and sent your Word made flesh to dwell with us and to teach and heal. Thank you for this gift of love! Open our ears and hearts today. Stir up faith in us, and help us to live as Jesus' disciples. In his name we pray. Amen.

TELLING THE STORY (15 MINUTES)

You or your designated storyteller should now turn to telling the portion of the story that is highlighted in session 10. Incorporate any or all of the Background File notes in the participant book (p. 92) as part of the telling. Use one of the following three options for telling the story, or devise your own.

See the storytelling tips on p. 10 of this guide.

1. Read through, summarize, and comment on the story as provided in the participant book.
2. Ask for volunteers to tell portions of the story.
3. Read the story script provided below.

At the end of the storytelling time, summarize the Story Keys for this session.

The Story Script for Session 10

Today we turn to the New Testament portion of the greatest story, beginning with the books of Matthew, Mark, Luke, and John. Right from the start, these books called *Gospels* tell us that something new and truly amazing is happening. Mark 1:1 says this book is "the beginning of the good news [or gospel] of Jesus Christ, the Son of God." John introduces Jesus in a different way: "In the beginning was the Word, and the Word was with God, and the Word was God . . . All things came into being through him . . . And the Word became flesh and lived among us" (John 1:1-14). Jesus was God, and Jesus was human. Jesus was God in human flesh, connecting heaven and earth in a dynamic way! The Gospel of Matthew begins by tracing Jesus' family from his Jewish parents, Joseph and Mary, all the way back to Ruth, David, and Abraham, showing his roots in the line of David.

Many people are surprised to learn that only the Gospels of Matthew and Luke tell the story of Jesus' birth. In Matthew the story focuses on Joseph, who was unsure about Mary and the child she was carrying. In Luke the focus is on Mary, who obediently and humbly accepted the angel's word that a child would be conceived in her by God's Spirit, making her son also "the Son of the Most High."

Late in Mary's pregnancy, she and Joseph had to travel to be counted among Joseph's kin for a Roman census. They went from Nazareth in the north to Bethlehem in the south, at a time when most travel meant walking or riding on a donkey's back. Imagine what this meant for Mary, who was about to give birth to her first child! To make matters worse, when they got to Bethlehem, all the hotels were full. Jesus was born in a cold, dank cattle stall. His first crib was a straw-filled feedbox!

Angels announced the good news of the Messiah's birth to shepherds, who were in the fields with their sheep. Later on, wise men or astrologers came from the east to honor Jesus. But this made Herod, the king of Judea, jealous. What was this talk of another king? According to Matthew's Gospel, Herod had all the boys in Bethlehem who were two years or younger killed. But in the meantime, an angel had told Joseph to flee to Egypt with Mary and the baby. They stayed in Egypt until Herod was dead.

The Gospels include only one story about Jesus' childhood, from when he was twelve. Jesus and his family went to Jerusalem to celebrate the Passover. When the family started to return home, his parents realized Jesus was missing. They finally found him back in the temple, teaching the teachers of Israel!

Then the Gospels jump to a story about Jesus as an adult, wading into the waters of the Jordan River. His cousin John baptized him. John had been telling people that someone "mightier" than he was coming. It seems odd that the Son of God would need to be baptized, but Jesus claimed it was necessary in order for him to fully identify with the world so that he could save the world from its sin. During his baptism, Jesus received the Holy Spirit as God declared from heaven, "This is my Son, the Beloved." When we are baptized, we too receive the gift of the Spirit and become children of God.

Jesus immediately went into the wilderness, where he was tested by Satan for 40 days. (Remember the testing of the Israelites in the wilderness for 40 years?) Satan tempted Jesus to turn rocks into bread, to rule the world, and finally, to jump from the top of the temple. But Jesus trusted God completely and showed Satan he didn't need to prove his divine power.

Jesus visited his hometown synagogue one day and read from Isaiah about someone who was anointed by the Spirit to bring good news to the poor, release captives, give sight to the blind, and free the oppressed. Then he said that this Scripture was coming true right at that time! This was a rough sell, especially in his hometown, where people knew him as Joseph's boy. Maybe that's why Jesus recruited twelve followers to help spread this good news.

The Story Script for Session 10 (continued)

Jesus' followers, or disciples, were common people who showed both incredible courage and disheartening lack of faith. They were fishermen, tax collectors, and even included one who later betrayed Jesus. But all of them left other things behind when he said, "Come, follow me!"

The Gospels are full of stories of Jesus healing people. He healed people who had illnesses, diseases, and disabilities of many kinds. In one instance, he cast a "legion" of demons out of a man and into a herd of pigs. The pigs then plunged into the sea and drowned. People didn't know what to think about healings like this, and some wanted Jesus to go away.

In another instance, Jesus was on his way to heal the daughter of a synagogue leader when a woman with a terrible hemorrhage simply touched his robe and was healed. By the time he reached the synagogue leader's home, the girl had died. But Jesus raised her to life again, amazing everyone around him.

As the Son of God, Jesus could do other miraculous things. Large crowds often showed up wherever he went. On one occasion, his teaching lasted all day. Of course, the crowd was hungry. Rather than telling the people to leave, Jesus fed them all with just a few loaves and fishes. But Jesus was not simply a miracle-worker. His miracles were simply demonstrating the kingdom of God.

In the Gospel of John, Jesus expands on this story by saying that he is the "living bread from heaven" which gives eternal life to all who eat it. This is what happens when we receive the bread in Holy Communion. Christ, the living bread, is there with us at the table, and he brings us all into his one body, the church.

PICTURING THE STORY (20 MINUTES)

Go through the reflection questions listed in this section in the participant book (p. 92). Then play the segment called The Word Became Flesh (session 10) on the course DVD. Encourage the participants to watch the story unfold as artist Joe Castillo depicts the scenes of the story. Participants may be invited to write down their own questions.

When the segment is done, address the questions together as a large group or ask the participants to discuss in smaller teams. Invite participants to share their own questions or observations. What difference did it make to see the story in this way?

SINGING AND PRAYING THE STORY (10 MINUTES)

Use one or both of the psalms provided in the participant book to help address the story and its themes. Psalms are best read aloud. You may have one volunteer read the entire psalm or portion of a psalm. Or you may wish to have the psalm read responsively, verse by verse or line by line. Use a solo reader with the group responding, or read responsively using different groups.

As time allows, discuss the observations and questions provided.

Psalm 91 is a liturgy celebrating God's protection for the people. The psalmist says God will be a fortress and refuge to those who live lives faithful to God. God will protect the people, even amid terror and destruction. Neither armies nor evil shall overcome them, because God has become their "dwelling place." God's promise of protection and salvation for the people concludes the liturgy.

Psalm 113 is a hymn of praise inviting all people to join in honoring God. The psalmist says God should be praised each day, everywhere, and forever because God blesses and protects all people, especially those who are poor and needy.

LOOKING AHEAD (5 MINUTES)

Briefly introduce the next chapter of the story that appears in session 11.

Mark it

You are encouraged to do the "Mark it" exercise as well.

Encourage participants to read and mark one or more of the passages listed in this section during the week ahead. Let the group know that at the start of next week's session you will ask volunteers to share any insights they have from this exercise.

Next time

You may find it helpful to take some notes or highlight items in the readings to share next week as part of Telling the Story.

In the next session, we will continue the story of Jesus told in the Gospels. To review this week's story and to help prepare for the next session, you and your group are encouraged to read introductions to the following in a study Bible:

- The New Testament
- The Gospels
- Matthew
- Mark
- Luke
- John

OUR STORY

WELCOME

Whether Our Story is done consecutively along with the Core Session Plan, or planned for a separate time or location, consider providing hospitality in the form of refreshments.

- Arrange the room comfortably for small group discussion.
- Introduce newcomers in the group.
- Begin with prayer, using the session prayer on p. 119 or another prayer of your choice. Ask volunteers to provide prayers, if they feel comfortable doing so.
- You may wish to begin by asking if anyone has a particular question or thought to share from the large group session. As an alternative to discussing those questions, simply note them or write them down on newsprint. Small groups may decide to discuss further.

Ideas for optional settings and schedules for this time are provided in the introduction on page 13 of this leader guide.

CONVERSATION

The reflection questions are intended to help participants connect their own stories to the key themes of the greatest story. These questions can be used for personal reflection while reading or used to guide group discussion. It is unlikely that a group could discuss all the questions in one discussion period. Don't be concerned about this. Here are some options for approaching the questions:

See the tips for leading and participating in small group discussion on page 17 of this guide. Make available to all participants copies of the reproducible Guidelines for Small Group Discussion.

1. As leader, you may choose to focus on certain questions from the list.
2. Ask participants to suggest questions to discuss.
3. Have participants form smaller groups, assign the groups a designated number of questions to discuss, and then have each group report back to the large group.
4. If participants have the time and interest, you could assign each person a question or two to think about and prepare a response during the week. These responses could be shared as discussion starters when the group meets for Our Story discussion time.

Questions and Responses

The questions below are designed with personal reflection and response in mind. They do not require a certain amount of prior knowledge in order to respond. Responses may vary according to individual insights and context. Even so, a few guiding thoughts are provided for some of the questions.

- *Explain the phrase "the Word became flesh" in your own words. Is it easier to imagine Jesus as human or as God? Why?*

The Gospel of John takes a more cosmic approach in looking at Jesus' divinity and humanity when it says that Jesus, the Word, was with God from the very beginning of creation. We use the term "incarnation" when we talk about Jesus becoming human in order to fully embody the depth of God's love for all God's people. At Christmas we celebrate the incarnation, when Jesus became human and was born to Mary.

- *In what ways can families be channels of hope and promise? What is most surprising to you about Jesus' family?*

In many ways, Jesus' entire lineage was a channel of hope and promise. God made a covenant with King David that through him a blessed dynasty, or house, would be established. God also showed that ordinary and sometimes surprising people, like Mary, a young unwed mother, can be used by God to fulfill a promise.

- *When he discovered Mary was already pregnant, Joseph was no longer obligated to marry her. It took courage and trust to go through with the marriage. Where did he get that courage and trust?*

In the Gospels, both Mary and Joseph display courage and trust in God in the way they respond to the angels' announcements. In the Old Testament, God called Moses, the prophets, and others and then empowered them to do what they were called to do.

- *What do you think of Mary's response to the news that she would be the mother of God's Son?*

- *Theologian and reformer Martin Luther called the Bible the manger that holds the Christ child. What do you think this means?*

When you take a wide-angle look at the entire Bible, the greatest story, you begin to realize that it all points to Jesus Christ. Not only does he fulfill Old Testament prophecies, but he is directly descended from many of the more significant characters that we meet there. The Bible holds the promise and the truth of Jesus' identity as the Son of God.

- *John the Baptist prepared the way for Jesus. Who has prepared the way to Jesus for you?*

- *Complete this sentence: Because Jesus was baptized, I . . .*

Questions and Responses (continued)

- *If you could ask Jesus anything about temptation or facing evil, what would you ask?*

- *What do you think about the idea that God allows us the freedom to choose good or evil? What would life be like if we couldn't choose?*

Throughout the Old Testament we see that God allowed the people to make their own decisions, even if they chose poorly at times. The freedom to make these kinds of decisions also offers us the freedom to choose God over everything else. Any relationship is a two-way street and requires making decisions. God strongly desires to be in relationship with us!

- *How would you describe what Jesus' mission was and is?*

- *What role do Jesus' disciples play in that mission?*

- *How do you hear Jesus' invitation to "Come, follow me"?*

- *What kinds of limits have you faced in your life? Do you need healing?*

- *Imagine being present when Jesus heals someone. What emotions would you feel? What questions would run through your mind?*

- *Jesus had power over illness and death. Christians believe he still does. How is this true?*

In dying and being raised from the dead, Jesus conquered all illness and death for all times. Human beings will still get sick and die, but Jesus has defeated the power of death for all eternity.

- *What does the miracle of the loaves and fish say to you about Jesus? What does it say to you about food in our world?*

- *What question do you have for Jesus today?*

Creative Corner

Depending on how your schedule is organized, you may wish to assign this activity for individuals or small groups.

With one or more partners, think about the phrase, "the Word became flesh and lived among us." How can you illustrate or describe what this phrase means in a creative way?

Provide colored markers, paper, construction paper, poster board, magazines, scissors, or other materials that may be used to complete this creative assignment.

WHO DO YOU SAY I AM?

The Gospels, Part 2

History kneels at the foot of the cross and rejoices at the empty tomb

Materials for this session available on the Leader Reference CD:

- Jesus' Ministry: Miracles, Parables, and Teachings (CHART)
- The Roman Empire (MAP)
- Palestine in Jesus' Time, 6-30 C.E. (MAP)
- City of Jerusalem in Jesus' Time (MAP)
- The Temple in Jerusalem and Antonia Fortress, New Testament Times (ILLUSTRATION)
- The Temple in New Testament Times (exterior) (DIAGRAM)
- The Temple in New Testament Times (interior) (DIAGRAM)

STORY KEYS

- Jesus demonstrated God's power over nature.
- Jesus was a master teacher and often used parables to point to God's kingdom.
- Jesus is the resurrection and the life.
- Jesus is put to death after a council of his own people pressures Pilate to kill him.
- Jesus conquers death and appears to his disciples.

SESSION PREPARATION

OVERVIEW

In the previous session we entered the New Testament and took an initial look at the four Gospels that speak about Jesus Christ, God's Son. Christians believe he is the Messiah who was promised in the Old Testament. Now we'll take an in-depth look at Jesus' power over nature, his teachings, death, and resurrection, all of which finally proved that he is indeed the Messiah.

Scenes in this Session

Jesus Stills the Storm (Luke 8:22-25)
Jesus Teaches (Matthew 5:1-12; Matthew 22:34-40; Luke 15:11-32)
Jesus Raises Lazarus (John 11:1-44)
Jesus Enters Jerusalem (Mark 8:27—9:1; Luke 19:28-40)
A Long Night (Luke 22:1-65)
A Dark Day (Luke 22:66—23:56)
Resurrection! (Luke 24; John 20–21; Matthew 28:16-20)

What's the Story?

Mark, the first Gospel written, was likely intended for a Christian community in the Roman Empire around 70 C.E., when Jerusalem was destroyed. This fast-paced Gospel was written to share stories about Jesus and interpret his role as God's Son. Mark uses three main events to do this: Jesus' baptism, his transfiguration, and his crucifixion. Mark says that it is only after the crucifixion that people will truly understand that Jesus is the Messiah.

Matthew was written for an unknown community during the mid-80s C.E., when Christians and Jews debated who they were and how they related to one another. So even though the Gospel used Mark as its foundation, it reflects the conversations and struggles of Matthew's time. Like Luke, Matthew also used "Q" as a source, along with other unique material. Matthew included stories that refer back to God's covenant with Israel alone, and others that talk about the inclusion of Gentiles. Matthew also included a lot of Jesus' teachings.

Luke was written between 80 and 90 C.E. and used both Q and other unique sources. A central theme in this Gospel is how Jesus fulfills the Jewish expectation of a coming Messiah. Because of this, a lot of action revolves around the temple, and the story shows Jesus both starting and ending his ministry in Jerusalem. In Luke the Messiah comes to save all people, not just the Jews. This Gospel is the only one that has a second part, the book of Acts, which we'll talk about in the next session.

John was probably written at the end of the first century. It is very different from the other Gospels. John has two sections: the Book of Signs (1:19—12:50), which describes Jesus' miracles; and the Book of Glory (13–21), which describes the final events of Jesus' life and his resurrection. This Gospel is a more theological or spiritual account which places Jesus' identity as one who is both divine and human at center stage.

What's the Message?

What Jesus does and what he says help to point out who he is. In the previous session, we learned that Jesus' ministry included healing. In this session, we see that Jesus' ministry also included power over nature, teaching, and raising people like Lazarus from the dead. Jesus demonstrated power over nature with miracles like turning water into wine, stilling storms, and feeding a large crowd of people with a few fish and loaves. (See the chart called "Jesus' Ministry" for a list of miracles showing control of nature.) In the Old Testament, only God has power over nature, so these miracles clearly demonstrated that Jesus was one with God. They helped to identify him as the Son of God.

Jesus was a good teacher who knew how to hold the attention of his listeners. He told stories or parables related to daily living to teach people about the kingdom of God or kingdom of heaven. These stories may have seemed simple on the surface, but they often had a surprising point that prodded listeners to see life and God's promises in new ways. We find parables in the Synoptic Gospels: Matthew, Mark, and Luke.

The story about the raising of Lazarus (John 11:1-44) is a turning point in John and a significant part of the story of Jesus in the Gospels. Jesus tells Martha,

"I am the resurrection and the life." Martha recognizes his true identity, saying, "I believe that you are the Messiah, the Son of God, the one coming into the world." Then Jesus demonstrates his power over life and death by calling Lazarus out of the tomb. In the Gospel of John, this dramatic event also sets the religious authorities against Jesus.

We might wonder why the religious authorities were so worried about Jesus. Keep in mind that when Jesus healed people, performed miracles, taught, and raised Lazarus from the dead, lives were changed. This meant that Jesus' following grew rather quickly. Religious leaders worried that they would lose their followings if people began to believe that Jesus was indeed the Messiah. All four Gospels make it clear that these leaders took action to ensure that this didn't happen. The religious authorities plotted to put Jesus to death—to end things before they really got out of hand.

The depth of God's love for humanity was shown through the life, death, and resurrection of Jesus, God's Son. Here God fulfilled the promises made throughout the Old Testament, especially the covenant with the house of David. The resurrection gave new meaning to Jesus calling himself "the resurrection and the life." He is, indeed, the one who saves us and gives us the gift of eternal life.

PREPARE

1. Review chapter 11 in the participant book.
2. Review the overview and session plan for session 11 in the leader guide.
3. Watch the DVD segment for session 11.
4. Have extra Bible available for those who did not bring one.
5. Have equipment for projecting or viewing the DVD set up and ready to go.
6. Consider distributing handouts or projecting images of reference materials (see list on p. 126) in the session. You might want to do this during Telling the Story or discussion of the Background Files.
7. If you are having the class do the Creative Corner activity, gather any materials suggested.
8. Pray for your class members and for God's presence and guidance as you gather in God's Word.

MATERIALS NEEDED

- Extra copies of the Bible
- Participant books
- Computer or DVD player; projector or TV monitor
- Course DVD
- Reference materials
- Creative Corner materials (optional)
- Name tags
- Refreshments (optional)

LEADER PRAYER

Lord Jesus, through your ministry you taught and inspired your followers to love and honor God. Bless me as I prepare this session. Be with the group as we meet. Teach us and inspire us to love and honor God. Amen.

CORE SESSION PLAN

GATHERING (10 MINUTES)

The Core Session Plan is designed for use in one 60-minute period. The Core Session Plan can be extended 45-60 minutes by incorporating the group reflection time called Our Story, found at the end of the Core Session Plan.

Welcome and check-in

Provide name tags again as you welcome participants to the session. If you are serving refreshments, have them set out ahead of time. Spend a few minutes asking if anyone wants to share any thoughts or insights from their personal "Mark it" reading for the week. You won't be able to spend much time on this, but hearing a couple of testimonials will encourage more in the group to make this weekly reading and devotional reflection a part of their routine.

Scripture and prayer

Read the following verse and prayer, or ask a volunteer to do so.

The women were terrified and bowed their faces to the ground, but the men said to them, "Why do you look for the living among the dead? He is not here, but has risen." (Luke 24:5)

Loving God, we give you thanks that through Jesus Christ you fulfilled your promise to send a Messiah to save a broken humanity from its sins. We live in awe of the incredible depth of your love for us. Thank you for giving your Son to die and then ultimately conquer death, so that we might live eternally in you. Empower us to live lives that reflect this profound love and honor you with our whole being. In Jesus' name. Amen.

TELLING THE STORY (15 MINUTES)

You or your designated storyteller should now turn to telling the portion of the story that is highlighted in session 11. Incorporate any or all of the Background File notes in the participant book (p. 101) as part of the telling. Use one of the following three options for telling the story, or devise your own.

See the storytelling tips on p. 10 of this guide.

1. Read through, summarize, and comment on the story as provided in the participant book.
2. Ask for volunteers to tell portions of the story.
3. Read the story script provided below.

At the end of the storytelling time, summarize the Story Keys for this session.

The Story Script for Session 11

In the previous session, we began the gospel or good news story of Jesus. Today we continue that story and hear about major events in the greatest story.

Jesus demonstrated the very same power over nature that God demonstrated in the Old Testament. He commanded a storm at sea to stop, walked on water, turned water into wine, and enabled the disciples to haul in a huge catch of fish. When these things happened, people began to pay attention!

Jesus was also a wise teacher. One of the most popular sets of his teachings is the Sermon on the Mount. These teachings deal with topics like anger, worry, and prayer, and included the Beatitudes, a series of blessings. Jesus also summarized the entire law of Israel in the commandment to love God and love your neighbor as yourself.

Jesus often taught using stories called parables, which described what the kingdom of God is like. On the surface, these stories seemed very simple, but each one had a point that surprised and even prodded listeners to see God and God's promises in new ways. One of Jesus' stories is often called the Parable of the Prodigal Son. In this story, the younger of two sons begs his father for an early inheritance and then squanders it all. He returns home starving and expecting the worst from his father, but receives a warm welcome instead. Meanwhile, the older son can't believe there is so much fuss over his good-for-nothing brother and refuses to join the "welcome home" party.

Now, how does this parable grab you? If you feel like you've wandered so far away from God that you can never go "home," there's great news for you: God welcomes sinners! If, like the older son in the story and the religious leaders who heard Jesus tell this parable, you believe that you've worked hard and you should have "dibs" with God, the news might not seem so great: God welcomes sinners! This is how Jesus' parables can grab us and work on us.

Even more amazing than the healing and teaching and power over nature, Jesus showed God's power over life and death. One day Jesus received word that his friend Lazarus was dying, but didn't arrive at Lazarus' home until he had been dead four days. Jesus told Martha, one of Lazarus' sisters, "I am the resurrection and the life. Those who believe in me, even though they die, will live, and everyone who lives and believes in me will never die" (John 11:25-26). Then he went to the tomb where Lazarus had been buried and called him out of the tomb. Lazarus emerged, still wrapped up in burial cloths, but he was alive!

People had a lot of different ideas about who Jesus was and what he was up to. The Gospel of Mark tells us that Jesus asked his followers what people were saying about him. Then he asked, "Who do you say I am?" Peter said, "You are the Messiah." Jesus then told the disciples that this meant he would suffer, die, and rise from the dead. The disciples did not want to hear this! But this is what happened.

The Story Script for Session 11 (continued)

At the beginning of the last week of Jesus' life, he rode on a donkey into Jerusalem. The crowd surrounding him hailed him as the Messiah. This reaction from the crowd made the religious leaders worry that this might cause Rome, the ruling power, to clamp down on the Jewish people.

It was the time of the Festival of Unleavened Bread, also known as Passover. Jesus and his disciples shared the Passover meal together. As he broke bread and passed it around Jesus said, "This is my body given for you." As they drank the wine for Passover he said, "This is my blood shed for you." Meanwhile. Judas, one of Jesus' disciples, plotted with the religious leaders to hand over Jesus to the authorities for thirty pieces of silver.

While Jesus was praying in a garden called Gethsemane, Judas arrived with soldiers. Jesus was arrested and taken before a council made up of elders, chief priests, and scribes. Then he was beaten and humiliated, and all of his disciples abandoned him.

The council sent Jesus on to Pilate, the Roman governor of Judea, hoping to sway him into condemning Jesus. But Pilate wanted nothing to do with this case and sent Jesus to Herod, the governor of Galilee, the area Jesus came from.

Herod sent Jesus back to Pilate. This time the leaders persuaded Pilate to crucify Jesus and release a known criminal named Barabbas instead. Jesus was led through crowds of people shouting insults at him, then put to death on a cross between two thieves on a hill named Golgotha. Above him a sign read, "King of the Jews." His last words were "Father, into your hands I commend my spirit."

The body of Jesus was taken away by one of the council members, Joseph of Arimathea, who secretly followed Jesus. Jesus' body was wrapped according to Jewish custom and laid in a new tomb provided by Joseph.

Well, of course, everyone thought that was the end of the story! But very early Sunday morning some women took spices to the tomb for the body. But when they arrived at the tomb, a large stone that had blocked the entrance was rolled away, revealing two angels who said, "He is risen!" The women ran from the tomb and told the disciples.

Peter and another disciple ran to the tomb to see for themselves, and only found Jesus' burial clothes. Could it be that Jesus really had risen from the dead?! Jesus, in fact, appeared to the disciples several times after he was raised from the dead. He walked with some disciples along the road to Emmaus, a small town outside Jerusalem, and then revealed himself when he broke bread.

He appeared to the disciples when they were afraid and locked inside a house. Thomas wasn't there and refused to believe that Jesus was alive until he could see Jesus. The next time Jesus appeared, Thomas saw and felt the scars on Jesus' hands and side. Then Thomas said, "My Lord and my God!" Jesus replied, "Blessed are those who have not seen and yet have come to believe" (John 20:28-29).

Jesus commanded the disciples to "Go therefore and make disciples of all nations, baptizing them in the name of the Father and of the Son and of the Holy Spirit" (Matthew 28:19), and assured them that he would be with them always. Then, leading them out to the town of Bethany, he blessed them and ascended in glory to heaven.

The disciples returned to Jerusalem, praising God and awaiting "power from on high" to equip them to "go and make disciples" everywhere.

PICTURING THE STORY (20 MINUTES)

Go through the reflection questions listed in this section in the participant book (p. 101). Then play the segment called Who Do You Say I Am? (session 11) on the course DVD. Encourage the participants to watch the story unfold as artist Joe Castillo depicts the scenes of the story. Participants may be invited to write down their own questions.

When the segment is done, address the questions together as a large group or ask the participants to discuss in smaller teams. Invite participants to share their own questions or observations. What difference did it make to see the story in this way?

SINGING AND PRAYING THE STORY (10 MINUTES)

Use one or both of the psalms provided in the participant book to help address the story and its themes. Psalms are best read aloud. You may have one volunteer read the entire psalm or portion of a psalm. Or you may wish to have the psalm read responsively, verse by verse or line by line. Use a solo reader with the group responding, or read responsively using different groups.

As time allows, discuss the observations and questions provided.

Psalm 25 is an acrostic psalm that asks God for guidance, forgiveness, and deliverance. (Lines in an acrostic psalm begin with consecutive letters in the Hebrew alphabet.) The psalmist starts off with a statement of trust in the Lord, then asks for guidance in living according to God's covenant. He also asks for forgiveness for his sins and asks for God's blessing in the midst of loneliness and suffering.

Psalm 72 is a royal psalm asking for God's blessings to be bestowed upon the king. The psalmist asks God to allow the king to rule all people justly, especially those in need, and to give the king a long life and victory over all nations.

LOOKING AHEAD (5 MINUTES)

Briefly introduce the next chapter of the story that appears in session 12.

Mark it

Encourage participants to read and mark one or more of the passages listed in this section during the week ahead. Let the group know that at the start of next week's session you will ask volunteers to share any insights they have from this exercise.

You are encouraged to do the "Mark it" exercise as well.

Next time

In the next session we will see and hear about the spread of Christianity in Acts. To review this week's story and to help prepare for the next session, you and your group are encouraged to read introductions to the following in a study Bible:

- The New Testament
- Acts

You may find it helpful to take some notes or highlight items in the readings to share next week as part of Telling the Story.

OUR STORY

WELCOME

Whether Our Story is done consecutively along with the Core Session Plan, or planned for a separate time or location, consider providing hospitality in the form of refreshments.

- Arrange the room comfortably for small group discussion.
- Introduce newcomers in the group.
- Begin with prayer, using the session prayer on p. 129 or another prayer of your choice. Ask volunteers to provide prayers, if they feel comfortable doing so.

Ideas for optional settings and schedules for this time are provided in the introduction on page 13 of this leader guide.

- You may wish to begin by asking if anyone has a particular question or thought to share from the large group session. As an alternative to discussing those questions, simply note them or write them down on newsprint. Small groups may decide to discuss further.

CONVERSATION

See the tips for leading and participating in small group discussion on page 17 of this guide. Make available to all participants copies of the reproducible Guidelines for Small Group Discussion.

The reflection questions are intended to help participants connect their own stories to the key themes of the greatest story. These questions can be used for personal reflection while reading or used to guide group discussion. It is unlikely that a group could discuss all the questions in one discussion period. Don't be concerned about this. Here are some options for approaching the questions:

1. As leader, you may choose to focus on certain questions from the list.
2. Ask participants to suggest questions to discuss.
3. Have participants form smaller groups, assign the groups a designated number of questions to discuss, and then have each group report back to the large group.
4. If participants have the time and interest, you could assign each person a question or two to think about and prepare a response during the week. These responses could be shared as discussion starters when the group meets for Our Story discussion time.

Questions and Responses

The questions below are designed with personal reflection and response in mind. They do not require a certain amount of prior knowledge in order to respond. Responses may vary according to individual insights and context. Even so, a few guiding thoughts are provided for some of the questions.

○ *Imagine what it might be like to witness one of Jesus' miracles over the forces of nature. Would this experience make you more or less certain that God exists?*

○ *What do you think the miracles over the forces of nature say about Jesus?*

The Old Testament portrayed God, from the very beginning of creation, as the only one who had control over nature. God formed the heavens and earth, separated the Red Sea, and fed the people with manna. It's significant that the nature miracles show Jesus also exercising control over nature by stilling storms and turning water into wine. This points to the fact that Jesus and God are intimately connected and reveals Jesus' identity as God's Son.

Questions and Responses (continued)

○ *Why are stories such a powerful way to teach?*

Think about the best sermons that you've ever heard. Are they filled with confusing and obscure theological language, or did the preacher tell a story that you'd remember and possibly even retell? We remember stories that connect with our lives.

○ *What would you say is the point of the Parable of the Prodigal Son?*

○ *Name a powerful thing that you have learned. What teacher or teachers have influenced you the most? Why?*

○ *How do you hear Jesus' words about the resurrection?*

○ *Why do you think some fear Jesus' power over life and death?*

○ *How do you answer Jesus' question: Who do you say I am?*

○ *What do you think it means to carry Jesus' cross?*

We often presume that being a disciple means that things will get easier for us, not harder. Check out the assumptions of James and John in Mark 10:35-45. They think to be closer to Jesus means they will receive glory and greatness. This question really gets to the heart of what it means to be a disciple of Christ. Explore with the participants examples of people they know who have "carried Christ's cross." They might be examples as diverse as Mother Theresa or a next-door neighbor.

○ *What do Jesus' words, "This is my body and blood," mean to you?*

○ *What do you think of Jesus' prayer in the garden of Gethsemane?*

○ *How do you face difficult times?*

○ *Politics, religion, God's purposes—all had a role in the death of Jesus. How would you describe the main reason or reasons that Jesus was crucified?*

Jesus lived in a volatile time when the Romans occupied Palestine and forced the Jews to live according to Roman laws. This caused great anxiety for the people, especially for those like members of the religious council, who wanted to live according to God's law, but had Roman law thrust upon them. Jesus was a threat in this unstable situation.

Questions and Responses (continued)

From a broader perspective, Jesus died because of our sins. Like people in today's story, sometimes we go along with the crowd and cheer for Jesus, sometimes we turn our backs on him, and sometimes we want him out of our lives for good.

- *What question would you like to ask someone in this part of the story?*
- *The cross may be the most common symbol of the Christian faith. What does the cross mean to you?*
- *Imagine what it must have been like to find Jesus' tomb empty. What might go through your head? What goes through your head and heart today when you think about the resurrection?*
- *How do you recognize Jesus?*
- *How are the chapters of the story of Jesus still being written?*

Provide colored markers, paper, construction paper, poster board, magazines, scissors, or other materials that may be used to complete this creative assignment.

Creative Corner

Depending on how your schedule is organized, you may wish to assign this activity for individuals or small groups.

The church developed faith statements we call creeds to summarize the key Christian beliefs regarding Jesus. Reflect back on the story of Jesus told in the Gospels. Create a personal faith statement about Jesus and illustrate it somehow. Be prepared to share this statement with at least one other person.

YOU WILL BE MY WITNESSES

12

Acts

Spirit-led followers make sure the Word is heard

SESSION PREPARATION

OVERVIEW

In the last session we looked at Jesus' ministries of teaching and healing, and his death and resurrection, which finally proved that he was the Messiah promised in the Old Testament. Now we'll look at Luke, part two, also known as the Acts of the Apostles. It explores the birth of a church in Jesus' name. The stories we find here tell of the ministries of Jesus' early followers, especially Peter and Paul.

Scenes in this Session

You Will Be My Witnesses! (Acts 1)
Souls on Fire (Acts 2:1—5:16)
Death Threats (Acts 5:17—9:2)
A New Vision (Acts 9:3—11:18)
Gospel Roads (Acts 13–20)
Gospel On Trial (Acts 21–26)
Last Stop Rome (Acts 27–28)

What's the Story?

The book of Acts is a continuation of the story about Jesus begun in Luke. Both of these books are addressed to Theophilus, which means "friend of God," who may or may not have been a real person. Another name for this book is the Acts of the Apostles. An apostle is "one who is sent out." The apostles included Jesus' disciples and other followers who took the good news of the gospel to their known world. The book of Acts chronicles the apostles' activities following Jesus' ascension and the coming of the Holy Spirit. Once the Spirit filled the disciples, there was no stopping them from sharing the story of Jesus' life,

Materials for this session available on the Leader Reference CD:

- Synopsis of Events in History, Literature, and Philosophy, 4 B.C.E.-200 C.E. (CHART)
- Paul's Missionary Journeys (MAP)
- The Early Church and Key Locations in Acts (MAP)
- Cities and Countries Included in Acts 2 (MAP)
- Key People in Acts (CHART)

STORY KEYS

- The Holy Spirit empowers and guides the early Christian church.
- The early church was persecuted because of its belief in the risen Christ.
- The church expands its witness to include both Jews and Gentiles.
- Paul plants many churches when he hits the road to share the good news about Jesus.

death, and resurrection. This "spirited" bunch was empowered to preach and heal, all in Jesus' name.

Peter and Paul are the two central characters in Acts. Peter takes center stage at Pentecost when he interprets how Jesus' resurrection has changed everything. His speech was compelling and people immediately asked to be baptized. A faith community known as The Way began to form, and the apostles had to begin to organize their lives as followers of Jesus.

Paul is first introduced in Acts 8 as Saul, a Jewish leader who persecuted the early Christians. But Saul had a spectacular encounter with the risen Christ on a trip to Damascus, and he was called to preach the good news to the Gentiles. He used his Greek name, Paul, as he carried out this special calling. The majority of the book of Acts is an account of Paul's gospel road show, in which he is accompanied at first by Barnabas, and later by Timothy and Silas. Together Paul and his assistants planted faith communities as they traveled across Asia Minor, going as far as Greece and Rome.

In Acts, Jerusalem is the hub of this growing network of faith communities and important decisions are made there. But Acts portrays the early church as both formed and directed by the Holy Spirit. That same Spirit forms and directs faith communities today!

What's the Message?

Beginning at Pentecost, the new church, fueled by the Spirit, became a tight-knit community. But things soon changed. The very early days of the church were not easy, as the followers of Jesus were persecuted for preaching about the risen Christ. The persecution caused many to leave Jerusalem to seek sanctuary elsewhere. This scattering of the church launched the development of a network of believers with Jerusalem at its hub.

Acts also demonstrates the power of the Holy Spirit through somewhat turbulent times. God was at work in spite of the challenges and persecution early Christians endured. Lives were changed and the Jesus movement continued to spread. God used what the world saw as a shameful, crushing defeat (Jesus' death on a cross) to show God's continued faithfulness and love for the people. While humans had killed God's only Son, God raised him from the dead to conquer death for all time. While humans persecuted the fledgling church formed in Jesus' name, God called one of the worst offenders, Saul, and turned him into one of most famous missionaries for Christ. As we saw in the Old Testament,

God's love for humanity is so deep that it can overcome evil. The Holy Spirit witnesses to Jesus Christ and empowers Jesus' followers to do the same.

The gradual spread of Christianity also meant that Gentiles began to believe and be baptized. Acts serves as an explanation as to how and why the Gentiles were first permitted, and then later openly invited, into the church. Acts 15 is an important turning point in the story. At a key meeting of early Christian leaders in Jerusalem, decisions were made about the inclusion of Gentiles that dramatically affected the future of Christianity. The message was clear: sharing the good news about Jesus was not intended to simply create a new sect within Judaism; instead, it was a global movement to reach all people, even the outcast. This message was in tune with Luke, which emphasized the inclusion of those formerly considered to be outcasts. That's how broad and deep God's love is for all people.

Women held a much lower status than men in the Jewish faith, but Acts portrays them in a very different light. Lydia and Priscilla were both friends of Paul and active participants in the growth of the church in their communities. Those of lower social status were now welcomed in Jesus' church, and also granted positions of leadership.

PREPARE

1. Review chapter 12 in the participant book.
2. Review the overview and session plan for session 12 in the leader guide.
3. Watch the DVD segment for session 12.
4. Have extra Bibles available for those who did not bring one.
5. Have equipment for projecting or viewing the DVD set up and ready to go.
6. Consider distributing handouts or projecting images of reference materials (see list on p. 137) in the session. You might want to do this during Telling the Story or discussion of the Background Files.
7. If you are having the class do the Creative Corner activity, gather any materials suggested.
8. Pray for your class members and for God's presence and guidance as you gather in God's Word.

MATERIALS NEEDED

- Extra copies of the Bible
- Participant books
- Computer or DVD player; projector or TV monitor
- Course DVD
- Reference material
- Creative Corner materials (optional)
- Name tags
- Refreshments (optional)

LEADER PRAYER

O God, thank you for the gift of your Holy Spirit, which empowers the church and its witness. Stir up the Spirit's power and presence in me as I prepare for this session, and help me to encourage others to reflect on their faith and the depth of your love for them. Amen.

CORE SESSION PLAN

The Core Session Plan is designed for use in one 60-minute period. The Core Session Plan can be extended 45-60 minutes by incorporating the group reflection time called Our Story, found at the end of the Core Session Plan.

GATHERING (10 MINUTES)

Welcome and check-in

Provide name tags again as you welcome participants to the session. If you are serving refreshments, have them set out ahead of time. Spend a few minutes asking if anyone wants to share any thoughts or insights from their personal "Mark it" reading for the week. You won't be able to spend much time on this, but hearing a couple of testimonials will encourage more in the group to make this weekly reading and devotional reflection a part of their routine.

Scripture and prayer

Read the following verse and prayer, or ask a volunteer to do so.

Then Peter began to speak to them: "I truly understand that God shows no partiality, but in every nation anyone who fears him and does what is right is acceptable to him." (Acts 10:34)

O Holy Spirit, your coming on Pentecost infused Jesus' disciples with new power to proclaim the good news of the risen Christ. Because of you, people followed Christ and their lives were changed. Stir up in each of us that same drive to witness to others about our Lord and Savior, Jesus Christ. Help us to do so in a way that is inclusive of all people, especially those whom society considers to be outcasts. In Jesus' name. Amen.

TELLING THE STORY (15 MINUTES)

See the storytelling tips on p. 10 of this guide.

You or your designated storyteller should now turn to telling the portion of the story that is highlighted in session 12. Incorporate any or all of the Background File notes in the participant book (p. 111) as part of the telling. Use one of the following three options for telling the story, or devise your own.

1. Read through, summarize, and comment on the story as provided in the participant book.
2. Ask for volunteers to tell portions of the story.
3. Read the story script provided below.

At the end of the storytelling time, summarize the Story Keys for this session.

The Story Script for Session 12

Before Jesus ascended to heaven, he promised to send the disciples out into the world equipped with the Holy Spirit. While the disciples waited for the Spirit to come to them, they replaced Judas, the one who betrayed Jesus, with Matthias. Now big things were about to happen!

The birth of the church started off with a burst of wind that filled the entire house where the disciples had gathered. They were filled with the Holy Spirit, who led each of them to speak in a different language. This caused a stir among the many Jews who were in town from all over the world.

A crowd gathered. Some thought the disciples were drunk. But Peter pointed to the prophecy of Joel who said the "day of the LORD" would come with the Spirit being poured out on old and young, slave and free, alike. He even compared Jesus to Israel's "superstar" king, David. Peter told the crowds that Jesus was the fulfillment of God's promise to Abraham and Sarah and that Jesus was glorified by God, but many refused to believe in him.

The Spirit was so powerful that day that 3,000 people stepped forward to be baptized. These new believers shared much time together in the temple, during meals, and in fellowship.

The Spirit equipped the disciples with the power to heal, but their main work was preaching the good news about Jesus. The religious leaders continued to resist the good news and threw Peter and John in jail. Peter and John simply said, "We cannot keep from speaking about what we have seen and heard."

The apostles felt honored to serve Jesus in spite of opposition and torture. One of these was Stephen, who was called a man of "grace and power." Stephen's message stirred up jealousy and hatred among some, especially when he spoke of Israel's past unfaithfulness. And so Stephen was dragged out of the city and stoned to death as he cried out, "Lord, do not hold this sin against them" (Acts 7:60).

One of the witnesses to Stephen's stoning was a Pharisee named Saul. He was especially zealous in searching out and persecuting followers of Jesus. On his way to Damascus, Saul was intercepted by a flash of light that knocked him to the ground. The voice of Jesus told Saul to stop the persecution.

Blinded by this event, Saul obeyed Jesus and went to Damascus to wait for further instructions. After three days, a follower named Ananias came and laid his hands on Saul, who was then able to see again! This began the long and fruitful preaching and teaching journeys of Saul, now called Paul. He had once persecuted others for following Jesus, but became one of the greatest missionaries for Christ.

As the early church continued to grow despite persecution, the apostle Peter had a vision which told him to go to a Roman centurion and put aside food restrictions that separated Jewish believers from Gentiles.

The Story Script for Session 12 (continued)

But this vision was about more than food laws—it meant that the message about Jesus was for all people, both Jews and Gentiles! The debate on this matter continued, especially within the council at Jerusalem, but Paul was convinced that God had called him to preach the gospel to the Gentiles.

This was an exciting and challenging time for Jesus' followers. Their preaching was very successful in Jewish synagogues and in Greek and Roman temples. The famous duo of Paul and Barnabas traveled all across Asia Minor and Greece. But opposition was never far behind.

In Philippi, Paul, Timothy, and Silas converted a wealthy woman to faith in Christ, but were later thrown into prison. An earthquake broke open their chains and provided an opportunity for them to convert the jailer and his entire family! In Athens, a center of great learning and debate, Paul preached a strong message about the God in whom "we live and move and have our being" (Acts 17:28). This was in contrast to a monument in the city dedicated to an "unknown god."

As he traveled and preached, Paul created more and more new communities of faith in places like Corinth and Ephesus. Many New Testament books are actually letters Paul wrote to encourage and inspire these fledgling churches. (See the "Synopsis of Events in History, Literature, and Philosophy, 4 B.C.E.-200 C.E.," which includes Paul's journeys and letters.)

After three long trips spreading the good news, Paul returned to Jerusalem where the opposition stirred up a riot and had him arrested. Given a chance to speak, Paul testified to his excellent Jewish credentials and to his vivid conversion. Realizing that Paul was a Roman citizen and that conditions had become too dangerous for him in Jerusalem, a Roman officer had him taken to Caesarea to plead his case before the Roman governor Felix. Making no decision about Paul's fate, Felix had Paul put under house arrest. He was followed by Festus, who sent Paul to Rome to appear before the Emperor.

While Paul was headed to Rome on board a prisoner ship, the ship was nearly sunk by a terrible storm. It managed to drift to the island of Malta with no loss of life. On Malta, Paul continued to demonstrate the healing powers of the Spirit. After three months, he finally arrived in Rome. Here he told his story to Jewish leaders, causing more debate and argument between those who believed and those who didn't.

Acts tells us that Paul stayed in Rome for two years preaching and teaching, but gives no indication of whether he was put to death there or set free.

PICTURING THE STORY (20 MINUTES)

Go through the reflection questions listed in this section in the participant book (p. 111). Then play the segment called You Will Be My Witnesses (session 12) on the course DVD. Encourage the participants to watch the story unfold as artist Joe Castillo depicts the scenes of the story. Participants may be invited to write down their own questions.

When the segment is done, address the questions together as a large group or ask the participants to discuss in smaller teams. Invite participants to share their own questions or observations. What difference did it make to see the story in this way?

SINGING AND PRAYING THE STORY (10 MINUTES)

Use one or both of the psalms provided in the participant book to help address the story and its themes. Psalms are best read aloud. You may have one volunteer read the entire psalm or portion of a psalm. Or you may wish to have the psalm read responsively, verse by verse or line by line. Use a solo reader with the group responding, or read responsively using different groups.

As time allows, discuss the observations and questions provided.

Psalm 138 is a psalm of thanksgiving for God's faithfulness and protection. The psalmist describes the depth of his gratitude for God's faithfulness in answering his prayers. Even though God is exalted, God pays attention to those who are humble in spirit. Because of this, God deserves to be praised by all the nations. The psalm closes with the assurance that God's faithfulness will continue.

Psalm 96 is a psalm of praise and an enthronement psalm that praises God as king. The psalmist calls upon the people to sing praises to God for God's marvelous deeds and superiority over all nations. God is a king who will judge all creation with fairness.

LOOKING AHEAD (5 MINUTES)

Mark it

Encourage participants to read and mark one or more of the passages listed in this section during the week ahead. Let the group know that at the start of next week's session you will ask volunteers to share any insights they have from this exercise.

You are encouraged to do the "Mark it" exercise as well.

You may find it helpful to take some notes or highlight items in the readings to share next week as part of Telling the Story.

Next Time

Briefly introduce the next chapter of the story that appears in session 13. In the next session we will explore the letters Paul wrote to a number of early Christian churches and to individuals. The letters give us several pictures of how the story of Jesus was being told and interpreted in the early church. You might not be surprised to find out that controversies and disagreements went hand in hand with bold witness and faithfulness to the gospel. To review this week's story and to help prepare for the next session, you and your group are encouraged to read introductions to the following in a study Bible:

- The Letters of Paul
- Romans
- 1 Corinthians
- 2 Corinthians
- Galatians
- Ephesians
- Philippians
- Colossians
- 1 Thessalonians
- 2 Thessalonians
- Philemon

OUR STORY

Ideas for optional settings and schedules for this time are provided in the introduction on page 13 of this leader guide.

WELCOME

Whether done consecutively along with the Core Session Plan or planned for a separate time or location, consider providing hospitality in the form of refreshments.

- Arrange the room comfortably for small group discussion.
- Introduce newcomers in the group.
- Begin with prayer, using the session prayer on p. 140 or another prayer of your choice. Ask volunteers to provide prayers, if they feel comfortable doing so.
- You may wish to begin by asking if anyone has a particular question or thought to share from the large group session. As an alternative to discussing those questions, simply note them or write them down on newsprint. Small groups may decide to discuss further.

CONVERSATION

The reflection questions are intended to help participants connect their own stories to the key themes of the greatest story. These questions can be used for personal reflection while reading or used to guide group discussion. It is unlikely a group could discuss all the questions in one discussion period. Don't be concerned about this. Here are some options for approaching the questions:

See the tips for leading and participating in small group discussion on page 17 of this guide. Make available to all participants copies of the reproducible Guidelines for Small Group Discussion.

1. As leader, you may choose to focus on certain questions from the list.
2. Ask participants to suggest questions to discuss.
3. Divide the groups into smaller teams, assign the teams a designated number of questions to discuss, and then have each group report back to the large group.
4. If you have a group that has the time and interest, you could assign each participant a question or two to think about and prepare a response during the week. These responses could be shared as discussion starters when the group meets for Our Story discussion time.

Questions and Responses

The questions below are designed with personal reflection and response in mind. They do not require a certain amount of prior knowledge in order to respond. Responses may vary according to individual insights and context. Even so, a few guiding thoughts are provided for some of the questions.

- *Why would you say the promise of the Holy Spirit was so important to the disciples?*

- *How would you have felt to be chosen as the new disciple?*

- *How did Peter make it clear that the story of Jesus was part of the story God had begun long before?*

In our study of the Gospels, we learned that it was very important to Jesus' early followers to draw the connection between God's promises made to the people in the Old Testament and Jesus' coming as that promised Messiah. Because of this, the authors of the Gospels referred back to Old Testament prophecy to prove the point. We see this in the Pentecost story, too. The coming of the Holy Spirit changed everything. Peter interprets this event for the crowd using a prophecy from Joel.

Questions and Responses (continued)

- *Imagine that you are someone in the crowd on the day the Holy Spirit came upon the disciples. Describe what you hear and see.*

- *Why was being a witness to the story of Jesus no easy task? What makes being a witness to this story challenging today?*

Early Christians were persecuted for their beliefs in the Risen Lord, which threatened the religious leaders of the day and government authorities who wanted to maintain control of the people. Explore some of the things that control our lives today that make it challenging to be a follower of Christ and witness to our belief in him.

- *How do you think you might react if you were threatened with imprisonment or even death for speaking up for Jesus? What's the bravest thing you have ever done?*

- *Have you ever felt persecuted? Have you ever persecuted or made fun of someone else because of what he or she believed?*

- *What a turnaround Saul had on the road to Damascus. Do you know of anyone whose life has been turned around? How did this turnaround happen?*

God is a God of turnarounds who can make anything happen!

- *Why would anyone want to put limits on the gospel? Do you think the gospel is meant for everyone? Why or why not?*

The early church struggled with its newfound identity as a body called together in Jesus' name by the Holy Spirit and the relationship this new calling had to their Jewish origins. This discernment required a lot of prayer and conversation. Acts 15 is a real turning point for the early church. Reread it in preparation for your discussion.

- *What kind of vision do you think might be needed in the church today? How would you know such a vision was coming from God?*

- *Imagine traveling with Paul as part of his gospel road show. What would have been most exciting? Most scary?*

Questions and Responses (continued)

- *How do you think the message of the gospel can reach people today? What has changed since the time of Paul? What, if anything, is still the same?*

The Gospel stories of Jesus hold real clues on how to reach people today. Jesus told stories and spoke in ways that were very relevant to the people of his day. He met them in ways that made his message very accessible. This is something we need to reflect upon today. Where do people gather and how can we make our gospel witness more accessible?

- *What do you think of Paul's statement that God is the one in whom we live and move and have our being?*

- *Paul had many identities—he was an expert in Jewish law, a Roman citizen, a follower of Jesus, missionary to the Gentiles. Which one of these do you think he thought was most important? Why?*

- *How do you identify yourself? Which part of that identity is most important? Why?*

- *How would you describe the journey you are on? How is it like or unlike Paul's journey?*

- *The church today traces its roots back to the church described in the story of Acts. What do you think has changed? What is still the same?*

Creative Corner

Depending on how your schedule is organized, you may wish to assign this activity for individuals or small groups.

Working in groups of three or four, choose a story from the book of Acts. (There are many colorful scenes to choose from.) Then imagine that one or two of you are reporters for a local newspaper or TV station. Conduct an interview with one or more of the main characters in the story. After practicing, do your interviews for the rest of the group.

Provide colored markers, paper, construction paper, poster board, magazines, scissors, or other materials that may be used to complete this creative assignment.

13 THE POWER OF GOD FOR SALVATION
The Letters of Paul

The man, the mission, and the message

SESSION PREPARATION

Materials for this session available on the Leader Reference CD:

- Synopsis of Events in History, Literature, and Philosophy, 4 B.C.E.-200 C.E. (CHART)
- Paul's Missionary Journeys (MAP)
- The Early Church and Key Locations in Acts (MAP)

OVERVIEW

In the previous session we looked at the emergence of the early church in Jerusalem and the persecution endured by early believers. We also learned about Paul's gospel road show that carried the faith across Asia Minor and as far as Greece and Rome. This session takes a broad look at the letters of Paul, which were written to support and encourage the churches he planted.

Scenes in this Session

A New Man with a New Message (Galatians 1:11—2:21; Philippians 3:2-11)
To All God's Beloved (Paul's letters to churches)
I Am Not Ashamed of the Gospel
Powerful Messages (selected passages from Paul's letters)

What's the Story?

What we know about Paul comes from Acts and from details he shared in his epistles or letters. We know that he was a Jew from Tarsus in Cilicia, and that he originally persecuted the early followers of Jesus. However, because of a radical conversion experience, he became one of Jesus' most devout followers. Through intense missionary work, he founded churches as he traveled throughout Asia Minor and Europe. Paul wrote letters to guide these fledgling faith communities from afar as they struggled with important issues. Paul may not have written all of the letters attributed to him, but we do know that he wrote Romans, 1 and 2 Corinthians, Galatians, Philippians, 1 Thessalonians, and Philemon.

STORY KEYS

- Each of Paul's letters deals with an important issue in the life of a faith community or an individual.
- God's salvation is for both Jews and Gentiles.
- Christ alone has the power to save us.
- It is by grace that we are set free to love and serve our neighbor.

Romans (written around 56-57 C.E.) is the one letter Paul wrote to a faith community that he did not plant. Paul wrote this letter when he was in transition, and intended to head to Rome in the near future.

1 Corinthians (53-55 C.E.) was probably the second of Paul's letters to the church in Corinth, the first having been lost. Along with 2 Corinthians, this letter demonstrates the intensity of the two-way conversation between Paul and the church in Corinth and shows us the church's struggles and debates. Because of some rocky transitions in tone and context, many scholars believe 2 Corinthians is an anthology of several letters pieced together sometime after 1 Corinthians.

Galatians (50-55 C.E.) was written to support Gentile converts to the Christian faith.

Philippians (mid-late 50s C.E.) was a collaboration between Paul and Timothy, addressed to the first church Paul started in Europe.

1 Thessalonians (45-50 C.E.) is the earliest surviving document of the early church. It was written to the church in Thessalonica, in modern-day Greece, which was probably persecuted for believing that Jesus, not the Roman Emperor, was God.

Philemon (55 C.E.) is a letter asking Philemon, a leader in the Colossian church, to reconcile with Onesimus, his slave and recent convert to Christianity.

What's the Message?

Together these letters give us a picture of the early church as it worked out its theology based in a variety of church contexts addressed by Paul.

Theologian and reformer Martin Luther saw the letter to the Romans as a lens for interpreting the whole Bible because it boiled down the gospel message so well, connecting the Old Testament and the New Testament. In this letter, Luther discovered a key for his own gospel interpretation: we are saved by God's grace and are "justified apart from works of the law." In Romans, Paul also seeks to reconcile the relationship between Jewish and Gentile Christians in Rome.

In 1 Corinthians, Paul denounces the social ranking system of the day that divided people rather than uniting them. He reminds the church that in Christ we are all one body and therefore interdependent and necessary. In doing this, Paul drives home the point that Christian love is what the Corinthians should strive for, not that which further divides. Second Corinthians has rough transitions because it contains several messages. Paul both defends himself and seeks reconciliation with the church at Corinth. He also describes what it means to be a generous giver.

In Galatians, Paul describes the meaning of Christian freedom for followers of Christ. Through Christ, we are justified by faith purely through God's grace. Freed by Christ, we are no longer slaves to the law. We are set free to love and serve our neighbor. This letter also highlights the inclusivity of Christ's church, in which there is "no longer Jew or Greek" (Gentile), but all are made one.

Philippians is a four-chapter thank-you note to the church at Philippi. This is Paul's most upbeat letter, which is a little surprising because he was in prison at the time. Paul uses an early hymn of the church to remind the Philippians why Christ entered human form and deserves thanks and praise. Paul also invites the believers in Philippi to celebrate their heavenly citizenship.

In 1 Thessalonians, Paul encourages and celebrates the church which has turned from worshipping idols to serving the one true God. Paul reminds his readers that through Christ they are united with him at all times.

In Philemon, Paul condemns the practice of social ranking which places some people in places of higher respect than others. In this letter, he seeks to persuade his friend, Philemon, both to reconcile with his slave Onesimus and change the way he looks at relationships and social status.

PREPARE

1. Review chapter 13 in the participant book.
2. Review the overview and session plan for session 13 in the leader guide.
3. Watch the DVD segment for session 13.
4. Have extra Bibles available for those who did not bring one.
5. Have equipment for projecting or viewing the DVD set up and ready to go.
6. Consider distributing handouts or projecting images of reference materials (see list on p. 148) in the session. You might want to do this during Telling the Story or discussion of the Background Files.
7. If you are having the class do the Creative Corner activity, gather any materials suggested.
8. Pray for your class members and for God's presence and guidance as you gather in God's Word.

MATERIALS NEEDED

- Extra copies of the Bible
- Participant books
- Computer or DVD player; projector or TV monitor
- Course DVD
- Reference materials
- Creative Corner materials (optional)
- Name tags
- Refreshments (optional)

LEADER PRAYER

Lord Jesus, I thank you for Paul and his ability to address the issues and concerns of his day in ways that people could understand. As I prepare to lead this session, help me to listen to Paul's messages and glorify your name above all others. Amen.

CORE SESSION PLAN

GATHERING (10 MINUTES)

The Core Session Plan is designed for use in one 60-minute period. The Core Session Plan can be extended 45-60 minutes by incorporating the group reflection time called Our Story, found at the end of the Core Session Plan.

Welcome and check-in

Provide name tags again as you welcome participants to the session. If you are serving refreshments, have them set out ahead of time. Spend a few minutes asking if anyone wants to share any thoughts or insights from their personal "Mark It" reading for the week. You won't be able to spend much time on this, but hearing a couple of testimonials will encourage more in the group to make this weekly reading and devotional reflection a part of their routine.

Scripture and prayer

Read the following verse and prayer, or ask a volunteer to do so.

For if while we were enemies, we were reconciled to God through the death of his Son, much more surely, having been reconciled, we will be saved by his life. (Romans 5:10)

O loving Jesus, through you we are reconciled to God and receive true salvation and eternal life. Thank you for bearing the burden of our sins, freeing us from their deadly weight, and assuring us of your constant presence, now and forever. Amen.

TELLING THE STORY (15 MINUTES)

You or your designated storyteller should now turn to telling the portion of the story that is highlighted in session 13. Incorporate any or all of the Background File notes in the participant book (p. 118) as part of the telling. Use one of the following three options for telling the story, or devise your own.

See the storytelling tips on p. 10 of this guide.

1. Read through, summarize, and comment on the story as provided in the participant book.
2. Ask for volunteers to tell portions of the story.
3. Read the story script provided below.

At the end of the storytelling time, summarize the Story Keys for this session.

The Story Script for Session 13

We learned a lot about Paul in the book of Acts. (Use "Synopsis of Events in History, Literature, and Philosophy, 4 B.C.E.-200 C.E." to note approximate dates for Paul's journeys and letters.) Paul's letters help us learn even more about Paul, his faith, and how he applied that faith to building up the churches he founded.

Paul is named as the writer of thirteen of the twenty-seven books in the New Testament. These books are actually letters written to churches and also to individuals such as Paul's friend Philemon and coworker Timothy. They were written to a particular church or person for a particular reason. Due to some differences in writing style, wording, and ideas, however, we can't be certain that Paul wrote all thirteen of these letters. One of his closest students may have written some of them. What we do know for certain is that all of these letters point to Jesus as the Risen Lord.

Paul wrote to the Galatians about his upbringing in the Jewish tradition and his training as a teacher of the law, but he declared that Gentiles did not have to follow Jewish customs in order to be part of God's people. God's message was for both Jews and Gentiles. There was much resistance to this radical new idea at the time, but Paul could not be swayed. He clearly stated that "a person is justified not by works of the law but through faith in Jesus Christ" (Galatians 2:16).

Paul wrote about his background in his letter to the Philippians, too. In spite of everything that he had gained in his former life, he said, it was all nothing compared to Jesus. Suffering—and even death—no longer mattered to him, because he knew that in Christ Jesus he would be raised from the dead.

In writing to the Corinthians, Paul addressed an attitude among some that their spiritual gifts were better than others. Paul stated instead that each gift was an equally valuable asset in building up the body of Christ.

Paul wrote his longest letter to Rome. Although he had not visited or started a church there, it seems that he planned to visit Rome soon. In his letter, Paul laid out his testimony and beliefs very carefully. He declared that the gospel is "the power of God for salvation to everyone who has faith, to the Jew first and also to the Greek [Gentile]" (Romans 1:16). There is no separation, no inequality, for if you belong to Christ you are one in Christ.

Going further, Paul said that sin came into the world with the first man, Adam, but with Jesus the free gift of God's grace is given for all. Now, this doesn't mean that we no longer struggle with sin. Paul described our ongoing struggle with sin like this: "I do not do the good I want, but the evil I do not want is what I do" (Romans 7:19). Sounds a bit familiar, doesn't it? There's nothing we can do to stop sinning or escape sin. We can't make ourselves right with God by praying hard enough, or following the law strictly enough, or by doing thousands and thousands of good works. Only Jesus can make us acceptable to God. God's grace in Christ saves us. This is the powerful message in Paul's letters, and Paul was not at all ashamed to preach and teach it.

PICTURING THE STORY (20 MINUTES)

Go through the reflection questions listed in this section in the participant book (p. 118). Then play the segment called The Power of God for Salvation (session 13) on the course DVD. Encourage the participants to watch the story unfold as artist Joe Castillo depicts the scenes of the story. Participants may be invited to write down their own questions.

When the segment is done, address the questions together as a large group or ask the participants to discuss in smaller teams. Invite participants to share their own questions or observations. What difference did it make to see the story in this way?

SINGING AND PRAYING THE STORY (10 MINUTES)

Use one or both of the psalms provided in the participant book to help address the story and its themes. Psalms are best read aloud. You may have one volunteer read the entire psalm or portion of a psalm. Or you may wish to have the psalm read responsively, verse by verse or line by line. Use a solo reader with the group responding, or read responsively using different groups.

As time allows, discuss the observations and questions provided.

Psalm 121 is both a liturgy and trust psalm. (Liturgy psalms were generally composed so that various people could speak different parts, often for a specific purpose such as entering the temple, asking for God's help, or thanking God.) The psalmist responds to the opening question: "From where will my help come?" by reminding us that God will protect and keep all the faithful in a deep, abiding relationship to insure that no harm befalls them.

Psalm 131 is a trust psalm. The psalmist quiets his soul and takes a humble approach in drawing near to God. The psalm also calls upon Israel to depend on and hope in God forever.

LOOKING AHEAD (5 MINUTES)

Briefly introduce the next chapter of the story that appears in session 14.

Mark it

Encourage participants to read and mark one or more of the passages listed in this section during the week ahead. Let the group know that at the start of next week's session you will ask volunteers to share any insights they have from this exercise.

You are encouraged to do the "Mark it" exercise as well.

You may find it helpful to take some notes or highlight items in the readings to share next week as part of Telling the Story.

Next time

In the next session we will explore more writings of the New Testament. They are called letters, but some read more like sermons or teachings. To review this week's story and to help prepare for the next session, you and your group are encouraged to read introductions to the following in a study Bible:

- General Letters
- Hebrews
- James
- 1 Peter
- 2 Peter
- 1 John
- 2 John
- 3 John
- Jude

OUR STORY

Ideas for optional settings and schedules for this time are provided in the introduction on page 13 of this leader guide.

WELCOME

Whether done consecutively along with the Core Session Plan or planned for a separate time or location, consider providing hospitality in the form of refreshments.

- Arrange the room comfortably for small group discussion.
- Introduce newcomers in the group.
- Begin with prayer, using the session prayer on p. 151 or another prayer of your choice. Ask volunteers to provide prayers, if they feel comfortable doing so.
- You may wish to begin by asking if anyone has a particular question or thought to share from the large group session. As an alternative to discussing those questions, simply note them or write them down on newsprint. Small groups may decide to discuss further.

See the tips for leading and participating in small group discussion on page 17 of this guide. Make available to all participants copies of the reproducible Guidelines for Small Group Discussion.

CONVERSATION

The reflection questions are intended to help participants connect their own stories to the key themes of the greatest story. These questions can be used for personal reflection while reading or to guide group discussion. It is unlikely a group could discuss all the questions in one discussion period. Don't be concerned about this. Here are some options for approaching the questions:

1. As leader, you may choose to focus on certain questions from the list.

2. Ask participants to suggest questions to discuss.
3. Divide the groups into smaller teams, assign the teams a designated number of questions to discuss, and then have each group report back to the large group.
4. If you have a group that has the time and interest, you could assign each participant a question or two to think about and prepare a response during the week. These responses could be shared as discussion starters when the group meets for Our Story discussion time.

Questions and Responses

The questions below are designed with personal reflection and response in mind. They do not require a certain amount of prior knowledge in order to respond. Responses may vary according to individual insights and context. Even so, a few guiding thoughts are provided for some of the questions.

○ *What kinds of things do you learn from reading letters or personal e-mails?*

For many people, reading letters or e-mail messages leaves out part of the communication process—the visual cues and body language. Yet you can still pick up a lot from a person's writing, choice of words, and tone. What can you tell from Paul's choice of words and the tone in his letters?

○ *Why do you think Paul's message angered some and gave great hope to others? How does his message strike you?*

In Paul's time, the early church was struggling with its identity, especially related to its Jewish origins. As this struggle went on, Paul brought the good news to Gentiles within the Roman Empire. The Gentiles had no previous relationship with the God of Israel. They were more accustomed to worshiping the Emperor as god. In the midst of these major transitions, Paul took a strong stand that God's salvation was for both Jew and Gentile, stating that salvation came only through Jesus Christ.

○ *What do you think it means to gain Christ?*

○ *What thoughts or questions do you have about whether Paul actually wrote all the letters that bear his name?*

In Paul's day, writing under the name of a respected teacher was not uncommon and was actually considered a way to honor the teacher. Those who did this were acting to promote the faith, not to undermine it.

Questions and Responses (continued)

- *Why do you think Paul's personal letters to churches and to individuals became part of the Bible?*
- *What kind of a letter would you like Paul to send to you or to your church?*
- *How does Paul help connect the beginning of the greatest story to Jesus? How does he help you see yourself in the story?*

The letter to the Romans (chapters 4-5) discusses the deep connections between the Old Testament and the New Testament.

- *How does it make you feel to know that Paul struggled with sin each day?*
- *How would you define the word* grace*?*
- *How do you see the connection between God's grace and our freedom?*
- *How does the armor of God fit you? What may need to be strengthened, tempered, tightened, or added?*

Provide colored markers, paper, construction paper, poster board, magazines, scissors, or other materials that may be used to complete this creative assignment.

Creative Corner

Depending on how your schedule is organized, you may wish to assign this activity for individuals or small groups.

Consider these questions: How is your relationship with God going? How are your personal relationships going? What issues are you dealing with in your life? How about faith? What's happening, or not happening, with that? Think about the whole story you have been experiencing. What is making sense? What is still hard to understand?

With all these questions—or others—in mind, write yourself a letter, like Paul would have written to his friends. This letter doesn't have to sound like Paul or even include his teachings. Just stand back and look at what is going on in your life. What do you want to say to yourself?

Start with something like, "Dear (your name): I see that you . . . ." When you are done with your letter, talk with someone about it, if you wish.

SO GREAT A CLOUD OF WITNESSES

General Letters

14

Keeping the faith, running the race, living in love

SESSION PREPARATION

OVERVIEW

In the previous session, we took a broad look at the letters attributed to Paul. In this session, we'll talk about the seven General Letters. Unlike Paul's epistles, these letters were not directed to a specific church context. Instead they addressed broad issues facing the early Christians as they awaited Jesus' second coming.

Materials for this session available on the Leader Reference CD:

- Synopsis of Events in History, Literature, and Philosophy, 4 B.C.E.-200 C.E. (CHART)
- The Early Church and Key Locations in Acts (MAP)

Scenes in this Session

Linking Past and Future
A Cloud of Witnesses (Hebrews)
Doers of the Word (James)
God's Own People (1, 2 Peter)
Truth and Love (1, 2, 3 John; Jude)

What's the Story?

While Paul's letters are contextual, dealing with specific community issues and concerns, the General Letters are more universal, addressing common issues faced by early believers as they awaited the return of Jesus. Written in the names of several of Jesus' disciples, the General Letters portray the theological viewpoints the authors thought these key leaders would have for a new generation of believers.

Hebrews (70 C.E.), originally composed in Greek, is more like an eloquent sermon than a letter. It was most likely written in Rome. Although the letter was attributed to Paul, it's doubtful that he wrote it. Hebrews is a "two-edged

STORY KEYS

- The General Letters were written to connect a new generation of Christians with the witnesses of the past.
- Jesus creates a new covenant with God's people, making them holy.
- James provokes us to be doers of the Word.
- The Lord will return, but in the meantime watch out for false teachers!
- Christians are called to abide in God's love.

sword" that addresses judgment and promise. As you read this letter, pay attention to the intricate dance between the two.

James (most likely written between 130 and 140 C.E.) was originally thought to have been written by Jesus' brother James, but many scholars think it was written much later and then attributed to him. The first part of the letter holds the Christian accountable in his or her daily living and exhorts believers to be "doers of the word." Then James compares the wisdom from below with God's higher wisdom, which is pure.

Although 1 and 2 Peter were originally attributed to Jesus' disciple Peter, it is more likely that these letters were written in his name after he died. Themes in 1 Peter include the rebirth of the Christian through Jesus' resurrection, and the call to holy living, even amid persecution and false prophets.

Because of common language and themes, the writer of 1, 2 and 3 John was believed to be the writer of the Gospel of John as well. However, it's more likely that these letters were written in a faith community that was deeply connected to the Gospel of John. 1 John is the longest of the three letters and focuses on what it means to be children of God dwelling in God's love. Like the other two letters, it warns against false teachers.

Jude (probably written in the late first century C.E.) is an exhortation against false teachers and how to stand fast against them.

What's the Message?

Although these letters were written under the names of Jesus' disciples, they were most likely written a generation or two after these men died. This was a time of uncertainty for the young church. Christians began to see themselves as living in the time in between Jesus' resurrection and his promised second coming. They had to discern what living during this indefinite time period should be like. At the same time, they continued to face persecution. The General Letters address these issues and more.

Both Hebrews and 1 Peter look at the Christian faith community as one body with whom God has created a new covenant through Jesus' death and resurrection, fulfilling all the promises of the Old Testament. Hebrews especially draws on Old Testament references to make a strong connection between God's new covenant and that of the past. Through Christ we are connected to a great "cloud of witnesses." Both letters (along with some of the others) address what the community's new identity as "God's own people" means in light of persecution. Jesus' resurrection gives the people new life and hope, even amid difficult times. Second Peter reminds the early Christians that "the day of the Lord" will come, but its timing is not predictable.

James discusses what it looks like to live as "doers of the word" in these in-between times. Doers are those who live lives that produce good works as a result of their faith. James also talks about the practical wisdom that comes with Christian living and identifies wisdom as a gift from God.

Several of the General Letters deal with false teachers who preach in opposition to the more established biblical tradition. First John talks about false teachers who say that Jesus was merely a spiritual being, and not really human. This teaching directly opposes the Gospel of John, which identifies Jesus as fully divine from the beginning of creation, who then became flesh at the appointed time. Those who opposed the Christian tradition and the story about Jesus as revealed through his disciples were considered "false prophets."

PREPARE

1. Review chapter 14 in the participant book.
2. Review the overview and session plan for session 14 in the leader guide.
3. Watch the DVD segment for session 14.
4. Have extra Bibles available for those who did not bring one.
5. Have equipment for projecting or viewing the DVD set up and ready to go.
6. Consider distributing handouts or projecting images of reference materials (see list on p. 157) in the session. You might want to do this during Telling the Story or discussion of the Background Files.
7. If you are having the class do the Creative Corner activity, gather any materials suggested.
8. Pray for your class members and for God's presence and guidance as you gather in God's Word.

MATERIALS NEEDED

- Extra copies of the Bible
- Participant books
- Computer or DVD player; projector or TV monitor
- Course DVD
- Reference materials
- Creative Corner materials (optional)
- Name tags
- Refreshments (optional)

LEADER PRAYER

O God, thank you for the great cloud of witnesses that has gone before us. Help the group to know the deep connection that you have had with all your people throughout time. Amen.

CORE SESSION PLAN

The Core Session Plan is designed for use in one 60-minute period. The Core Session Plan can be extended 45-60 minutes by incorporating the group reflection time called Our Story, found at the end of the Core Session Plan.

GATHERING (10 MINUTES)

Welcome and check-in

Provide name tags again as you welcome participants to the session. If you are serving refreshments, have them set out ahead of time. Spend a few minutes asking if anyone wants to share any thoughts or insights from their personal "Mark it" reading for the week. You won't be able to spend much time on this, but hearing a couple of testimonials will encourage more in the group to make this weekly reading and devotional reflection a part of their routine.

Scripture and prayer

Read the following verse and prayer, or ask a volunteer to do so.

The Lord is not slow about his promise, as some think of slowness, but is patient with you, not wanting any to perish, but all to come to repentance. (2 Peter 3:9)

O God of all time and space, like the early Christians we, too, live in the time in between Jesus' resurrection and his promised return. Empower us to boldly witness to your love, so that those who need to hear your gospel word of hope and promise may enter into a relationship with you. In Jesus' name we pray. Amen.

TELLING THE STORY (15 MINUTES)

See the storytelling tips on p. 10 of this guide.

You or your designated storyteller should now turn to telling the portion of the story that is highlighted in session 14. Incorporate any or all of the Background File notes in the participant book (p. 127) as part of the telling. Use one of the following three options for telling the story, or devise your own.

1. Read through, summarize, and comment on the story as provided in the participant book.
2. Ask for volunteers to tell portions of the story.
3. Read the story script provided below.

At the end of the storytelling time, summarize the Story Keys for this session.

The Story Script for Session 14

Eight letters in the New Testament are known as General Letters: Hebrews; James; 1 and 2 Peter; 1, 2, and 3 John; and Jude. These letters were probably written one or two generations after the disciples of Jesus had died. (Look at "Synopsis of Events in History, Literature, and Philosophy, 4 B.C.E.-200 C.E." and the approximate dates when these letters were written and other historical events happening at the time.) They served as guides for the early Christians, who were trying to move forward in faith while facing persecution from outside the church and false teaching from within. Hebrews was originally thought to be written by Paul, but modern scholars doubt this connection. The other seven letters are named after James (a brother of Jesus), the disciple Peter, the disciple John; and Jude (another brother of Jesus). Building upon these pillars of faith gave strength to the early church as it tried to move forward and speak to a new generation.

Hebrews connected second-century Greek-speaking Christians with the rich traditions of their ancestors in faith: "Long ago God spoke to our ancestors in many and various ways by the prophets, but in these last days he has spoken to us by a Son" (1:1-2). Hebrews makes many more references to the Old Testament, demonstrating the rich line of history and God's faithfulness from Abraham and Sarah through Jesus Christ. In Hebrews, Jesus is compared to Old Testament figures, but is seen as worthy of more glory than all of them. Jesus, the great high priest, does not offer animal sacrifices. Instead, he offers himself for the forgiveness of the sins of all. The suffering world is saved through the sacrifice of God's own Son. God's grace is shown on the cross—the most unexpected, unlikely place for finding out about God's will and purpose.

Hebrews also gave encouragement to believers by talking about a great "cloud of witnesses" made up of faithful ancestors like Abel, Noah, Rahab, Samson, and David. Hebrews pictures these faithful ones as a crowd at a big sporting event, cheering on new followers who are running the "race of faith." We can think of these ancestors in faith, as well as faithful friends and family members who have gone before us, in the same way—surrounding us and cheering us on as we live and share our faith.

The letter of James was probably written and dedicated to this great hero of the faith many years after he had been put to death. It is addressed to "the twelve tribes in the Dispersion." This probably referred to Jewish people who had been forced to move away from their homeland, and reminded them of the strong ties they still had to the twelve Israelite tribes.

James tells readers to be doers of God's Word. Doers of the Word are those who live lives that produce good works as a result of their faith. James also reminds believers to give their lives to God, purify their hearts, fight temptation, recognize false teaching, and be patient and continue to pray for the coming of the Lord. This letter tells us that God's gift of wisdom is planted in us through God's word. We are free to use God's gifts to change the things that can and should be changed.

The Story Script for Session 14 (continued)

The letters of 1 and 2 Peter were addressed to churches throughout Asia Minor. These letters deal with issues like living as God's people, dealing with suffering and hardship, combating false teachers, and preparing for Jesus' return. The key theme is that believers have been given "a new birth into a living hope through the resurrection of Jesus Christ from the dead" (1 Peter 1:3). This new birth calls believers to be "a holy priesthood," with lives that reflect the light of God, rather than the darkness of the world.

The writer of 2 Peter reminds readers to watch out for false teachers, stay on the lookout for the final days, and wait patiently for Christ to come again. The Lord is not slow in returning, 2 Peter says, but is patiently giving everyone time to repent.

Due to similar key themes and wording, the letters of 1, 2, and 3 John appear to be written by members of a faith community closely associated with the Gospel of John. One key theme in 1 John is clarifying who Jesus is and what he has done. Jesus is "the atoning sacrifice for our sins, and not for ours only but also for the sins of the whole world" (1 John 2:2). Against the false teaching that Jesus was a spiritual being who only appeared to be human, the writer of 1 John says, "The Word became flesh and lived among us," a theme we have also heard in the Gospel of John. First John repeats the commandment that Jesus gave his disciples to love one another, and tells us that shining God's light by loving others penetrates the darkness of hatred.

Three very short letters follow 1 John. Second John was written by an unknown church elder to the "elect lady" (either a congregation or a woman who hosted a house church in her home). It again lifts up the themes of walking in love and rejecting false teachers. Third John joyfully points to the teaching of the truth and warns against false teachers. False teaching is also the theme of Jude. Because God is forgiving and gracious, apparently some were teaching that people can live however they choose, and this was causing divisions. Jude tells believers to pray and continue in God's love, keeping their eyes on Jesus and his promise of eternal life.

PICTURING THE STORY (20 MINUTES)

Go through the reflection questions listed in this section in the participant book (p. 127). Then play the segment called So Great a Cloud of Witnesses (session 14) on the course DVD. Encourage the participants to watch the story unfold as artist Joe Castillo depicts the scenes of the story. Participants may be invited to write down their own questions.

When the segment is done, address the questions together as a large group or ask the participants to discuss in smaller teams. Invite participants to share their own questions or observations. What difference did it make to see the story in this way?

SINGING AND PRAYING THE STORY (10 MINUTES)

Use one or both of the psalms provided in the participant book to help address the story and its themes. Psalms are best read aloud. You may have one volunteer read the entire psalm or portion of a psalm. Or you may wish to have the psalm read responsively, verse by verse or line by line. Use a solo reader with the group responding, or read responsively using different groups.

As time allows, discuss the observations and questions provided.

Psalm 111 is both a hymn of praise and an acrostic psalm. (Lines in an acrostic psalm began with consecutive letters in the Hebrew alphabet.) The psalmist gives praise for God's gracious love and "wonderful deeds" on behalf of the people. God is faithful to the covenant and should be praised forever. In Hebrew, the lines of this psalm begin with consecutive letters in the Hebrew alphabet.

Psalm 141 is a prayer for help. It recounts God's rescue of the people through their exodus from Egypt. The psalmist calls upon the people to worship God for demonstrating power over all of creation.

LOOKING AHEAD (5 MINUTES)

Briefly introduce the next chapter of the story that appears in session 15.

Mark it

Encourage participants to read and mark one or more of the passages listed in this section during the week ahead. Let the group know that at the start of next week's session you will ask volunteers to share any insights they have from this exercise.

You are encouraged to do the "Mark it" exercise as well.

Next time

In the next session we will explore the book of Revelation. To review this week's story and to help prepare for the next session, you and your group are encouraged to read an introduction to the following in a study Bible:

- Revelation

You may find it helpful to take some notes or highlight items in the readings to share next week as part of Telling the Story.

OUR STORY

Ideas for optional settings and schedules for this time are provided in the introduction on page 13 of this leader guide.

WELCOME

Whether done consecutively along with the Core Session Plan or planned for a separate time or location, consider providing hospitality in the form of refreshments.

- Arrange the room comfortably for small group discussion.
- Introduce newcomers in the group.
- Begin with prayer, using the session prayer on p. 160 or another prayer of your choice. Ask volunteers to provide prayers, if they feel comfortable doing so.
- You may wish to begin by asking if anyone has a particular question or thought to share from the large group session. As an alternative to discussing those questions, simply note them or write them down on newsprint. Small groups may decide to discuss further.

See the tips for leading and participating in small group discussion on page 17 of this guide. Make available to all participants copies of the reproducible Guidelines for Small Group Discussion.

CONVERSATION

The reflection questions are intended to help participants connect their own stories to the key themes of the greatest story. These questions can be used for personal reflection while reading or used to guide group discussion. It is unlikely a group could discuss all the questions in one discussion period. Don't be concerned about this. Here are some options for approaching the questions:

1. As leader, you may choose to focus on certain questions from the list.
2. Ask participants to suggest questions to discuss.
3. Divide the groups into smaller teams, assign the teams a designated number of questions to discuss, and then have each group report back to the large group.
4. If you have a group that has the time and interest, you could assign each participant a question or two to think about and prepare a response during the week. These responses could be shared as discussion starters when the group meets for Our Story discussion time.

Questions and Responses

The questions below are designed with personal reflection and response in mind. They do not require a certain amount of prior knowledge in order to respond. Responses may vary according to individual insights and context. Even so, a few guiding thoughts are provided for some of the questions.

○ *Imagine living in the second or third generation of Christians after Jesus had lived, died, was raised from the dead, and ascended to be with God. What kinds of issues or questions do you think you might be dealing with?*

The themes of the General Letters give us a glimpse into the time in which they were written. Being patient with God and remaining faithful are issues dating back to the Old Testament. The General Letters show that this hasn't changed. They encourage believers to be patient and remain faithful to the witness established by the apostles. Explore with your group what it would have been like to be an early Christian in this in-between time.

○ *In what way is the church always built on and linking the past with the future?*

○ *Think back to earlier chapters. How do you see Hebrews tying parts of the greatest story together?*

Hebrews draws rich connections between the Old Testament and Jesus, God's Son. Consider having the group skim Hebrews for Old Testament references, and see how many you can find.

○ *What's new about the covenant that Jesus brings?*

The Old Testament covenant was based on laws and commandments. God remained faithful to this covenant, while the people often fell short and rebelled. The new covenant is based on God's grace shown in the life, death, and resurrection of Christ. Through this covenant, believers receive the gifts of salvation, eternal life, and more!

○ *Who makes up the "cloud of witnesses" in your life? Who is cheering you on and encouraging you in your faith walk or run?*

○ *God gives wisdom (Proverbs 2:6), and wisdom leads to right living. How do you see this kind of wisdom in James?*

○ *What do you think it means to be a "doer of the Word"? What things can and should be changed in the world?*

The gift of faith leads naturally to living out faith in words and actions. Explore with your group the kinds of things that could and should be changed by individual Christians and by believers working together.

Questions and Responses (continued)

- *Is a person's identity based more on who he or she is, or what he or she does? Why?*

- *What do you think is meant by false teaching in these letters? Can you think of an example?*

- *What do you hope it will be like when Jesus returns?*

This topic will be covered in more detail in the next session on Revelation. If participants are hesitant to respond to the question, you might discuss how Jesus' return has been described or pictured in books, articles, and movies.

- *What is the truth about Jesus? What is the truth about us?*

- *In your opinion, why was showing God's love so important in the early church? Why is it still important?*

- *When you think of false teaching, what comes to mind? How can you know what is false and what is true?*

Provide colored markers, paper, construction paper, poster board, magazines, scissors, or other materials that may be used to complete this creative assignment.

Creative Corner

Depending on how your schedule is organized, you may wish to assign this activity for individuals or small groups.

Choose one of the following themes or concepts that appear in the General Letters:

- The truth about Jesus
- The race of faith
- Faith and works
- Love one another
- Watch out for false teachers

Using poster board and markers, or other materials provided, create a visual image and message that expresses this theme or concept. You may also use a key verse to get your message across.

COME, LORD JESUS!
Revelation

15

Ending with a new beginning

SESSION PREPARATION

OVERVIEW

In the previous session we looked at the General Letters in the New Testament, which deal with general concerns of the early church living in-between Jesus' resurrection and his promised second coming. This session explores the book of Revelation. This book concludes the written portion of the greatest story by revealing the visions of John of Patmos.

Materials for this session available on the Leader Reference CD:

- Churches Addressed in Revelation (MAP)
- Bible History Timeline (CHART)
- The Roman Empire (MAP)

Scenes in this Session

It's a Revelation! (Revelation 1)
Seven (Revelation 2–3)
Worthy Is the Lamb (Revelation 4–7)
The Cosmic Battle (Revelation 8–20)
Making All Things New (Revelation 21–22)

What's the Story?

Revelation, also known as the Revelation to John, was written by a man named John, most likely in the first century C.E. John is believed to have been a leader of one or more faith communities in Asia Minor during a time when the Roman Empire commanded all people to worship the Emperor as a god. Christians typically wouldn't have agreed to this. And so John says his leadership and Christian activities got him into trouble and he was banished to an island (Revelation 1:9). On this island, John had a series of visions, which make up the entire book of Revelation. These visions include violent battles, joyous celebrations, and some wonderful hymns celebrating God's victories.

STORY KEYS

- Revelation is comprised of the visions John had while on the island of Patmos.
- Revelation addressed the current situation of churches in John's day.
- Revelation challenges people to remain faithful to God.
- God sticks to the promise to make all things new.
- Jesus is the beginning and the end of the greatest story!

Revelation is written in the style of *apocalyptic* writing, which talks about end times and includes intense conflict and often bizarre images that can appear to be difficult to understand. Because of these images, some have tended to read this book as a detailed vision of things that will happen in the future. Revelation is not meant to be read that way, however. Like Paul's letters, written to address either specific issues facing an individual or church, Revelation addresses a particular situation—the suffering and persecution endured by the church in John's day. The book concludes with God's glorious victory over evil.

What's the Message?

Over the years there has been a lot of controversy about the book of Revelation. Some people interpret it as a literal series of events that God will use to bring history to a cataclysmic end. They try to match it up with current events and even predict when the last days will arrive. Throughout the greatest story, however, God always acts out of love and faithfulness on humanity's behalf, but generally doesn't do what people expect or want. And more importantly, God usually turns things around and surprises us in marvelous ways, as in raising Jesus from the grave!

Like Paul, who wrote letters to particular individuals and churches to address particular situations, John writes to address a pressing situation of his day. In the first century C.E., the Roman Empire dominated areas across Asia Minor. The church may have experienced persecution at this time. All people were required to worship the Roman emperor as god. Many Christians like John refused to do this. Some of the imagery in Revelation (the beast, for example) was probably interpreted by the people of John's day to represent the Roman Empire. And the number 666 or 616 in some ancient manuscripts, was probably a code for the Roman emperor Nero, known for torturing and slaughtering Christians. The imagery in Revelation, which at times seems confusing or even bizarre to us, undoubtedly spoke directly to the people of John's day.

One of the main themes in Revelation is the battle between good and evil, Jesus and Satan. In the end, God prevails and establishes a new heaven and new earth. The past, present, and future are all centered in Jesus, the Alpha and Omega, the beginning and the end of the greatest story. Jesus the Lamb is there at the end, renewing all things and making a home among God's people.

PREPARE

1. Review chapter 15 in the participant book.
2. Review the overview and session plan for session 15 in the leader guide.
3. Watch the DVD segment for session 15.
4. Have extra Bibles available for those who did not bring one.
5. Have equipment for projecting or viewing the DVD set up and ready to go.
6. Consider distributing handouts or projecting images of reference materials (see list on p. 167) in the session. You might want to do this during Telling the Story or discussion of the Background Files.
7. If you are having the class do the Creative Corner activity, gather any materials suggested.
8. Pray for your class members and for God's presence and guidance as you gather in God's Word.

MATERIALS NEEDED

- Extra copies of the Bible
- Participant books
- Computer or DVD player; projector or TV monitor
- Course DVD
- Reference materials
- Creative Corner materials (optional)
- Name tags
- Refreshments (optional)

LEADER PRAYER

Lamb of God, the book of Revelation reveals your love and devotion to your people continuing through the end of time and beyond. Come, Lord Jesus, into this session, into our lives, and into the world. Amen.

CORE SESSION PLAN

The Core Session Plan is designed for use in one 60-minute period. The Core Session Plan can be extended 45-60 minutes by incorporating the group reflection time called Our Story, found at the end of the Core Session Plan.

GATHERING (10 MINUTES)

Welcome and check-in

Provide name tags again as you welcome participants to the session. If you are serving refreshments, have them set out ahead of time. Spend a few minutes asking if anyone wants to share any thoughts or insights from their personal "Mark it" reading for the week. You won't be able to spend much time on this, but hearing a couple of testimonials will encourage more in the group to make this weekly reading and devotional reflection a part of their routine.

Scripture and prayer

Read the following verse and prayer, or ask a volunteer to do so.

Then [the one seated on the throne] said to me, "It is done! I am the Alpha and the Omega, the beginning and the end. To the thirsty I will give water as a gift from the spring of the water of life. (Revelation 21:6)

Lord Jesus, be with us and bless us today. Through the Bible we hear the story of God's great love for us, most fully revealed in you. You are the center of this story. Be the center of our lives also. Live in us as we wait for your glorious second coming. Amen.

TELLING THE STORY (15 MINUTES)

See the storytelling tips on p. 10 of this guide.

You or your designated storyteller should now turn to telling the portion of the story that is highlighted in session 15. Incorporate any or all of the Background File notes in the participant book (p. 136) as part of the telling. Use one of the following three options for telling the story, or devise your own.

1. Read through, summarize, and comment on the story as provided in the participant book.
2. Ask for volunteers to tell portions of the story.
3. Read the story script provided below.

At the end of the storytelling time, summarize the Story Keys for this session.

The Story Script for Session 15

In the late first century, John, a Christian leader in Asia Minor, was banished to the island of Patmos because of his Christian beliefs and activities. On the island, John had a series of visions about the end of the ages.

Revelation is a complicated and intriguing book that records John's visions and brings the written portion of the greatest story to a grand finale. Written in an *apocalyptic* style, it uses John's visions and imagery to reveal the end times to the Christian community.

John saw someone like the Son of Man, or Jesus, who said, "I am the first and the last, the living one." Jesus holds the whole story together, from beginning to end.

Seven lamp stands represented the seven churches in Asia addressed by John. Each church was challenged to remain faithful to Christ. The church at Ephesus was told to love; the church at Smyrna was promised the "crown of life" if it remained faithful through persecution; and the churches at Pergamum and Thyatira were warned not to adopt Roman practices. John sent a wake-up call to the church at Sardis, which had become lackadaisical in worship, and stung the church at Laodicea with a sharp message: "Because you are lukewarm, and neither cold nor hot, I am about to spit you out of my mouth" (3:16). Finally, the church at Philadelphia was encouraged to endure through poverty and persecution.

The Story Script for Session 15 (continued)

Next, John's visions turned to heaven, where a great host of creatures and white-robed elders were praising God night and day. This was a reminder that the One who is the end of all things also created all things.

John's next vision was of a Lamb (Jesus) and a scroll with seven seals that no one but Jesus could open. Jesus was praised as the Lamb who was slaughtered and the one who has wisdom, power, and might. The Lamb opened the first four seals, revealing four horsemen and four riders. Their message was about security that cannot be found in governments, defenses, social rules, or wealth. The fifth seal revealed those who had died for the faith, and the sixth seal revealed that death will come to everyone.

Yet, suddenly, a new vision appeared in which John saw a perfect number of servants, 144,000, joined in singing praises to God! It was a huge multitude from every nation, tribe, and people, worshiping God continually. The Lamb would be their shepherd and God would wipe away every tear from their eyes.

When the Lamb opened the seventh seal, seven devastating visions were revealed. Seven trumpets blew forth seven judgments of God, with mountains crashing, stars falling, darkness increasing, and armies of locusts and a cavalry killing a third of humanity.

Other bizarre creatures appeared. A beast, probably representing the Roman Empire, opposed the Lamb. The seventh trumpet unleashed a round of singing praise to God. Then came visions of a woman, her child, and a dragon, perhaps referring to the church, Jesus, and Satan. One of the beasts marked everyone's foreheads with the number 666 (or 616), probably a code for the savage emperor Nero who ordered the torture and slaughter of many Christians.

Things grew worse as John's vision unveiled seven bowls of wrath being poured out. God's judgment turned on Rome, referred to as an evil woman and as Babylon, the destroyer of ancient Israel. A funeral song was sung for Babylon, followed by songs of rejoicing in heaven.

Finally, a white horse appeared with its rider, The Word of God. The rider defeated all the armies that opposed him, an angel swooped down to plunge the dragon into the bottomless pit, and many who had given their lives because of their faith were raised to rule with Christ for a thousand years. After a thousand years passed, Satan was released but defeated and burned in a lake of fire forever, along with those whose names were not recorded in the book of life.

The great cosmic battle between God and all evil was ended!

Now a new heaven, a new earth, and a new Jerusalem appeared. God would dwell with God's people, wiping out death, pain, and tears forever. An angel showed John a river of life and healing, a tree of life for the healing of the nations, and the brightness of God shining in place of the sun and moon. It's like the story has come full circle. Heaven and earth are reunited, as are God and people, just as it was at the beginning of creation.

Finally, God declared, "I am the Alpha and the Omega" (22:13). The message of Revelation for believers then and now is that Jesus is the beginning and the end of the story. God controls history, and the center of Christian life is Jesus. The terrifying visions in Revelation are meant to tell those falling away to make Christ central again. And the visions of triumph offer encouragement and hope to people who are oppressed, persecuted, or powerless in the world.

Revelation ends with an invitation and a prayer. Jesus invites us to "Come . . . take the water of life as a gift" (22:17). Come and follow, receive all of God's gracious gifts. Our prayer is "Come, Lord Jesus!" (22:20). We pray for Jesus to come again, to make all things new, to make us part of God's kingdom now and for all time.

PICTURING THE STORY (20 MINUTES)

Go through the reflection questions listed in this section in the participant book (p. 136). Then play the segment called Come, Lord Jesus! (session 15) on the course DVD. Encourage the participants to watch the story unfold as artist Joe Castillo depicts the scenes of the story. Participants may be invited to write down their own questions.

When the segment is done, address the questions together as a large group or ask the participants to discuss in smaller teams. Invite participants to share their own questions or observations. What difference did it make to see the story in this way?

SINGING AND PRAYING THE STORY (10 MINUTES)

Use one or both of the psalms provided in the participant book to help address the story and its themes. Psalms are best read aloud. You may have one volunteer read the entire psalm or portion of a psalm. Or you may wish to have the psalm read responsively, verse by verse or line by line. Use a solo reader with the group responding, or read responsively using different groups.

As time allows, discuss the observations and questions provided.

Psalm 149 is a hymn of praise that glorifies God for continued faithfulness to the people. Those who are faithful in return are called upon to praise God with all of their actions and being, especially through music, song, and dance.

Psalm 130 is a penitential psalm that asks for God's forgiveness. The psalmist calls upon God from the depths of pain and guilt and asks for mercy, knowing that it will be granted because God is a loving God.

LOOKING AHEAD (5 MINUTES)

Briefly introduce the next chapter of the story that appears in session 16.

Mark it

Encourage participants to read and mark one or more of the passages listed in this section during the week ahead. Let the group know that at the start of next week's session you will ask volunteers to share any insights they have from this exercise.

You are encouraged to do the "Mark it" exercise as well.

Next time

In session 16 we will review some of the key themes of the New Testament and celebrate our journey through the Bible. We will think about how each one of us is included in the greatest story. To review this week's story and to help prepare for the next session, you and your group are encouraged to read or review an introduction to the following in a study Bible:

- The New Testament

You may find it helpful to take some notes or highlight items in the readings to share next week as part of Telling the Story.

OUR STORY

WELCOME

Whether done consecutively along with the Core Session Plan or planned for a separate time or location, consider providing hospitality in the form of refreshments.

- Arrange the room comfortably for small group discussion.
- Introduce newcomers in the group.
- Begin with prayer, using the session prayer on p. 170 or another prayer of your choice. Ask volunteers to provide prayers, if they feel comfortable doing so.
- You may wish to begin by asking if anyone has a particular question or thought to share from the large group session. As an alternative to discussing those questions, simply note them or write them down on newsprint. Small groups may decide to discuss further.

Ideas for optional settings and schedules for this time are provided in the introduction on page 13 of this leader guide.

CONVERSATION

See the tips for leading and participating in small group discussion on page 17 of this guide. Make available to all participants copies of the reproducible Guidelines for Small Group Discussion.

The reflection questions are intended to help participants connect their own stories to the key themes of the greatest story. These questions can be used for personal reflection while reading or used to guide group discussion. It is unlikely a group could discuss all the questions in one discussion period. Don't be concerned about this. Here are some options for approaching the questions:

1. As leader, you may choose to focus on certain questions from the list.
2. Ask participants to suggest questions to discuss.
3. Divide the groups into smaller teams, assign the teams a designated number of questions to discuss, and then have each group report back to the large group.
4. If you have a group that has the time and interest, you could assign each participant a question or two to think about and prepare a response during the week. These responses could be shared as discussion starters when the group meets for Our Story discussion time.

Questions and Responses

The questions below are designed with personal reflection and response in mind. They do not require a certain amount of prior knowledge in order to respond. Responses may vary according to individual insights and context. Even so, a few guiding thoughts are provided for some of the questions.

○ *What have you heard about the book of Revelation?*

Responses to this question can give you some idea of where people are coming from with their own understanding of this book. It's a good idea to reflect upon your own background and understanding of Revelation, too, as you prepare for this session.

○ *John was banished because of his faith. What would that be like?*

○ *What do you think you would do if you met Jesus face-to-face, even in a vision?*

○ *Which church would you say faced the biggest challenge? Why?*

The issues the churches faced included persecution, lack of commitment, and in some cases, actually turning from the faith to follow Roman rituals. What does John's vision say to each church? What kind of tone does he use to address them?

Questions and Responses (continued)

- *In your opinion, what are the biggest challenges facing your community of faith or the Christian church in general?*

While most people do not suffer persecution for their faith like the early Christians did, we do experience challenges to our faith today. Many of us struggle with our level of commitment to Christ, and with putting other things in God's place in our lives. Allow some time for participants to consider challenges facing congregations and the larger Christian church today.

- *Why do you think people are so interested in visions of future destruction?*

- *What truth about life was revealed when the first six seals were opened?*

- *If you were being persecuted for your faith in Jesus, how might this part of the vision give you hope? Do you see hope in it for your own life today?*

A lot of people get caught up in the violent nature of parts of Revelation, and miss out on how God's love is expressed through Jesus, the Lamb, who even here works for the good of all the faithful so that God's kingdom might ultimately be fulfilled.

- *Is the battle between good and evil in Revelation what you expected? Why or why not?*

- *What have you heard about the end of the world? What do you believe?*

- *What part of John's vision of a new heaven and a new earth stands out for you? Why?*

- *Why do you think so many people use Revelation to try to interpret current events?*

Throughout the greatest story we've seen that God's people struggle with wanting to be in control. We have trouble waiting for God to do things in God's own time. In many ways, attempts to predict the end times are a continuation of that. As part of your discussion, you might reflect upon how God has surprised humanity with unexpected acts of love and faithfulness throughout the greatest story.

- *Do you see Revelation as more of a warning or a promise? Why?*

In the Bible we find the significance of both law—judgment that accuses us—and gospel—grace that saves us. This means that any one text or book in the Bible isn't just judgment or just gospel, but could actually be both, depending on the situation and context.

Provide colored markers, paper, construction paper, poster board, magazines, scissors, or other materials that may be used to complete this creative assignment.

Creative Corner

Depending on how your schedule is organized, you may wish to assign this activity for individuals or small groups.

Think about the big posters at a movie theater that pitch upcoming or currently featured movies. Sometimes these posters picture part of the action in a movie. Sometimes they focus on the main characters. Sometimes they have one single message, or even just a word or phrase. With a partner, create a poster for "Revelation: The Movie."

JESUS PEOPLE
The New Testament Story for Us

Discovering our place in the greatest story

SESSION PREPARATION

OVERVIEW

In the last session we took a detailed look at the last book in the Bible, Revelation, a collection of the visions of a man named John. These visions can be hard to understand if not looked at through the lens of John's own time period. This last session gives us an overview of the New Testament message and connects us to the greatest story.

Materials for this session available on the Leader Reference CD:

- Thirty Key New Testament Stories (CHART)

Scenes in this Session

By Grace through Faith in Christ (Ephesians 2:1-10)
Go! (Matthew 28:16-20; Romans 12:4-8)
Love! (1 Corinthians 13; Luke 10:25-37; Romans 13:8-10)
Forgive! (Matthew 18:21-22; Romans 12:9-21)
Shine! (Matthew 5:14-16)
Pray! (Luke 11:1-10; Philippians 4:6)
Hope! (Matthew 6:25-24; Romans 8:31-38)

What's the Story?

The New Testament is a continuation of the story which began at creation. God intended the world to be holy and good, but things went awry when sin and evil entered the picture. Because of humanity's rebellion, God instructed Noah to build an ark. Everything that wasn't on the ark was destroyed by floodwaters. After the flood, God promised Noah that it wouldn't happen again. But God was left with the continuous dilemma of dealing with a disobedient people. The New Testament tells about God's ultimate and surprising response to the presence of sin.

STORY KEYS

- The greatest story is a story of God's everlasting love and faithfulness, and we are part of it.
- Jesus tells all his disciples to go, baptize, teach, and tell.
- The power of love and forgiveness comes from God and is given to us.
- Nothing can ever separate us from God's love.

The Gospel of John tells us the Word, present with God at creation, took on flesh to dwell with humanity. We know him as Jesus, the Messiah foretold by the prophets. Jesus preached about the coming of God's imminent kingdom, performed incredible miracles of nature, healed people, and even raised the dead to life. But God's power over death was ultimately demonstrated when Jesus was raised three days after dying on the cross. God's decisive response to humanity's rebelliousness was to destroy the power of sin and death over humanity! God is a seeker of faithful relationships also, so things didn't end there. God sent the Holy Spirit, which fueled Jesus' disciples for preaching, teaching, and healing in Jesus' name.

Acts records the early days of the Christian church and the identity crisis and persecution it endured. Acts also introduces us to some early leaders of the Christian movement, especially Peter and Paul. An enemy-turned-hero of the faith, Paul took numerous mission trips to start new churches throughout Asia Minor and Europe. Paul wrote letters to these churches, especially as they struggled with issues that arose from their particular contexts.

God's love for humanity never ends! Now we're the Jesus People who are part of this continuing story.

What's the Message?

At its very heart, the New Testament is an incredible salvation story, demonstrating the depth of God's love for a fallen humanity. Throughout the greatest story, humanity is sinful and rebellious while God is faithful. That faithfulness is now demonstrated most profoundly in Jesus' death and resurrection, which reconcile us to God and destroy our bondage to sin and death. God loves us so much that God became human to live and die for us!

The New Testament tells us about God's amazing grace. We can't make ourselves right with God, but God does that for us. God does this as a gift, out of love for us! And God's love and forgiveness free and empower us to love and forgive others, too. These are gifts that just keep on giving.

The New Testament tells us about the undying hope we have through Christ. This is especially clear in the letters written by Paul and others to support the early communities of faith as they struggled with persecution and other issues. And it is a central message of Revelation, which paints a clear picture that even in troubled times God is—and always will be—present and actively working to heal and restore!

From the very beginning, the greatest story is about God's love for people and the world. Because of that love, God showers us with grace and gives us hope. Amazing as this is, the story doesn't end there. God wants us to participate in spreading the word about Jesus' life, death, and resurrection. Like the disciples, we are called to go, baptize, teach, and tell, and we are empowered by the Holy Spirit to do just that! We can't keep the good news of Jesus to ourselves—we need to spread it. We become part of the greatest story when the story comes alive in us and when we pass it on to others.

PREPARE

1. Review chapter 16 in the participant book.
2. Review the overview and session plan for session 16 in the leader guide.
3. Watch the DVD segment for session 16.
4. Have extra Bibles available for those who did not bring one.
5. Have equipment for projecting or viewing the DVD set up and ready to go.
6. Consider distributing handouts or projecting images of reference materials (see list on p. 177) in the session. You might want to do this during Telling the Story or while discussing the Background Files.
7. If you are having the class do the Creative Corner activity, gather any materials suggested.
8. Pray for your class members and for God's presence and guidance as you gather in God's Word.

MATERIALS NEEDED

- Extra copies of the Bible
- Participant books
- Computer or DVD player; projector or TV monitor
- Course DVD
- Reference materials
- Creative Corner materials (optional)
- Name tags
- Refreshments (optional)

LEADER PRAYER

O God, you are the author of all life and of your greatest story, woven throughout time as a sign of your love for your children. Bless me as I prepare this session. Bless the group and fill each person with the passion to be an active participant in your continuing story. Amen.

CORE SESSION PLAN

GATHERING (10 MINUTES)

Welcome and check-in

Provide name tags again as you welcome participants to the session. If you are serving refreshments, have them set out ahead of time. Spend a few minutes asking if anyone wants to share any thoughts or insights from their personal "Mark it" reading for the week.

The Core Session Plan is designed for use in one 60-minute period. The Core Session Plan can be extended 45-60 minutes by incorporating the group reflection time called Our Story, found at the end of the Core Session Plan.

Scripture and prayer

Read the following verse and prayer, or ask a volunteer to do so.

But you are a chosen race, a royal priesthood, a holy nation, God's own people, in order that you may proclaim the mighty acts of him who called you out of darkness into his marvelous light. (1 Peter 2:9)

Gracious God, thank you for your faithfulness throughout the generations. You have made us your holy people. May your Holy Spirit stir up your greatest story within us so that we, too, might serve as witnesses to the power of your love and forgiveness, which unites you and your people now and for all eternity. In Jesus' name. Amen.

TELLING THE STORY (15 MINUTES)

See the storytelling tips on p. 10 of this guide.

You or your designated storyteller should now turn to telling the portion of the story that is highlighted in session 16. Incorporate any or all of the Background File notes in the participant book (p. 146) as part of the telling. Use one of the following three options for telling the story, or devise your own.

1. Read through, summarize, and comment on the story as provided in the participant book.
2. Ask for volunteers to tell portions of the story.
3. Read the story script provided below.

At the end of the storytelling time, summarize the Story Keys for this session.

The Story Script for Session 16

Our journey with the greatest story has covered a lot of ground. It started in the Old Testament, at the beginning with God and creation, with Adam and Eve, Jacob, Joseph, Moses and Miriam, Abraham and Sarah, Deborah, Samson, Samuel, David, Solomon, and the prophets. The story continued in the New Testament, with the coming of Jesus—the fulfillment of Old Testament prophecies—and his life, death, and resurrection. The story went on in Acts and the letters of Paul and others, showing us how early believers lived out their faith and told others the good news about Jesus. Then, in Revelation, the biblical story wrapped up with visions of the end times, with God in control of all things and Jesus the Lamb ruling over all creation.

The Story Script for Session 16 (continued)

What are we to make of all this? One thing we see over and over in the greatest story is God's grace and faithfulness to the people. Even when the people waver and turn away, there is grace. And once and for all, through Jesus' death and resurrection, God did for us what we can't do for ourselves. God saved us from the power of sin and death. Our relationship with God depends on what God has done through Christ, and not on anything we do or don't do. That's amazing, and that's grace!

So now, where do we go from here? Our time together with the greatest story is ending, but the story is far from over! We are Jesus' followers or disciples in the world today. And Jesus calls us, like the first disciples, to "Go therefore and make disciples of all nations, baptizing them in the name of the Father and of the Son and of the Holy Spirit, and teaching them to obey everything that I have commanded you" (Matthew 28:19-20). Jesus is always with us and sends the Holy Spirit to equip and empower us for this mission.

The Holy Spirit gives us gifts like prophecy, teaching, generosity, leadership, compassion, and more. Although all gifts come from God and can be used in godly ways, Paul said one gift is the best of all—love. By sending Jesus to die for us, God shows the kind of love that we are called to share with others, with our neighbor. In the eye-opening Parable of the Good Samaritan, Jesus told about a Samaritan, an outsider, who had compassion for someone who had been robbed and nearly beaten to death. The point of the parable is that our neighbor is anyone in need. Set free by grace in faith through Christ, we can show God's love to our neighbor in what we say and do.

Now, sharing God's love with others isn't easy. People hurt us, and we hurt them. And yet, Jesus calls us to forgive as many times as needed. Paul, too, is straightforward about forgiveness. He says, "Do not repay anyone evil for evil, but take thought for what is noble in the sight of all. If it is possible, so far as it depends on you, live peaceably with all. Beloved, never avenge yourselves" (Romans 12:17-19a).

Following Jesus' call to love and forgive allows the light of God's love to shine through us. Jesus says, "You are the light of the world...let your light shine before others, so that they may see your good works and give glory to your Father in heaven" (Matthew 5:14-16). God called Abraham and Sarah to shine the light with the promise that their descendants would be a blessing to the nations. We receive this call at baptism. Letting your light shine means living in a way that gives glory and honor to God.

We give glory and honor to God when we pray. Throughout the Bible, God's people pray. Jesus prayed and taught his followers how to pray. In the Lord's Prayer, we address God as Father, as the ideal parent who provides, protects, nurtures, and loves us. We "hallow" God, meaning we honor God's holiness. We cannot fully understand God's holiness, but we pray in complete trust that God's kingdom will come. We pray for our daily bread—all the things we need to live our lives each day and all the ways we can help others. We pray for forgiveness. We pray for God's help against temptation and trials.

The Story Script for Session 16 (continued)

As we face the temptations and trials of life, it's easy to lose hope. But Jesus says, "Do not worry about your life, what you will eat or what you will drink, or about your body, what you will wear . . . [God] knows that you need all these things. But strive first for the kingdom of God and his righteousness, and all these things will be given to you as well" (Matthew 6:25, 32-33). Through Jesus, we have a powerful hope. According to Paul, "If God is for us, who is against us? . . . [nothing] will be able to separate us from the love of God in Christ Jesus our Lord" (Romans 8:31, 38-39). God created us, and through Jesus Christ, God also saved us. And the God who created and saved us will never let us go. The greatest story, therefore, is a story filled with hope from beginning to end.

And now, the greatest story continues on in those who hear the story and tell it to others. We can't keep the good news of Jesus to ourselves—we need to spread it. We become part of the greatest story when the story comes alive in us and we pass it on to others!

PICTURING THE STORY (20 MINUTES)

Go through the reflection questions listed in this section in the participant book (p. 146). Then play the segment called Jesus People (session 16) on the course DVD. Encourage the participants to watch the story unfold as artist Joe Castillo depicts the scenes of the story. Participants may be invited to write down their own questions.

When the segment is done, address the questions together as a large group or ask the participants to discuss in smaller teams. Invite participants to share their own questions or observations. What difference did it make to see the story in this way?

SINGING AND PRAYING THE STORY (10 MINUTES)

Use one or both of the psalms provided in the participant book to help address the story and its themes. Psalms are best read aloud. You may have one volunteer read the entire psalm or portion of a psalm. Or you may wish to have the psalm read responsively, verse by verse or line by line. Use a solo reader with the group responding, or read responsively using different groups.

As time allows, discuss the observations and questions provided.

Psalm 65 is a psalm of praise thanking God for answered prayers and for salvation, forgiveness of sins, and deliverance. God alone has power to both control and care for nature and God creates overflowing bounty for all.

Psalm 136 is a liturgical psalm calling the people to celebrate God's faithfulness shown throughout history. The psalmist celebrates that God has not only created all things, but shown dominion over them through continued acts of salvation on behalf of the Israelites. God's steadfast love does indeed endure forever.

LOOKING AHEAD (5 MINUTES)

Celebrate! You've covered a lot of ground in reviewing God's greatest story and the best part is you've discovered that you're part of the story too. Take time to discuss in your group how this journey has transformed you!

Mark it

Encourage participants to read and mark one or more of the passages listed in this section during the week ahead.

You are encouraged to do the "Mark it" exercise as well.

OUR STORY

WELCOME

Whether done consecutively along with the Core Session Plan or planned for a separate time or location, consider providing hospitality in the form of refreshments.

- Arrange the room comfortably for small group discussion.
- Introduce newcomers in the group.
- Begin with prayer, using the session prayer on p. 180 or another prayer of your choice. Ask volunteers to provide prayers, if they feel comfortable doing so.
- You may wish to begin by asking if anyone has a particular question or thought to share from the large group session. As an alternative to discussing those questions, simply note them or write them down on newsprint. Small groups may decide to discuss further.

Ideas for optional settings and schedules for this time are provided in the introduction on page 13 of this leader guide.

CONVERSATION

The reflection questions are intended to help participants connect their own stories to the key themes of the greatest story. These questions can be used for personal reflection while reading or used to guide group discussion. It is unlikely a group could discuss all the questions in one discussion period. Don't be concerned about this. Here are some options for approaching the questions:

See the tips for leading and participating in small group discussion on page 17 of this guide. Make available to all participants copies of the reproducible Guidelines for Small Group Discussion.

1. As leader, you may choose to focus on certain questions from the list.
2. Ask participants to suggest questions to discuss.
3. Divide the groups into smaller teams, assign the teams a designated number of questions to discuss, and then have each group report to the large group.
4. If you have a group that has the time and interest, you could assign each participant a question or two to think about and prepare a response during the week. These responses could be shared as discussion starters when the group meets for Our Story discussion time.

Questions and Responses

The questions below are designed with personal reflection and response in mind. They do not require a certain amount of prior knowledge in order to respond. Responses may vary according to individual insights and context. Even so, a few guiding thoughts are provided for some of the questions.

- *What do you think about the following statement: "The Bible is just a bunch of words on a page if no one reads or teaches or shares it"?*

- *What makes it easy, or hard, to believe that you are saved by grace?*

Our society values individualism and a strong work ethic that elevates those who work hard to achieve success. Grace doesn't work this way, however. Out of grace, God does what we can't do for ourselves. We are saved and set free from the power of sin and death only by grace in faith through Christ. Explore these and other factors that may make it difficult for us to believe in the power of God's grace.

Questions and Responses (continued)

- *What do you think it means to go and tell? Does this make you nervous, excited, confused, or something else? Why?*

Sometimes people are frightened to "go and tell" because they feel like they need to have the proper theological answers and responses to everything. Encourage participants to reflect upon the power of God's story throughout history and the effect it has on them personally. We're each called to share the good news about the Jesus we have encountered and who has transformed us.

- *What gifts do you think others might say you have? What part would you like to play in the greatest story?*

Group members have spent some time together, so consider asking them to name some of each other's gifts. What possibilities do they see in each other? What possibilities do they see in themselves?

- *Have you ever been a "good samaritan" to someone? Has anyone ever been one to you?*

- *Why do you think love is more about* do *than* who*?*

- *How do you understand the connection between the words* love, grace, *and* law*? How might you diagram the connection?*

Hand out paper and colored pencils or markers. Invite group members to make their own diagrams and then compare what they have done. What similarities and differences do you see between the diagrams?

- *When does not forgiving cost more than forgiving?*

Explore with participants what happens to us and to our relationships when we refuse to forgive. When we aren't able to forgive on our own, the love and forgiveness we receive from God through Christ empowers us to love and forgive others.

- *How has the light of God's love been shined into your life?*

- *How do you, or will you, shine?*

This is a good follow-up question for the conversation about identifying gifts.

- *What would you like to learn about prayer?*

- *How do we listen to God when we pray?*

- *What makes you worry? How can you reduce worry? How do Jesus' words help?*

Questions and Responses (continued)

- *What kinds of things might separate us from God?*

Reflect back upon the greatest story and some of the things that got in the way of the faithfulness of the children of God throughout the ages. What correlations does your group see in our contemporary times?

- *What gives you hope? What do you hope for?*

Provide colored markers, paper, construction paper, poster board, magazines, scissors, or other materials that may be used to complete this creative assignment.

Creative Corner

Depending on how your schedule is organized, you may wish to assign this activity for individuals or small groups.

Choose one of the theme words from today's session—go, love, forgive, shine, pray, hope—and create something to depict its meaning. You can draw something, build something, write a song or poem, take photos, and even produce a video. Use your imagination. Work on your own or work with others. Share your creations as a way to celebrate your time together exploring the Bible, the greatest story.

Located in Bexar County, San Antonio is currently home to more than a million people. More keep coming; it continues to be one of fastest-growing cities in the United States.

Although it lies at the southern edge of the Texas Hill Country, San Antonio is flat. The city's central downtown district is laid out like early Spanish settlements; it hugs the river and surrounds a church, the San Fernando Cathedral. San Antonio's downtown area is also home to the Alamo, Riverwalk, La Villita, and Tower of the Americas, as well as numerous hotels, businesses, and restaurants. It is not only the center of the city, but also the tourist hub.

San Antonio sprawls in all directions from downtown. Miles of suburbs envelop the central city, reflecting the spread of later growth. Northeast of the downtown area lie the airport and Brackenridge Park with its zoo, amusements, and ornamental gardens. Southeast of town the old Christian missions are strung like beads along the San Antonio River through a mostly Hispanic area. The southwest is dominated by Lackland Air Force Base and the former Kelly Air Force Base, which is being turned into an aviation industry park. Northwest of downtown is the newest growth, as well as the Six Flags Fiesta theme park. Highways encircle the central city and head off in all directions.

To the north and west of San Antonio is the central Texas Hill Country, which features gently rolling limestone hills, rivers,

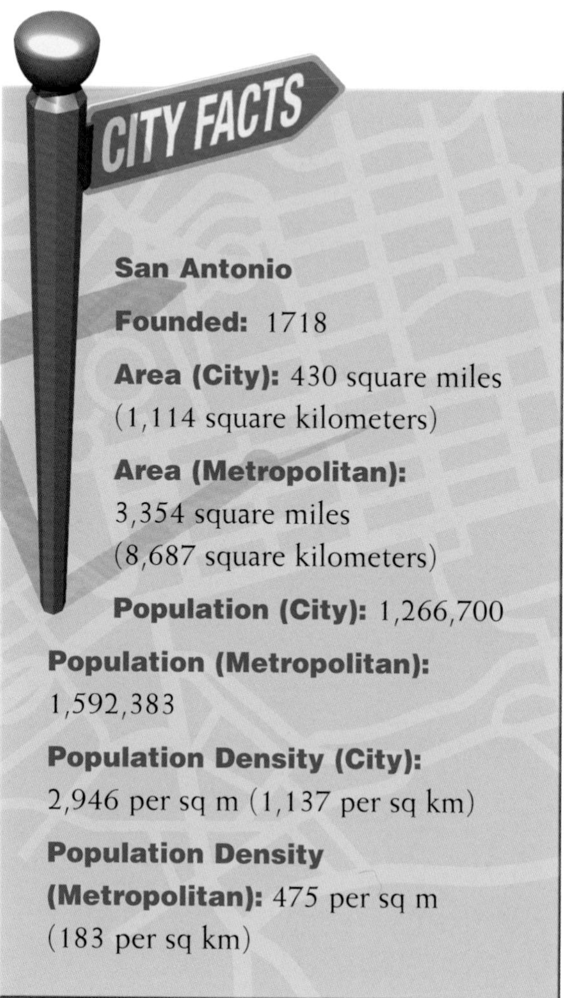

San Antonio

Founded: 1718

Area (City): 430 square miles (1,114 square kilometers)

Area (Metropolitan): 3,354 square miles (8,687 square kilometers)

Population (City): 1,266,700

Population (Metropolitan): 1,592,383

Population Density (City): 2,946 per sq m (1,137 per sq km)

Population Density (Metropolitan): 475 per sq m (183 per sq km)

"[San Antonio] is, and has been always, a meeting place, on the verge, between France and Spain, between Spain and England, between the Indian and the white, between the South and the West, the old and the new."

—Charles Ramsdell, author of *San Antonio: A Historical and Pictorial Guide*, 1976.

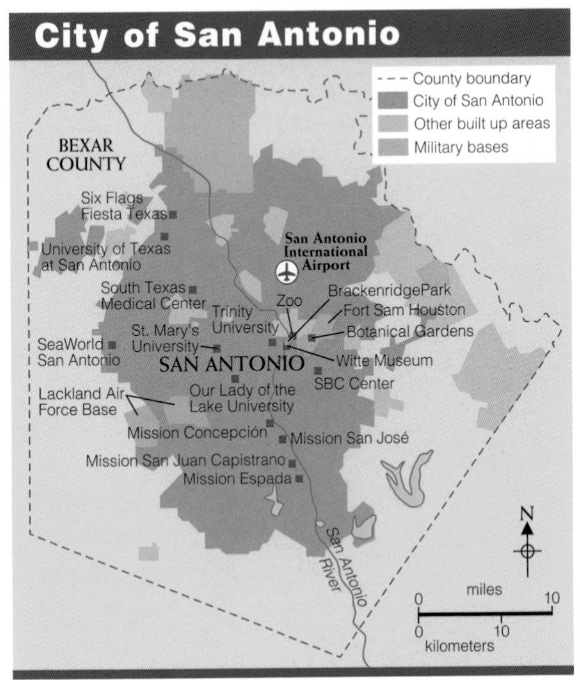

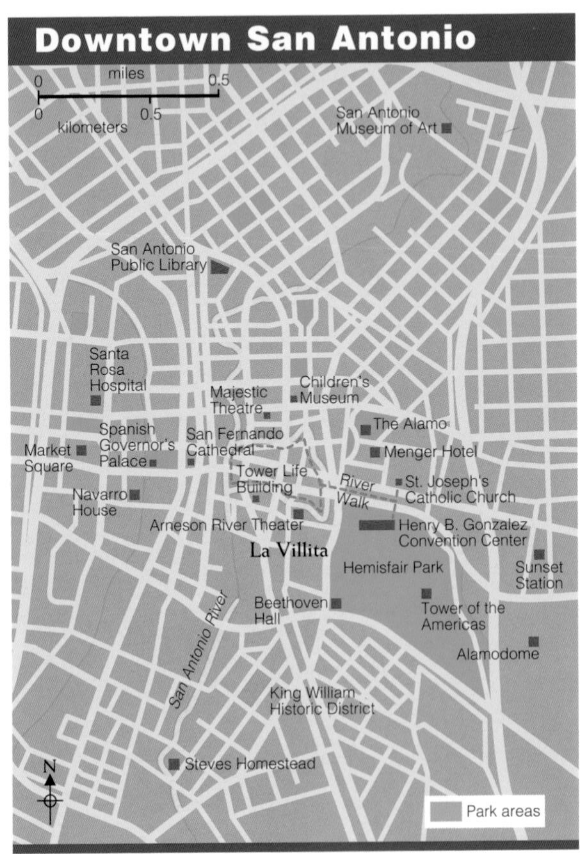

creeks, and oak trees side by side with mesquite trees and cactus. Historic towns settled by German immigrants, such as Fredericksburg, Boerne, and New Braunfels, can be found in the Hill Country, as well as many of the state's vineyards, parks, arts colonies and the Kerrville Folk Festival.

A Tourist Destination

The San Antonio River wanders through the center of the city. The beautiful walking paths and shops that have grown up alongside its waters are San Antonio's most popular tourist attraction—the River Walk, or Paseo del Rio.

Many tourists enjoy visiting "the place where the sunshine spends the winter." The climate is warm and subtropical, with hot, humid summers averaging 85° Fahrenheit (29° Celsius) and mild winters averaging 49° F (9° C) with little or no snowfall. The city's average annual temperature is 70° F (21° C).

San Antonio is also known as "Military City USA." It receives much government money because of the number of military bases and hospitals located there. The tourism and convention business also supports the local economy. Other key businesses for the city include producing transportation equipment, metal fabricating, business services, banking, and communication services.

A Spicy Mix

A population that is 59 percent Hispanic and proximity to the Mexican border give the city an unmistakable cultural flavor. A large Spanish-speaking population lives in San Antonio, and the city is growing as a gateway to Latin American trade.

In 1981, San Antonio became the first major U.S. city to elect a Hispanic mayor, Henry Cisneros. It is home to Tex-Mex cuisine, which is a combination of local and Mexican foods. San Antonio blends its long history with a colorful local Hispanic culture, a savvy Texas business sense, and a thoroughly modern American cityscape, making it one of the great and unique cities of the United States.

River Walk (Paseo del Rio)

Recognized as a key to the city's character, the Paseo del Rio, or River Walk (above), *was built along the banks of the San Antonio River. It provides people with the opportunity to walk along the city's beautifully landscaped riverside and offers access to many local shops, businesses, restaurants, and arts and crafts stores. Riverboat taxis transport people to riverside attractions. The river also features dining boats and even Marriage Island, where people can be married outdoors in a scenic downtown setting. The River Walk is the scene of many of the city's events, such as arts and crafts fairs, food-tasting fairs, canoe races, and even boat parades.*

CHAPTER 1

History of San Antonio

Native Americans once roamed the land that San Antonio now sprawls on. The Coahuiltecans were a diverse group of hunter-gatherer bands that ranged throughout southern Texas and northeastern Mexico. Following the seasonal availability of foods, the women gathered the fruits, nuts, beans, roots, and seeds that were the main diet of the band, while the men hunted bison, deer, rabbits, and other small animals. The bands organized along family lines and gathered in larger groups when food was abundant. They created their clothing from animal skins and made brush huts in their camps. Nomadic tribes who had horses, such as the Apaches and Comanches, often attacked the Coahuiltecans.

In 1691, Governor Domingo Terán arrived in San Antonio, sent by Spain to claim the Texas territory for the Spanish Empire. Terán and Father Damián Massanet, a missionary priest, named the place San Antonio de Pádua because it was June 13,

◀ *The chapel at San Juan Capistrano mission features the figure of San Juan Capistrano, dressed as a crusader from the Middle Ages, located in the middle above the altar. At one time, this mission's farms grew enough fruits, vegetables, and grain to support the entire town of San Antonio.*

Saint Anthony's feast day. Spanish settlers to the area did not arrive, however, until April 25, 1718, when they established a fort (Presidio de Béxar) on the San Antonio River. They built a village nearby, named Villa de Béxar, in 1731.

"I named this place San Antonio de Padua because it was his day. In the language of the Indians it is called Yanaguana."

—Father Damián Massanet
in his diary entry for June 13, 1691.

Mission Concepción

Mission Concepción, or Misión Nuestra Señora de la Purísima Concepción de Acuña (left), is the oldest Spanish church in the United States that has not been restored and is still being used as a church. As an example of Spanish colonial architecture, it is probably the most beautiful of the mission churches along the San Antonio River.

Originally founded in 1716 in eastern Texas to protect against French expansion from Louisiana, the religious organization of Mission Concepción moved to the San Antonio River in 1731. There, the priests and mission Indians began building the church. The Indians painted the limestone church in brilliant red, blue, orange, and yellow geometric designs, which are no longer visible. At one time, more than two hundred Native Americans lived inside the mission walls, raising corn, beans, watermelons, and pumpkins and keeping sheep and cattle.

In 1739, half the mission population died of disease. In 1767, Comanches stole the last of the mission's horses, so ranch operations were shut down. When the mission was secularized in 1794, its lands were given to the thirty-eight remaining Indians. The church fell into poor repair, and the government used it as a supply depot and a barn. In 1887, local people repaired the church and reopened it, dedicating it to Our Lady of Lourdes. Since then, it has been used and cared for.

The Mission Era

Two miles (3.2 kilometers) south along the river, the Spanish also established the mission San António de Valero, later called the Alamo. The mission priests welcomed the Coahuiltec Indians, who lived primarily on beans, cacti, and small animals, and taught them about the Christian religion, as well as how to raise corn and squash. Soon, the Spanish built other missions farther south until five missions lined the San Antonio River. These provided instruction—and protection to the Coahuiltecans against the raiding Lipan Apaches and later the Comanches.

Some Native Americans welcomed the safety and steady food supplies offered by the missions, even though they had to completely change their lifestyle to become farmers and were required to become Christians. The diseases brought by the Europeans took a heavy toll on the Coahuiltecans, and many of the mission dwellers died.

Troubled Times

In 1731, the Spanish government sent fifty-six Spaniards from the Canary Islands to make their homes on land granted from the king of Spain. The small group settled in the exact center of present-day San Antonio, calling it Villa San Fernando. The village did not grow, and the Lipan Apaches often raided it. When the village made peace with the Apaches, the Comanches began to raid the settlement. In the meantime, few Coahuiltec people became Christians, and many did not settle permanently at the missions. The missions were disbanded as the number of Native Americans dwindled, the priests left, and the lands were given back to the remaining Native Americans.

The Mexican fight for independence from Spain began in 1810, and in 1813, some revolutionaries from Mexico captured the settlement for three months. Then, the Spanish General Joaquin Arredondo came with a large force, defeated the rebels, and killed all the men. Mexicans won independence in 1821, however, and the Mexican flag again flew over San Antonio de Béxar, as the fort, mission, and village became known collectively.

American Settlers and the Mexican Government

Few Mexican settlers wanted to live north of the Rio Grande River, so the Mexican government decided to allow Americans to settle in what was then the Mexican territory of Texas if they would agree to become Catholics and citizens of Mexico. Around 1830, Mexican dictator General Antonio López de Santa Anna began to rule Mexico, he decided that the American settlers had to go. He established new laws governing the Texas citizens and prevented new Americans from settling there. All the Texans—American settlers and Mexicans alike—suffered equally and protested, refusing to obey the laws.

► *In this hand-colored woodcut, General Santa Anna's troops are in the Alamo mission compound attacking the church, where the Texans made their last stand in 1836. Note the flag of the Republic of Texas flying above the church.*

The Mexican government sent General Martín Perfecto de Cos and his troops to take over San Antonio de Béxar, the most important town in Texas. They took control of San Antonio, including the Alamo, in 1835. A group of Texan rebels, Europeans, Mexicans, and Indians defeated General Cos there after four days of fighting. Cos negotiated a truce with the rebels and gave them all the public property, guns, and ammunition in San Antonio in exchange for letting him and his men return to Mexico.

Colonel William Barrett Travis remained in San Antonio de Bexar with 110 men and was joined by James Bowie with 30 more men. General Santa Anna himself marched into San Antonio on February 23, 1836, with Mexican army troops numbering 1,500 and more on the way.

The Texan rebels holed up in the Alamo and encouraged anyone who wanted to leave to do so; indeed, more men sneaked into the Alamo to join the fight than left it. They also were able to send out calls for more men, stating that they were determined to stay and fight. Their motto: Victory or Death. The approximately 180 men fought hard for thirteen days but were no match for the Mexican army. They held off Santa Anna until March 6, when he

"We had not been in there long when a messenger came from Santa Anna calling for us to surrender. I remember the reply to this summons was a shot from one of the cannon on the roof of the Alamo."

—From the memoirs of Enrique Esparza, San Antonio native, age twelve at the time of the Alamo fight.

attacked the Alamo with between fifteen hundred and eighteen hundred men. After heavy fighting, the remaining Texans surrendered. Santa Anna ordered that all the men and boys who remained alive were to be killed. Stories still vary on the numbers killed that day. Jim Bowie and David Crockett were two famous Americans who died in the battle of the Alamo. Today, the Alamo has become a shrine to honor everyone who died fighting for independence.

A New Republic

Forty-six days after that battle, Sam Houston's company of Texans—shouting "Remember the Alamo"—beat Santa Anna at San Jacinto in April of 1836. A few months later, Texans formed the Republic of Texas, a nation independent of Mexico. The new republic was not an instant success; it had few people and a poor economy. Its only police force was a small group of men known as the Texas Rangers, who were hard pressed to protect Anglo and Mexican settlers from raids by Native Americans who viewed the intruders as fair game.

▼ *On February 19, 1846, the last president of the Republic of Texas, Anson Jones, lowered the Texan flag. He announced, "The Republic of Texas is no more," in a ceremony to commemorate Texas' entry into the United States. The U.S. Congress voted to make Texas the twenty-eighth state on December 29, 1845.*

The area did not flourish until Texas joined the United States as the twenty-eighth state in 1845. After statehood, many Germans settled in Texas, pouring into San Antonio, the capital and most important city in the state.

Texas was a Confederate state during the Civil War and sent thousands of troops to fight in the Confederate army. It remained relatively undamaged, however, compared to other Southern states. Although Union troops attacked Galveston, Brownsville, and Fort Griffin, San Antonio saw no action and served only as a supply base for the Confederate army.

After the Civil War, the cattle industry in Texas exploded, and San Antonio became the starting point for massive cattle drives that moved thousands of cattle to Abilene, Kansas, to be shipped back east for slaughter. The city's military role also grew when Fort Sam Houston was expanded in last quarter of the nineteenth century.

▼ *In the 1800s, the San Antonio River provided water for drinking, cooking, and irrigating crops. It also provided a faster and better means of transportation through town than horses and mules.*

▲ *In the Mexican section of San Antonio in 1939, homes often lacked such basic necessities as heat and running water.*

The railroads came to San Antonio in 1877 and provided shipping for the state's cattle industry, helped expand its military bases by bringing in troops and supplies, and touched off an increase in the city's population by bringing settlers.

The Twentieth Century and Beyond

During World War I (1914–1918), San Antonio became an important military training and supply center, and the city's Mexican immigration swelled. The Great Flood of 1921 devastated the city, but it was soon rebuilt. By 1929, San Antonio had more than 150,000 people, and skyscrapers were being built next to mission ruins.

Growth slowed in the worldwide economic depression of the 1930s, but

World War II turned San Antonio into a booming city. The military bases expanded; Lackland Air Force Base alone trained one-third of the air cadets involved in the war. The 1950s saw San Antonio expanding its land base by taking possession of surrounding areas, and in 1968, San Antonio hosted the World's Fair, bringing it international recognition.

By the 1970s, San Antonio's population was more than one-half million people; more than half of them were Hispanic. This segment of the population demanded adequate housing and services; low-cost housing and urban renewal projects became the focus of the city. In 1981, Henry Cisneros was elected mayor, becoming the first Mexican-American mayor of a major U.S. city. He was reelected three times and served until 1989.

During the 1990s, San Antonio was the second-fastest-growing large city in the United States, after Phoenix, Arizona; it focused on building and expansion to accommodate the rapid increase. The Alamodome, a venue for large sports events, concerts, and conventions, was completed in 1993 for $186 million.

As the twenty-first century begins, San Antonio seeks to improve the quality of life in the city. Such basics as public safety, street and sidewalk building and upkeep, and flood and sewage control are priorities. Crime has decreased. The city's International Affairs Department has worked with more than five hundred clients to establish international opportunities for the city's and foreign businesses, both in San Antonio and abroad.

► *Opened in 1995, San Antonio's main library building was designed by Mexican architect Ricardo Legorreta. This colorful sculpture, "Fiesta Tower," is the work of blown-glass artist Dale Chihuly.*

CHAPTER 2

People of San Antonio

The city of San Antonio is home to more than 1.2 million people. The fastest-growing ethnic group continues to be Hispanic. The vast majority of Texan Hispanics are of Mexican descent. More than one-third of the population of San Antonio speaks Spanish at home.

Mexican Americans

Since San Antonio began as part of Mexico, it is no surprise that Mexican settlers played a key part in its history and continue to do so today. They originally settled on the west side and spread west and south of San Antonio. The old Mexican market at Haymarket Plaza was a center of commerce for the city. Big stacks of melons, carrots, cabbages, onions, potatoes, and tomatoes were offered for sale at the market, along with flowers, woven baskets, herbs, molcajetes (mortars and pestles), and almost anything else imaginable.

One historic residence is the Navarro house, home of one of the two native Texans who signed the Texas Declaration of

◀ *At a local festival, people shop for cascarones, colorful eggshells filled with confetti used at many Mexican American celebrations. People crack cascarones over each other's heads, bringing good luck to those showered with confetti.*

▶ *The growth of the Hispanic ethnic group in the region has helped propel the state of Texas to replace New York as the second most populated state in the nation.*

Independence in 1836. Captured and sentenced to life in prison by Santa Anna, José Antonio Navarro escaped and came home to live in this house until his death. The building has been declared a state historical site.

Although always a part of San Antonio's history and culture, the Mexican Americans were never part of the city's powerful or upper class. Hispanics were excluded from city politics between World Wars I and II when corrupt businessmen often elected their friends to government positions. These friends would then give city contracts back to the businesses that supported them. After World War II, the Good Government League, formed primarily of white businessmen, supported candidates who wanted government reform and city growth. The work of the league and a reorganization of city government put an end to the corruption, but again, the Mexican Americans were left out. During the Civil Rights movement of the 1960s and 1970s, they became politically active, claiming their right to full participation in city government and life. Today, Mexican Americans have taken their place in all areas of life in San Antonio.

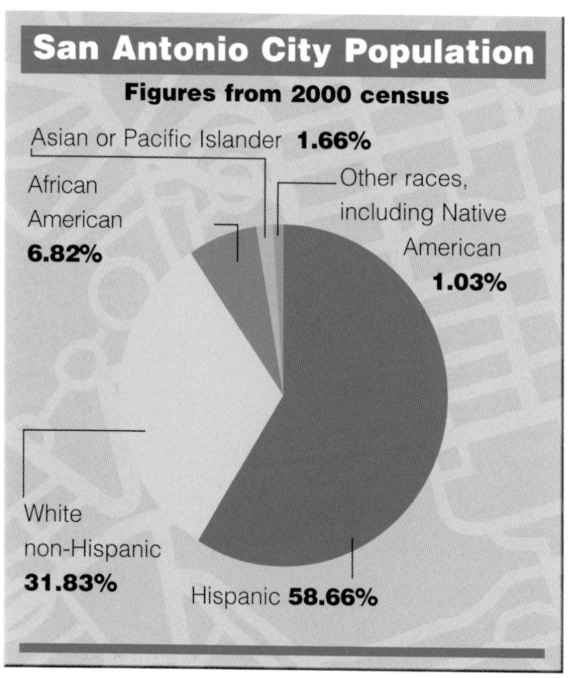

Day of the Dead

Dia de los Muertos, or Day of the Dead, is a major San Antonio celebration of its Mexican-American heritage. The purpose of the day is to honor family members who have died. People take food and flowers to the cemeteries; sometimes they make an altar there to honor a relative who died. Every November 1 and 2, hundreds visit the San Fernando Cemetery to decorate graves with balloons and flowers while picnicking and playing mariachi music for the dead. A special mass is celebrated in the cemetery. Elaborate altars are created in both homes and museums, and children are taught to make paper marigolds and sugar skulls to decorate gravesites.

Germans

Many Germans emigrated to Texas around 1845, settling in German colonies in the central Texas Hill Country. Many tired of rural living and came to San Antonio, where they settled east of the San Antonio River. They brought culture and music to the wild frontier town, opening the Menger Hotel in 1859, which still operates today.

The U.S. Army, which was using the Alamo as a supply depot, refused to let the immigrants use the Alamo church for worship. In response, the Germans built Saint Joseph's Catholic Church; it features stained glass windows from Munich, Germany.

They also built a neighborhood of lovely Victorian homes that stand today in an area now called King William Historic District. Old Beethoven Hall was built for operas, symphony orchestras, and local musical talent. The Germans dominated San Antonio society until World War I when anti-German feelings, combined with increasing Anglo and Mexican immigration, diminished their influence.

The Beethoven Maennerchor, a German singing society, was begun in 1867 and is still going strong today. It was organized to preserve German song, music, and language. Each October, members of the Beethoven Maennerchor organize an Oktoberfest, with German music, dancing, foods such as bratwurst and potato pancakes, and lots of beer.

▼ *A common feature in Mexican-American homes is a household altar or shrine honoring one or more saints. People light candles and say prayers here, asking for help. Although this altar features the Virgin Mary, many others are devoted to Our Lady of Guadalupe.*

▲ *The Alamo is San Antonio's heart and a center for many local celebrations. Here, a children's chorus sings Christmas carols in the brightly lit plaza in front of the old mission church.*

Migrants from the South

The Galveston, Harrisburg, and San Antonio Railway came to San Antonio in 1877, opening the way for a migration of European Americans from the South seeking to escape the destruction of the Civil War and begin a new life. By 1900, five railroads came to San Antonio, and the town began to boom. Fort Sam Houston continued to serve as a major military depot for the western United States. Many cavalry troops trained there, including the famous Buffalo Soldiers, African American cavalry who helped to settle the West after fighting in the Civil War. Both the European Americans and African Americans from the South found new lives in the newly prosperous Texas and joined the ranchers, cattlemen, and others to make a new home.

Religious Life

Metropolitan San Antonio has 845 churches, with more than one million people attending services in 2000. The primary religion in the city is Catholicism. The Catholic churches have the greatest number of worshipers, more than 600,000 of them, a reflection of both the Catholic origins of the city and the religion of the Mexican immigrants. A distant second place goes to the Southern Baptist Convention churches, a division of Protestant Christianity that is common in the southern United States.

San Fernando Cathedral has been the centerpiece of San Antonio life for centuries.

The Canary Island settlers and soldiers began building it in 1731; it was finished in 1755, though changes were made through 1873. When the missions became secularized in the eighteenth century, this cathedral became the only place of worship in the area. The original walls form the sanctuary in today's church. The first parish church in Texas, it is still used as a place of worship today, with more than five thousand people attending mass each weekend.

One of the largest churches in the San Antonio area is Saint Matthew's Catholic Church in Jourdanton, a suburb south of San Antonio. With an annual budget of more than $2 million, this church sponsors forty-seven parish organizations and a private school. Their project for fall 2004 was building a Habitat for Humanity house; they raised money for it by celebrating a special Czech Day with a Polka Mass and serving authentic Czech food.

San Antonio Chili Queens

As the 1900s began, San Antonio was the Wild West, and the dusty cowboys, railroad workers, businessmen, and soldiers would head over to the plaza for dinner. Since few restaurants were available—and most were in fancy hotels—the "chili queens," wives and daughters of the Canary Island and Mexican settlers, would set up their iron pots and cook up meat flavored with their traditional spices right out in the square. The men would buy a bowl of chili and sit at makeshift tables in the open, listening to local music. In today's San Antonio, the "Return of the Chili Queens" is a local chili cook-off competition that honors the original San Antonio Chili Queens.

Food

San Antonio's diverse population is reflected in the variety of hundreds of restaurants serving Texas barbecue, Gulf seafood, and German, Czech, Thai, Chinese, Japanese, Southern-style, Italian, and Indian foods. Not to be missed, however, is the Tex-Mex food. This American cuisine has developed from Mexican cooks adapting locally available foods to Anglo-American tastes. One of San Antonians' favorite dishes, cheese enchiladas consists of corn tortillas rolled around American cheeses and topped with a spicy red ranchero sauce. The enchiladas are usually served with rice flavored with chili powder and refried beans, which are boiled pinto beans that have been fried in lard. Other Tex-Mex favorites feature traditional Mexican foods that have been Americanized. The "puffy taco" features a meat filling inside a deep-fried, crispy, puffy tortilla. Fajita, which originally referred to a certain cut of beef in Mexico, now means a style of food preparation in which any type of meat is sautéed with onions and peppers.

Texas barbecue, another local food favorite, features slabs of beef brisket grilled on a mesquite wood fire. It is usually served with coleslaw, cooked pinto beans, and bread—a modern version of an old cowboy favorite.

▲ *Each April during the Fiesta San Antonio celebrations, the people of the city watch, or take part in, many colorful parades.*

Texans have also adopted chili and made it their own, with hundreds of chili cook-offs popping up all over the state. Locals of all ethnic backgrounds gather to cook their personal chili recipe and vie for a chili championship. It is a point of pride with Texans that their chili is a meat dish that doesn't include beans.

Food festivals in the German areas of town feature beers, bratwurst, sauerkraut, potatoes, and a huge variety of fine pastries. San Antonio's favorite food festivals feature dishes from all ethnic backgrounds.

Festivals, Celebrations, and Holidays

Fiesta San Antonio is held for ten days each April to honor the heroes of the Alamo and to celebrate the city's diverse cultures. This festival involves the whole town and many visitors. The festival began in 1891, when ladies in horse-drawn wagons paraded in front of the Alamo, throwing flowers at each other to remember the Battle of the Alamo. Modern celebrations still include a Battle of Flowers Parade but feature more than 150 other events: mariachi music, art shows, fun runs, an oyster bake, a masked ball, and an evening parade of boats carrying colorful lights floating down the San Antonio River.

Another big San Antonio event is the annual Texas Folklife Festival, held during the month of June and sponsored by the University of Texas Institute of Texan Cultures. It features foods, dances, and crafts from more than forty different ethnic groups. Here, you can learn how to rope a cow, dance a German polka, or make a piñata along with seventy thousand other people.

Chapter 3

Living in San Antonio

Mexican residents built the old neighborhoods, such as La Villita, in the center and west of the city. These neighborhoods consisted of adobe homes with flat roofs clustered around a square, or plaza. The plaza was the gathering place for the neighborhood, and various activities, including markets, took place there. Some of these neighborhoods still exist today.

When the Germans arrived in San Antonio, the successful ranchers and merchants built the King William neighborhood in the late 1800s and early 1900s. There, a variety of European architectural styles abound; the homes look like Italian villas or lacy Gothic castles. Looking out of place in the old Wild West, these homes were adorned by unusually detailed woodwork and ironwork, little towers called cupolas, arched windows, and other special touches.

As San Antonio began to grow and prosper, people moved out of the city and

◀ *Located in the Alamo Plaza, directly across from the Alamo, the museum section of the Cowboy Museum and Gallery displays artifacts related to the cowboys of the Old West and to San Antonio in the 1870s. Its gallery showcases a special collection of western art.*

▲ *El Mercado, a large, indoor shopping area, contains many specialty shops. Here is where people can buy Mexican candies, folk art, pottery, and piñatas. The custom of bargaining for a lower price continues in many shops here.*

into the surrounding suburbs, just as they did in most other cities in the United States. Groups of similar-looking, single-family homes, town homes, and apartments sprang up outside the city. Local stores, gas stations, and banks served those families that wished to live outside the city and work inside the city.

Shopping and Malls

Shopping in San Antonio is a combination of the ordinary and the unusual. Most of the people living in the suburbs shop for food at the local grocery stores and for clothing and other household goods at the local malls.

Downtown San Antonio, however, offers some unique shopping experiences in Market Square. El Mercado, built to resemble a public market in Mexico, has more than thirty shops that feature local handicrafts and Mexican imports. Right next to El Mercado in Market Square stands the Farmer's Market, with eighty shops selling fresh produce and tasty local dishes. Often the location for celebrations featuring mariachi music and folklorico dancers, visitors can choose from an enormous variety of Mexican candies and pan dulce (sweet bakery rolls and breads), clothing, pottery, jewelry, and craft items. Also located downtown, La Villita Historic Arts Village is a renovated historic neighborhood featuring art galleries, restaurants, and various arts and crafts shops, including glassblowers, weavers, jewelers, and painters.

▲ *In 1869, the CHRISTUS Santa Rosa Hospital—Downtown began as San Antonio's first private hospital and continues to provide health care services to city residents. The hospital mural reflects this Catholic hospital's philosophy of healing body, mind, and spirit in the local community.*

Architecture

San Antonio's immigrants have left their mark on the local architecture. The Spanish Governor's Palace, built in 1749, is a white, stucco-covered, adobe home with a flat roof. Vigas, or roof beams, accent the line of the roof, and iron grillwork covers the windows. The only remaining example of Spanish Colonial architecture, it once was the headquarters of the Spanish colony of Texas.

La Villita

Located on the south bank of the San Antonio River, La Villita is San Antonio's first (and oldest) neighborhood. It originally consisted of a collection of simple huts for the soldiers stationed at Misión San António de Valero (the Alamo). German and French immigrants lived in the area in the late 1800s, and the neighborhood became a reflection of many different cultural styles, with adobe homes sitting alongside Victorian houses. In the early twentieth century, it became a slum area. The city government sought to preserve it, however, because of its historical value when San Antonio began working on its River Walk in 1939. Today, La Villita is a colorful arts community, enjoyed by residents and visitors alike.

▲ *The George Kalteyer House, built in 1892, is a beautiful example of the homes built by early German immigrants in the King William area of San Antonio. A German pharmacist built this home, one of the most elaborate houses in the area.*

The Steves Homestead, an elegant Victorian home built on King William Street, was finished in 1878 in the German district known as "Sauerkraut Bend." Its limestone walls, imported mahogany woodwork, and arched windows look very much like an old European home. The active San Antonio Conservation Society has had a hand in saving and maintaining many of the city's beautiful old buildings.

James Wahrenberger, a native Texan, designed the main building of Our Lady of the Lake University and the administration building of St. Mary's University in the late 1800s. His German heritage is evident in these two striking buildings, which remind one of castles, even though they are all-American!

In the city, the Tower Life Building, originally the Smith Young Tower, is easy to locate at night with its lighted octagonal tower. Built in 1929 and 404 feet (123 meters) tall, it was the tallest building in San Antonio for nearly forty years.

When Hemisfair Park hosted the World's Fair in 1968, the city built many structures in preparation. One of these was the Tower of the Americas, which remains a unique part of the city's skyline. Today, people can ride to the top of the 750-foot (230-m)

▲ *The old and the new live together comfortably in San Antonio. The Marriott Hotel and Tower of the Americas loom over the squat, historic Alamo.*

tower, where a revolving restaurant treats them to the beauty of San Antonio as they dine.

Today, a large variety of architectural styles abound in San Antonio, although residents are serious about maintaining and celebrating their heritage. Perhaps that's why Mexican and southwestern styles of architecture are currently so popular.

Getting around—and Out of—San Antonio

Like residents of most of the western U.S. states, San Antonians travel a lot by car. Three interstate freeways lead to San Antonio, which is surrounded by two loop highways and numerous other highways and roads. San Antonians travel an average of forty-five minutes each day to get where they want to go in the city.

In addition, three railroads serve San Antonio. The city's VIA Metro Transit Service provides a bus service, with 479 buses running on eighty-one bus routes, including four downtown streetcar routes. The bus service covers 1,231 square miles (3,188 square kilometers), which is all of Bexar County, and transports about 37.6 million passengers each year. River taxis are also available for those who wish to travel along the San Antonio River.

The San Antonio International Airport, winner of an American Institute of

Architecture award, is located only 8 miles (13 km) from downtown. It offers airline services to fifty cities in the United States and Mexico.

Education

In 1854, the San Antonio City Council established the original San Antonio public schools. Today in Bexar County, fifteen public school districts provide schooling for children in kindergarten through twelfth grade (ages five to eighteen). Because the state requires children ages six to eighteen to attend school, these schools are free, paid for by tax dollars. Each school district has its own elected governing board and operates independently. More than three hundred elementary, middle, and high schools educate a total of more than 250,000 students. This includes schools on three military bases. In addition, there are about one hundred private schools in San Antonio.

One of the largest school districts is the San Antonio Independent School District, which has ninety-four different schools serving fifty-seven thousand students. The San Antonio district has recently completed a building program to improve all of its school buildings. It is also beginning a new program to add early childhood education centers to the elementary schools and music facilities to each of the high schools. They offer a free breakfast and lunch to all students, regardless of their family income.

Higher Education

San Antonio has six accredited colleges and universities: Trinity University, University of Texas at San Antonio, University of Texas Health Science Center, St. Mary's University, Our Lady of the Lake University, and Incarnate Word College. The Alamo Community College District, with four junior colleges, allows students to complete the first two years of their higher education. In addition, San Antonio has a branch campus of the National Autonomous University of Mexico, which is the largest Mexican university. At the University of Texas Health Science Center, over twenty-seven hundred students are working in the fields of medicine, dentistry, nursing, pharmacy, public health, and biomedical

Trinity University

Since 1869, Trinity has been one of the top private colleges in the United States. It currently offers undergraduate degrees in the liberal arts, communications, business, and education to twenty-seven hundred students from forty-six states and twenty-two countries. The campus is built on a hilltop on 117 acres (47 hectares) and features red brick buildings and towering oak trees. The college tries to build a sense of community with campus events and learning groups. A special lecture series brings in diverse worldviews, including those of a former British prime minister, a former mayor of New York, and a former president of Poland.

▲ *San Antonio Spurs Wheelchair Basketball team member Ross Davis (left), former Women's National Basketball Association star Clarissa Davis Wrightsil (center), and Spurs guard Steve Smith (right) read to Ms. Reeve's fourth grade class at Scobee Elementary. The children won the Spurs/SBC Slam Dunk Reading Challenge in 2002 by reading for 71,574 minutes. The three athletes also talked about their Olympics experiences and passed around their medals in this community-service event.*

sciences. They study and work in clinics in local hospitals, including military hospitals and neighborhood clinics.

Libraries and Museums

Students, citizens, and others can do their research at any one of San Antonio Public Library's twenty-one branches. The library system features a large Hispanic collection, with materials in both English and Spanish

"Our educational attainment is well below national averages—just 22% of us hold a BA, and Hispanic educational attainment is even lower—only 11% of Hispanics have a college degree."

—Mayor Ed Garza, in his 2004 "State of the City" address given January 30, 2004.

that focus on aspects of Texan Hispanic culture. Four more branches are planned; they are supposed to open between 2005 and 2007. The Hertzberg Circus Collection and Museum is housed in the old main library building and is the largest and oldest collection of circus memorabilia (posters, pictures, videos, records, and other items) in existence. Another notable museum, the Witte Museum of History and Science focuses on Texas' natural history and science, featuring four early Texan homes, including a log cabin built by early settlers. The Children's Museum features many fun, hands-on exhibits.

Issues and Problems

As one of the most rapidly growing cities in the United States, San Antonio shares the problems of its sister cities: crime, traffic congestion, pollution, a lack of good-paying jobs, and the struggle to maintain a kind of quality of life that keeps drawing people to the city. Major crime statistics have all decreased in San Antonio in the past few years, but the city still struggles with domestic-violence issues. The city's population is also less educated on average than that of other cities; many people are trapped in low-paying jobs.

Mayor Edward D. Garza, elected for a second term in 2003, also recently declared that the city must pay attention to its water needs. All of the growing communities in the southwestern United States, including San Antonio, will face difficulty in providing enough water for their citizens if they continue to grow without establishing an adequate supply of water.

▼ *In 2000, San Antonio contained 433,122 housing units. Of these, 54.42 percent were owner-occupied, 39.2 percent were rented, and 6.38 percent were vacant.*

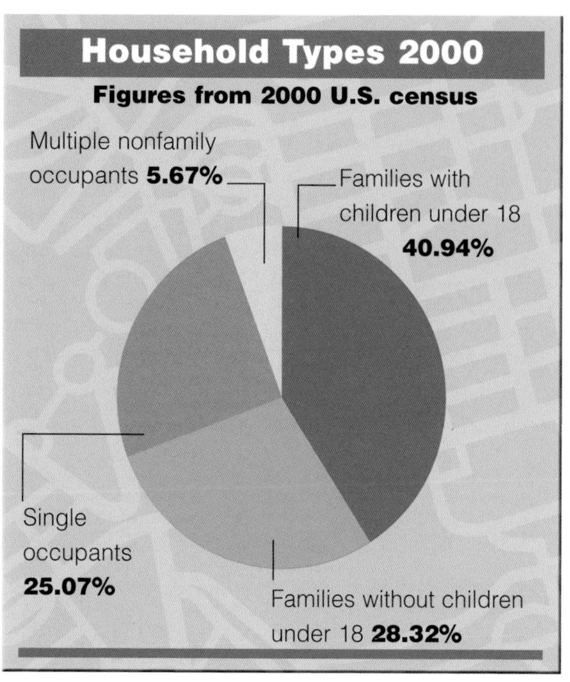

CHAPTER 4

San Antonio at Work

The San Antonio economy is diverse and owes its strength to several key industries. An important research and treatment center for cancer and other diseases, the South Texas Medical Center and other medical facilities contribute $11.5 billion annually to the local economy. They also provide many jobs in the health care and biotechnology fields.

Telecommunications and information security are two other areas of business where San Antonio is strong. The new aerospace and aviation industry is beginning to contribute a lot to the economy. In addition to military personnel, the four military bases employ many local civilians. San Antonio is a top visitor and convention destination, so tourism is important to the local economy. The city has also become a favorite retirement spot for military and other workers.

San Antonio's lack of high-paying manufacturing and financial-industry jobs has kept families' average income lower than those in other similar cities. A 2004 census

◀ *Historically, the military has always played a large part in boosting San Antonio's economy. Today, four military bases employ more than 73,000 people, both military and civilian.*

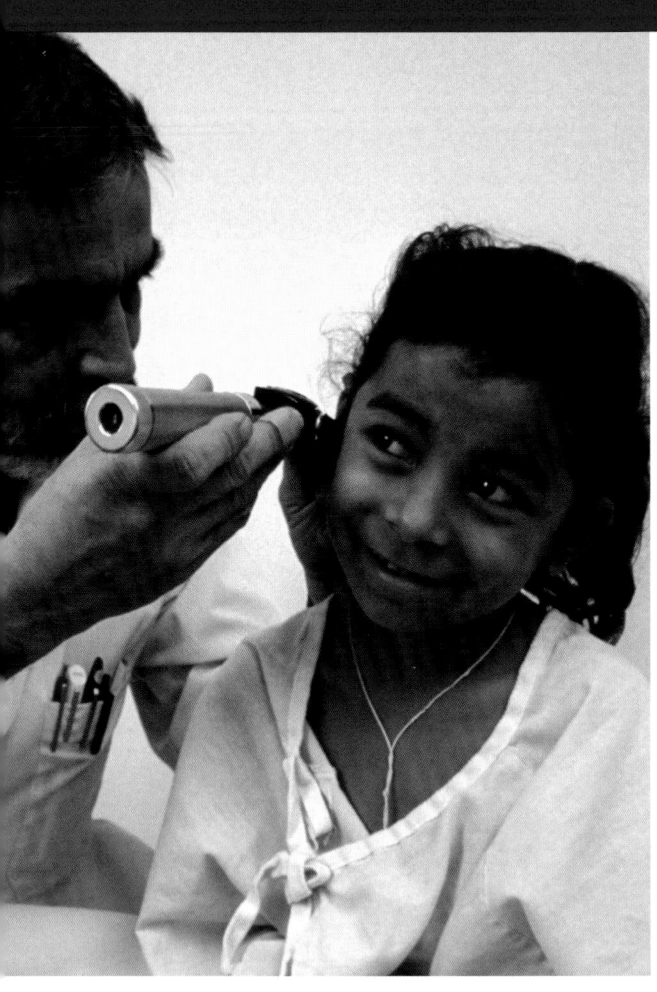

◀ *A Hispanic doctor makes sure that a child's ears are healthy at one of San Antonio's public health clinics.*

estimate shows that 27 percent of San Antonio households earn an income of less than $25,000 per year—a large number of low-income households.

The diversity of its economy, however, has made the city stable. The new Toyota factory currently being built will add some better-paying manufacturing jobs to San Antonio's military, medical, and tourism industry base.

The cost of living in San Antonio is 7 percent less than in other cities across the United States, and its home prices are among the most affordable in large urban areas in the nation. Its warm climate, many educational institutions, and state-of-the-art health research and care facilities all combine to make San Antonio an appealing place to live.

Toyota Tundra Plant

The San Antonio city officials worked closely with Bexar County and state of Texas officials to persuade Toyota, a Japanese car and truck company, to open a new manufacturing plant in San Antonio. The officials emphasized San Antonio's strong ties with its sister city in Japan. They showed that San Antonio could provide Toyota with wonderful resources and support. Toyota agreed and selected the city as the site of its new plant for manufacturing Tundra trucks. Open in 2006, the plant provides thousands of jobs for the people of San Antonio.

Major Employers

San Antonio is home to the largest military complex in the United States. The largest employer in San Antonio in 2003 was Fort Sam Houston, with 17,549 employees. In fact, three of the top five employers in San Antonio are military bases.

The United Services Automobile Association (automobile insurance and financing), H. E. B. Grocery Company, Methodist Healthcare System, SBC (telecommunications), the city of San Antonio itself, and two independent school districts round out the list of the top ten employers within the city. United Service Automobile Association, H.E.B. Food Stores, SBC, Taco Cabana, Frost National Bank, and other food, telecommunication, construction, and petroleum-industry companies all have their corporate headquarters in San Antonio.

San Antonio is an important center for shipping crops and produce from Mexico. Because it lies on highway, railroad, and airline routes to both Mexico and the rest of the United States, San Antonio has become an important shipper, packager, and distributor of Mexican vegetables, nuts, melons, and citrus fruits.

Many people in San Antonio work in the hotels, shops, and restaurants that depend upon visitors to the city. In turn, the city has supported the tourist industry by completing the Alamodome in 1993 and recently remodeling and expanding the Henry B. Gonzalez Convention Center. Bexar County, along with the San Antonio Spurs basketball team and several boards and businesses, opened the SBC Center in 2002, a huge community center. The city has also seen the improvement of the River Walk and new hotels opening in the heart of the city.

SBC Center

In 1999, Bexar County partnered with the San Antonio Spurs basketball team and corporate sponsor SBC to build a $175 million community center that would be the new home for the San Antonio Spurs and the San Antonio Livestock Exposition. The center also hosts many other shows and events. This "ranch tech" style community center opened in October 2002 with a state-of-the-art video and sound system, including live-action video screens and a display screen that encircles the entire arena.

Running the City

The city council is responsible for creating the policies that govern San Antonio. The whole city votes for the mayor who serves on the city council. Each of the ten city districts elects, for a two-year term, a representative who also serves on the city council. The city manager, who manages the city's twelve thousand employees, carries out the policies that are set by the city council.

Mayor Ed Garza was reelected in 2003 after his first term as mayor and two terms as a representative on the San Antonio City Council. A native of the city, Garza's priorities are to create more jobs in the high-tech and biomedical industries, modernize and streamline local government processes, and revitalize the older, rundown neighborhoods.

After the World Trade Center in New York was bombed on September 11, 2001, Mayor Garza worked with other city and county officials to create one of the country's first antiterrorism plans. Cable News Network (CNN) declared San Antonio the most-prepared city in the United States after New York.

▲ *San Antonio's Spanish speakers can enjoy newscasts and discussions in their own language, broadcast from studios in the city. There are twelve television stations within the San Antonio area, four of which are Spanish speaking.*

Inside City Government

San Antonio's city government provides police, fire, parks and recreation, libraries, housing and community development, planning, and economic development services. Altogether, there are thirty-eight different city departments within the city of San Antonio. The city manages the airport and the Alamodome, a $186 million venue where sporting events, concerts, conventions, and other entertainments take place. Since it opened in 1993, more than 13 million people have visited the Alamodome.

One of the most important daily services for San Antonio citizens is the customer service phone line. Citizens can dial an easy-to-remember number on any day, at any time, to report a pothole, stray dog, graffiti, or anything else that needs service. Trained city operators will relay the message to the correct city department so that the problem can be fixed.

Henry Cisneros

Born in San Antonio in 1947, Henry Cisneros grew up in the city and attended college in Texas. He went to Harvard for an advanced degree. In 1974, he began teaching in the Environmental Studies Division at the University of Texas at San Antonio. He was elected to the San Antonio City Council in 1975 and reelected twice more. In 1981, Cisneros was elected mayor of San Antonio. He served four terms as mayor. President Bill Clinton appointed Cisneros in 1993 to serve in his cabinet as the secretary for housing and urban development. He resigned this appointment in 1997 and was charged later that year with having lied on his background investigation. Cisneros pleaded guilty, paid his fine, and returned to private life in San Antonio, where he runs a business that helps low-income families finance the construction of their homes.

▲ *Henry Cisneros visits seniors at a church in 1979 while serving on the San Antonio City Council.*

A combination of property taxes, hotel taxes, alcoholic beverage fees, and other fees for various licenses and permits supports city services. Bexar County and the state of Texas also tax San Antonians. The city of San Antonio does not act alone but in partnership with the county, state, and federal government because the city is responsible to all these different governing bodies. Another example of partnership, the court system is a combination of city, county, state, and federal courts.

Torch of Friendship

Located in Convention Plaza, a 65-foot (20-m) tall sculpture called the "Torch of Friendship" reaches up toward the sky in a blaze of red. International sculptor Sebastian created the 50-ton (45.5-metric ton) red steel monument at the request of the Asociación de Empresarios Mexicanos, a group of Mexican businessmen. It honors the ties of history, friendship, and commerce that link San Antonio and Mexico. A day-long celebration marked the unveiling of the monument and the lighting of the torch when the sculpture was presented to San Antonio Mayor Ed Garza in June 2002.

The city of San Antonio supports numerous boards and commissions that act in an advisory capacity to the city government. More than six hundred San Antonio citizens serve on these boards at any time. Also, various neighborhood associations work with the city's planning department on ways to improve the quality of life in their area.

A problem shared with similar cities is that of dishonest city leaders and workers. The current Mayor's Commission on Integrity and Trust has made recommendations for changes to the current procedures. If these changes are adopted, they will establish a strong ethics code and reform how political campaigns are funded.

"On behalf of Mexico, I am proud to present to the City of San Antonio The Torch of Friendship. May it always stand tall to symbolize the ties of friendship that forever bind our countries."

—Dr. Jorge Casteneda, Mexico's foreign affairs minister, at the presentation of the sculpture to San Antonio Mayor Ed Garza in June 2002.

CHAPTER 5

San Antonio at Play

The citizens of San Antonio are enthusiastic supporters of the San Antonio Stock Show and Rodeo, held in February each year since 1950. When it began in 1854, it was called the Texas Agricultural Fair, and members of this cattle town were naturally interested in events such as judging livestock and contests of skill involving riding horseback or roping cattle. It is still one of the most popular sports events in town, and more than one million people attend each year.

San Antonio is perhaps best known for its professional National Basketball Association (NBA) basketball team, the San Antonio Spurs. The Spurs began as the Dallas Chaparrals. The team relocated to San Antonio in 1973, became the Spurs, and were soon included in the big league. Since then, they have won two NBA national championships in 1999 and 2003. Although they drew huge crowds in the Alamodome, they moved to the new state-of-the-art SBC

◀ *The first Saturday of the San Antonio Stock Show and Rodeo is Youth Day, when youngsters of all ages go to learn more about animals and participate in hands-on activities such as roping. There is even a Mutton Bustin' competition for four- to seven-year olds who try to ride a sheep for six seconds.*

▲ *Fans congratulate San Antonio Spurs player Manu Ginobili during a River Walk victory parade. The whole city celebrated after the Spurs won the 2003 National Basketball Association championship.*

Arena in 2002. The SBC Arena is also home to the Women's NBA team—the Silver Stars—and the American Hockey League team—the San Antonio Rampage. Both teams had their first year in the Alamo City from 2002 to 2003. Other professional sports teams include the San Antonio Missions baseball team and the San Antonio Racquets tennis team. The city also sponsors such sporting events as the Texas Open and the R. J. Reynolds PGA (Professional Golfers' Association) Seniors golf tournaments.

Charreria

A popular national sport in Mexico, charreria grew out of life in Spanish colonial Mexico. The San Antonio Charro Association keeps this centuries-old tradition alive with its special forms of dress, riding, and horse equipment. The charros (people who ride horses) have their own rodeo competition, called a charreada. Some of the events at a charreada are similar to an American rodeo, such as bullriding and riding on horses without a saddle. Women dressed in colorful, ruffled riding dresses ride sidesaddle in the escaramuza. During this event, they gallop their horses in complicated and dangerous patterns, barely missing each other as they dash around the arena.

Music Scene

San Antonio is home to the Tejano Conjunto Festival, held each May, featuring both conjunto and the more modern Tejano music that is native to this area. Conjunto music was born in the late 1800s when Mexicans in southern Texas began to use the accordion, which was brought by the German settlers. They added the Spanish guitar and invented a new kind of American music combining German polkas with traditional Mexican songs. Conjunto became popular in San Antonio beginning in the 1920s but was once considered the music of poor Mexican American migrants. A modern version of conjunto called Tejano (which is Spanish for Texan) adds rock and roll to the mix. Tejano has become popular throughout the United States, Europe, and Japan.

Reflecting the city's strong cowboy roots, many popular country western music and dance clubs entertain visitors and residents alike. Sunset Station is an entertainment venue in the remodeled Southern Pacific Railroad Depot building featuring two stages for live musical performances, restaurants, and upscale shopping under one roof.

Mariachi bands often play in San Antonio, primarily at restaurants, parties, and events. Consisting of trumpets, violins, guitar, vihuela (an early form of guitar), and guitarrón (a twenty-five string guitar), these bands perform lively music that includes polkas, waltzes, love ballads (boleros), and some country and popular songs. Often dressed as traditional Jalisco cowboys with boots, sombreros, and short jackets, the bands are historically from Mexico, although many San Antonio schools now have mariachi band programs.

Theater and the Arts

The Majestic Theatre, which originally opened in 1929, was an elaborate movie palace. Closed in 1974, it was restored and reopened in 1989 as the home of the San Antonio Symphony; other kinds of concerts and Broadway plays are often performed there as well. The San Antonio Performing Arts Association and the Arts Council of San Antonio regularly bring theater and arts performances into San Antonio, many of which can be seen at the old Majestic. The colleges have live theater groups, and many small local theater groups perform. The Ballet Folklorico de San Antonio dances at the Arneson River Theater.

In June 2003, the San Antonio Symphony was forced to shut down because

Folklorico Dancing

San Antonio has its own dance troupe, the Ballet Folklorico de San Antonio, which performs weekly during the summer months after touring all year long. The Ballet Folklorico preserves the heritage of regional Mexican dance by practicing and performing a huge variety of colorful dances based on Mexican history and folklore. The bright, vivid costumes resemble the traditional clothing of the various regions of Mexico.

of lack of funds and support. While city support has helped many economic development efforts, limited support is available for the arts. The symphony hopes to reopen in the future.

The San Antonio Museum of Art, located in the old Lone Star Brewing Company (built in 1884), opened in 1981 with a collection of Greek, Roman, Asian, and Egyptian art, and European and American painting and sculpture. Its massive Latin American art collection is probably the best collection of pre-Columbian, Spanish colonial, folk, and modern art of Latin America in the United States. It is now being featured in the new wing, the Nelson A. Rockefeller Center for Latin American Art, which opened in 1998.

An Historical Opening

In April 2004, the movie premiere of Disney's The Alamo, *starring Dennis Quaid, Billy Bob Thornton, Jason Patric, and others, opened at San Antonio's Majestic Theatre with many stars in attendance. This was a rerun for San Antonio; in 1960, the city premiered an earlier version of* The Alamo *starring John Wayne.*

▼ *Mexican food and drinks were served at the premiere of* The Alamo *at the Majestic Theatre in 2004. Mariachi bands played, and the colorful Ballet Folklorico dancers spun, whirled, and clapped as the Hollywood stars entered the theater.*

Parks

The San Antonio Botanical Gardens and Conservatory was established in 1980 on 33 acres (13 ha) of land that was once an old limestone quarry. It features a variety of Texan historic homes and plant life, including a Texas wildflower garden, an old-fashioned garden, an herb garden, and a children's garden that features edible plants. Perhaps the most beautiful is the Japanese garden, Kuamoto En, named for San Antonio's sister city in Japan, which sent their experts to create it. The conservatory houses plants from diverse locations from rain forests to deserts.

A San Antonio treasure for over one hundred years, Brackenridge Park is located at the head of the San Antonio River. Featuring recreational facilities, picnic areas, and miles of jogging paths, it is also home to the San Antonio Zoo. One of the best zoos in the United States, it showcases more than thirty-five hundred animals on 25 acres (10 ha) of land.

Of course, the city's development of the green space along the River Walk qualifies it

▼ *Used for all sorts of concerts, plays, dance performances, and other events, the Arneson River Theatre is a unique outdoor venue on the San Antonio River. The theater seats eight hundred people in the open area on the south side of the river; they watch events on the stage located across the river.*

▲ *Fiesta Texas, another San Antonio attraction, is known for its thrilling rides. "Die Fledermaus," a wave swinger ride, is tame compared to "Crackaxle Cragg," "Turbo Bungy," "Poltergeist," and "Der Twister."*

as a park as well. The city's Parks and Recreation Department keeps the area beautiful and attractive for strollers and joggers along the river.

Escapes

Visitors and residents alike can enjoy SeaWorld San Antonio, the world's largest marine life entertainment park. There are more than twenty-five shows, rides, and animal attractions on 250 acres (100 ha); trained killer whales and dolphins perform daily. In 2005, a new sea lion show will be added and the water park expanded to include 3.5 acres (1.4 ha) where guests will be able to float along a winding pool in inner tubes. Another San Antonio attraction is Six Flags Fiesta Texas, which features constant live entertainment and rides such as the "Rattler," the world's largest and fastest wooden roller coaster. A wave pool shaped like the state of Texas is also located in the former rock quarry that is now Six Flags.

Northwest of San Antonio lies the Texas Hill Country, famous for its lush, oak-covered hills and winding rivers. People often visit the German country towns of Fredericksburg and Gruene to sightsee and shop. North of San Antonio runs the San Marcos River, a popular place to ride down the river on inner tubes, floating along on a summer's day with foam coolers containing drinks and snacks tied to the tubes.

Chapter 6

Looking Forward

The city's residents approved a joint city/county resolution in 2003 for raising $250 million. This money will fund many future improvements, including renovating parks and libraries, repairing streets and sewage systems, and constructing a new history museum. A major investment of $426 million is also planned to improve the San Antonio International Airport over ten years. These improvements will not only add more parking and passenger gates but will also establish the airport as a hub for travel into Mexico.

The City South initiative is a major plan for future growth in San Antonio. To balance the rapid growth on its north side, the city has provided incentives for developers, businesses, and educational institutions in 57 square miles (148 sq km) on the south side of San Antonio. This planned development will include a wide variety of attractive homes and communities, plenty of open space, and a new campus of Texas A&M University.

The city continues to work to change the former Kelly Air Force Base, which closed recently, into an international aviation industry park. New employers such as Boeing,

◀ *The bright lights of downtown San Antonio at night show growth and development as far as the eye can see. San Antonio continues to be one of the fastest growing cities in the United States.*

▶ San Antonio is positioned to become a center of trade between Canada, the United States, and Mexico. Mexican, U.S., and Canadian ministers signed the North America Free Trade Agreement (NAFTA) at the Plaza San Antonio Hotel in 1992. Their respective heads of state, President Salinas de Gortari of Mexico, U.S. President George H.W. Bush, and Canadian Prime Minister Mulroney, look on.

Lockheed Martin, and others have turned the former air force base into a technology and business park that is employing thousands of San Antonio's citizens.

The Smithsonian Institution, with help from the city, plans to build a large museum in downtown San Antonio called Museo Americano. Through its exhibits and collections, the museum, which is currently under construction, will tell about the history of Hispanics in the United States.

"Our imagination—the future we see for San Antonio—truly does encircle the world. From Japan to Canada, from the Middle East to Mexico, San Antonio's businesses, partners, investors, and people are players on the global stage. Whether it's a Toyota truck or software for the United States military, we are making the future right here in San Antonio."

—Mayor Edward D. Garza, "State of the City" address, January 30, 2004.

A Historic Past, A Growing Future

San Antonio is a city that owes much to its history. The Spanish missions, the Alamo, and time spent as a Mexican state have all contributed to the flavor of the city. Often a city of clashing cultures, it was rocked by corruption, scandal, and racism. Over the years, the people of San Antonio have worked hard to cure these social ills.

Today, San Antonio is a vibrant "Fiesta City," a city that honors its roots by celebrating Dia de los Muertos, Oktoberfest, and rodeo days. Visitors and citizens alike can stroll down the River Walk, visit an old mission church, purchase colorful Mexican folk art, or eat a cowboy meal at a local saloon, all in a modern city with growing tourism, telecommunications, and health care industries.

Time Line

1691 Spanish explorers name San Antonio River after Saint Anthony of Padua on June 13.

1718 Spanish found Misión San António de Valero (Alamo) in May and establish Presidio de Béxar to protect it and other nearby missions.

1720 Spanish found Mission San José.

1731 Fifteen Canary Island families establish the first Spanish settlement in San Antonio, Texas—Villa San Fernando de Béxar. Missions Concepción, San Juan Capistrano, and Espada are relocated from East Texas to San Antonio area.

1793–94 The Catholic Church secularizes the missions.

1810 Mexican fight for independence begins.

1820 Moses Austin asks the Spanish governor in San Antonio for permission to allow American settlers in Texas.

1821 Mexico wins independence from Spain.

1835 The first battle in San Antonio for Texas' independence from Mexico ends in Mexico's defeat in the siege of Béxar.

1836 In February Mexican dictator Santa Anna marched in San Antonio to retake the city from Texan rebels. He attacked the Alamo in March and won the famous battle. In April Sam Houston's army drove the Mexicans out, and the new Republic of Texas gained its independence.

1837 San Antonio is incorporated as a city.

1845 Texas joins the United States as the twenty-eighth state.

1861 Texas secedes from the United States and joins the Confederate States of America during the Civil War.

1865 American Civil War ends.

1870 Previously a Confederate state, Texas is readmitted to the Union (United States).

1877 The railroad comes to San Antonio.

1880s German immigrants develop San Antonio's first suburb, King William.

1891 First Battle of Flowers Parade is held in San Antonio.

1939–40 San Antonio River Walk is built.

1968 World's Fair exposition comes to San Antonio.

1993 Alamodome is completed.

1998 Nelson A. Rockefeller Center for Latin American Art opens.

2002 SBC Center opens.

2004 *The Alamo* movie premieres at the San Antonio Majestic Theatre.

Glossary

adorn to decorate with beautiful things.

accredited recognized as maintaining high national standards.

biomedical involving biological, medical, and physical sciences.

biotechnology an industry using scientific techniques to change life forms to develop new or changed organisms.

cadets students in training for military or naval service.

commerce the business of buying and selling goods and transporting them from place to place.

corruption dishonest or bad behavior.

diverse differing from one another.

fabricating manufacturing.

folklorico describes performers and performances of traditional Mexican songs and dances.

Gothic relating to a style of building with pointed arches, tall thin walls, and large windows.

information security the business of protecting information from being stolen, changed, moved, or destroyed, especially regarding information stored on computers.

initiative a large, complicated, or difficult project that is launched to make major changes in an area or community.

Jalisco a state in west-central Mexico.

mariachi a kind of folk music performed by Mexican street bands.

missionary a person who tries to teach other people his or her religion.

nomadic not having fixed homes but instead traveling from place to place, usually in order to follow migrations of wild game or in search of good grazing for their animals.

piñata a container made of paper and glue holding candy and small toys. Blindfolded children take turns hitting the piñata, hoping to make it burst and release the treats inside.

revitalize to make new again; to give new life.

revolution a fight against one government or ruler to change to a different government.

sanctuary the holiest part of a religious building such as the area around the altar in a Christian church.

secularized transferred from religious control to control by the people.

telecommunications electronic systems used to transmit messages and information such as in telephone, cell phone, and computer communications.

territory a part of the United States that is not a part of any state but that has its own legislature; a number of U.S. states were first territories or part of a larger territory.

truce an agreement to stop fighting for a certain period of time.

urban renewal program for replacing or restoring old or run-down buildings or constructing new ones in a city.

venue place where special events are held.

Further Information

Books

Alpin, Elaine Marie. *Davy Crockett* (History Maker). Lerner Publishing Group, 2003.

Altman, Linda Jacobs. *Texas* (It's My State!). Benchmark Books, 2002.

Bednar, Chuck. *San Antonio Spurs* (Great Sports Teams). Lucent Books, 2003

Hanson-Harding, Alexandra. *Texas* (From Sea to Shining Sea). Children's Press, 2001.

McReynolds, Stacy. *San Antonio Zoo* (Great Zoos of the United States). PowerKids Press, 2003.

Murphy, Jim. *Inside the Alamo*. Delacorte Books for Young Readers, 2003.

Pelta, Kathy. *Texas: Hello U.S.A.* (Hello USA). Lerner Publications, 2001.

Riehecky, Janet. *The Siege of the Alamo* (Landmark Events in American History). World Almanac Library, 2002.

Web Sites

www.americansouthwest.net/texas/san_antonio_missions_/historical_park.html
This site covers the San Antonio Missions National Historical Park. It offers photographs and brief descriptions of the five missions.

www.isjunction.com/facts/missions.htm
Find out more about the San Antonio missions and their effect on life around San Antonio.

www.sanantonio.gov
Learn more about the government of San Antonio, cultural events, and other aspects of the city on the official web site of the city of San Antonio.

www.sazoo-aq.org
Meet the animals and learn more about the San Antonio Zoo on its official web site.

www.thealamo.org
The Alamo's web site contains history, descriptions, and educational resources relating to the mission and fort with a link to a special kids' section.

Index

Page numbers in **bold** indicate pictures.